Multidisciplinary Approaches to Culminating Student Experiences

Edited by

Michael G. Strawser
University of Central Florida

Robin G. Yaure
Penn State Mont Alto

Series in Education
VERNON PRESS

www.vernonpress.com

In the Americas:	*In the rest of the world:*
Vernon Press	Vernon Press
1000 N West Street, Suite 1200	C/Sancti Espiritu 17,
Wilmington, Delaware, 19801	Malaga, 29006
United States	Spain

Series in Education

Library of Congress Control Number: 2023952266

ISBN: 979-8-8819-0174-5

Also available: 978-1-64889-843-3 [Hardback]; 978-1-64889-899-0 [PDF, E-Book]

Cover design by Vernon Press with elements from Freepik.

Table of Contents

List of Tables and Figures   vii

Introduction   ix

Michael G. Strawser
University of Central Florida

Robin G. Yaure
Penn State Mont Alto

Section 1: Culminating Experiences in Higher Education   1

Chapter 1   **Defining Culminating Experiences**   3

Lindsay M. McCluskey
SUNY Oswego

Chapter 2   **Assessing Culminating Experiences: Balancing Rigor and Flexibility in the Design and Delivery of a Capstone Experience**   19

Patricia R. Payette
University of Louisville

Nisha Gupta
Centre College

Chapter 3   **Student Reflection**   45

Andrea Hamilton
Department of Defense at Wright-Patterson AFB

Susan Wildermuth
University of Wisconsin-Whitewater

Section 2: Examples of Culminating Activities   65

Chapter 4   **Thesis**   67

Amanda R. Martinez
Davidson College

Chapter 5   **Dissertation**   85

Karen Head
Missouri University of Science & Technology

Kevin Dvorak
Nova Southeastern University

Shirley O'Brien
Eastern Kentucky University

Russell Carpenter
Eastern Kentucky University

Chapter 6   **Applied Projects**   103

Ahmet Aksoy
Columbia College-South Carolina

Amber McCord
Texas Tech University

Chapter 7   **Comprehensive Exams**   123

Cassandra L. Carlson-Hill
City of Madison, Wisconsin

Danielle Johnson
University of South Florida

Chapter 8   **Portfolios**   141

Kathleen J. Kennedy
University of Arizona

Chapter 9   **Internships**   171

Amanda Joyce
Murray State University

**Section 3: Disciplinary Approaches to
Culminating Experiences**   187

Chapter 10 **Business**   189

Amanda M. Main
University of Central Florida

Chapter 11   **Humanities**   205

Javier Alvarez Jaimes
North Carolina Central University

Sharrah A. Lane
University of North Carolina, Chapel Hill

Chapter 12   **Natural and Applied Sciences**   217

Jacob Moore
Penn State Mont Alto

Chapter 13   **Social Sciences**   231

Nikki DiGregorio
Towson University

Amanda J. Rich
York College of Pennsylvania

Laura Evans
Penn State Brandywine

Contributors   245

List of Tables and Figures

Table 2.1.	Scaffolded Assessment Example	23
Table 5.1.	Dissertation Pathways	89
Table 5.2.	NACE Transferable Employability Skills	90
Table 5.3.	Sample Dissertation Skill Curriculum Map	92
Figure 5.1.	The Dissertation Writing Process	93
Table 6.1.	Job Outlook 2022, National Association of Colleges and Employers	105
Table 6.2.	Applied Project Tracking Document	113
Table 6.3.	Social Media Project Grading Rubric	114
Table 7.1.	Purpose of Doctoral Written Comprehensive Exam	126
Table 7.2.	Structures of Doctoral Comprehensive Exams	127
Table 8.1.	Common Uses of Portfolios	145
Table 8.2.	Portfolio Creation and Development Responsibilities	150
Table 8.3.	Effective Feedback Checklist	154
Table 8.4.	An Example of a Showcase Portfolio Planner	163
Table 8.5.	Plan for Completion	164
Table 10.1.	Culminating Experiences Planning Table	201

Introduction

Michael G. Strawser

University of Central Florida

Robin G. Yaure

Penn State Mont Alto

"Back in my day…"

More often than not Michael finds himself either living vicariously through his students or thinking deeply about the differences in their college experiences. He went to a small private university and completed a required senior research project as his 'culminating undergraduate experience', finishing his undergraduate degree in 2008. He then went on to his master's where he completed a thesis because he thought he might want to then go on and earn a Ph.D. He could have opted for comprehensive exams but was strongly urged to complete the typical thesis project. He was the student that needed, craved even, something different.

Robin also completed a research project, albeit much earlier than Michael, as a culminating experience for the psychology honors program at Temple University where she went as an undergraduate. Early in college, she knew she wanted to be a professor and she also enjoyed being challenged intellectually. She had to interview a few faculty in the department until she finally found one willing to work with her and whose work on intellectual development dovetailed with her own interests. She was delighted to be a part of weekly research team meetings where the level of discourse, including discussions on Piaget and Kant, was mind-blowing to her.

Both Michael and Robin were fortunate to have such high-quality research experiences. Such high-impact experiences became more popular as Kuh (2008) and others identified the significant benefits of real-world interactions and complex problem-solving for students. Culminating projects, those end-of-degree or end-of-school showcases or practical experiences, had been a staple in K-12 education and have gradually become more common at many universities. As such opportunities grow in popularity, more students are able to participate in valuable experiential learning. At the same time, however, the challenges for students to complete such projects have become more apparent.

Robin has been a faculty internship supervisor in the field of Human Development and Family Studies for about nine years and a professor for over

30. Observations she has made during the last few years along with some previously existing misgivings she had about the fundamental fairness of requiring full-time internships cemented the understanding that flexibility regarding culminating experiences is crucial from a social justice perspective as well as a practical matter.

Discussions with colleagues centered on what internships were really about and how they may not have been serving all students equally and fairly. What about those students who had to work a full-time job on top of an unpaid, full-time internship? What about the low- or no-paid internships that the students in human service agencies had compared with the well-compensated internships that business students had? What about the, thankfully rare, instances where interns were brought on board by companies or organizations which were merely aiming to avoid paying a full-time employee? What about when a student intern was employed doing menial tasks such as doing laundry and cleaning storage areas for an internship site? How much choice did a student intern have when an internship turned out not to be as planned or when a supervisor decided not to engage the intern in a meaningful experience? What if an internship site had colleagues who were hostile to interns working towards a degree when they themselves were in low-paying jobs with few prospects? How could we ensure that a student moved beyond stereotypes and biases that were well-ingrained about their clients and co-workers? What about when an internship site refused to take on a particular intern who was neuro-atypical?

In the past, we may have assumed that the mere existence of an internship was a panacea for moving the student beyond the classroom. Assumptions about internships and other culminating experiences need to be questioned. Understanding what students need and how they can achieve that must be at the forefront of the decisions made at institutional and program levels. Maximizing flexibility and tailoring culminating experiences to the individual student is paramount.

Recognizing that traditional theses and other written projects may not always be the most practical and applicable option for some students and being creative to move beyond these are challenges that we lay out for you as you read this volume. Understanding that there are myriad options, with benefits and costs to each, is a fundamental responsibility of the faculty advisor, academic program faculty, and institutional leaders. While few seem to question whether the role of the academy is to provide a training ground for future jobs or more as a fertile ground for developing critical thinking and creative accomplishments, this age-old debate comes to the forefront. Recognizing the importance of articulating programmatic goals embedded within the institutional values and objectives, assumptions must be challenged, and the status quo questioned.

This volume provides much food for thought as we move forward into a new "normal" for higher education institutions.

Despite the relatively recent popularity of culminating experiences, a multidisciplinary and practical resource that provides information for all types of culminating student experiences is not yet available. The idea for this volume arose because of the recognition that a holistic and applied resource for those looking to have general knowledge of different ways to assess student learning, especially at the undergraduate level, was lacking. This text seeks to fill a gap and provide a historical context for culminating experiences, suggestions for assessment, foundational knowledge for different types of projects, and finally approaches to using these experiences in various disciplines. Because of the information desired, experts in their field from a wide variety of disciplines were approached to be chapter contributors. This resource focuses predominantly on undergraduate students but many of the chapters can either be applied to both undergraduate and graduate students (e.g., thesis) or specifically focus on the graduate student population (e.g., dissertation).

The book is divided into three sections. The first section provides background information on experiences including definitions, assessment techniques, and valuable information related to student reflection. The second section includes chapters that dive deeply into various experience types including thesis, dissertation, applied projects, comprehensive exams, portfolios, and internships. This list is not exhaustive but representative of some of the more sought-after experiences. The third section focuses on different disciplines, specifically business, humanities, natural and applied sciences, and social sciences. These chapters are discipline-specific, providing information for readers on how to infuse culminating experiences at a programmatic and departmental level. For ease, chapter summaries are provided below.

Chapter Summaries

Chapter 1: Defining Culminating Experiences

The first chapter in this volume, authored by Lindsay M. McCluskey, sets the stage for the remainder of the text by providing definitions of and a contextual background for culminating experiences in higher education. McCluskey weaves together definitions by high-impact practice scholars while providing a holistic rationale for the importance of culminating experiences in university settings.

Chapter 2: Assessing Culminating Experiences: Balancing Rigor and Flexibility in the Design and Delivery of a Capstone Experience

Chapter Two, by Patricia Payette and Nisha Gupta, focuses on assessing culminating experiences. Their combined expertise, revealed in part by leading a large university Quality Enhancement Project aimed at enhancing culminating experiences for undergraduate students, provides a rare and unique perspective on demonstrating effectiveness in culminating experiences. Payette and Gupta build an argument based on the importance of assessment before diving into their institutional context. Their assessment resources are also invaluable and can be used as multidisciplinary resources across programs and departments.

Chapter 3: Student Reflection

In Chapter Three, Andrea Hamilton and Susan Wildermuth provide needed insight on student reflection as a means of encouraging deep learning as a result of culminating projects. Hamilton and Wildermuth not only provide a helpful historical context of student reflection as an instructional strategy but also establish reflection as a necessary way for students to debrief their culminating projects. Their rationale for incorporating reflection and their strategies for assessing reflection can be applied to varying degrees with undergraduate or graduate students.

Chapter 4: Thesis

Amanda Martinez, in Chapter Four, transitions the volume from general culminating approaches to a more detailed explanation of individual experiences. Martinez approaches the thesis from the perspective primarily of undergraduate students; however, much of the information explored could be applied at the graduate level. After defining the merits of a thesis, Martinez transitions to effective thesis writing, a section helpful not just for advisors or instructors but students as well. Helpful advice is offered to advisors as they are encouraged to be consistently attentive to student needs throughout the process.

Chapter 5: Dissertation

In a chapter unique to graduate populations, by Karen Head, Kevin Dvorak, Shirley O'Brien, and Russell Carpenter, exceptionally practical advice is granted from seasoned doctoral advisors. The authors do well to position the dissertations as a necessary manifestation of research while also positioning a framework for student-centered dissertation advising and writing.

Chapter 6: Applied Projects

Chapter Six, dovetailing with more traditional culminating experiences of thesis and dissertation, details a more recent conceptualization and applied projects. Ahmet Aksoy and Amber McCord use a 'next journey' analogy to discuss the value of applied projects and experiential learning. They also provide a solid rationale for why instructors, program directors, and future employers cannot ignore applied projects. To finish their chapter, they provide practical templates to help instructors or advisors track, manage, and ultimately assess applied projects.

Chapter 7: Comprehensive Exams

Cassandra L. Carlson-Hill and Danielle Johnson discuss an oft-overlooked approach to determining student mastery. Qualifying exams show student readiness to either enter the workforce or move on to a terminal degree or further research. This chapter offers expertise related to navigating the exam journey while effectively advising students through the process. They provide a rationale for why comprehensive exams can be beneficial and applicable for all programs, and identify best practices for effectively incorporating qualifying exams including diligently focusing on the role of the advisor.

Chapter 8: Portfolios

Kathleen J. Kennedy, author of chapter eight, dutifully explores portfolios as a valuable culminating experience for students. In this chapter, Kennedy provides practical suggestions for using portfolios, a versatile and effective tool to assess student learning. Portfolios allow students to not just collect and categorize their deliverables but also showcase these creations for future employers. An engaging exercise, portfolios can be helpful for all students, especially those in creative disciplines. Kennedy's chapter provides a rationale for why instructors should consider portfolios as a culminating tool and provides examples of integral and strategic student portfolios.

Chapter 9: Internships

Chapter nine delves into one of the more experiential culminating activities, the internship. Amanda Joyce shows how internships provide unparalleled opportunities for students to apply knowledge gained during their program. In addition, this chapter explores not only the benefits of internships but gives detailed suggestions for creating a collaborative and engaging internship program for undergraduate students. This chapter is also the final chapter that highlights a specific project or culminating experience.

Chapter 10: Business

Amanda Main begins what is in essence the third and final section of this volume. Main focuses on the culminating experience as a useful evaluative tool for business programs. By providing information related to competency-based programming, faculty-student research collaborations, industry-sponsored projects, and internships, Main discusses how business programs can incorporate strategic student experiences to enhance the learning journey. An example project template is provided to help apply the shared principles.

Chapter 11: Humanities

In chapter eleven, the authors contextualize culminating approaches in the humanities. The authors, Javier Alvarez Jaimes and Sharrah A. Lane, apply expertise surrounding the study of human culture and society. The humanities, those academic programs that focus on ideas, stories, words, symbols and expressions, are well suited for project-based learning that showcases student work and individual thought. Jaimes and Lane differentiate between culminating concepts, like service learning, independent studies, and others and provide information for humanities instructors looking to build effective end-of-study experiences.

Chapter 12: Natural and Applied Sciences

Because of the sheer breadth of disciplines encompassed in the natural and applied sciences, Jacob Moore had a difficult task. Yet, Moore approaches culminating experiences at both the undergraduate and graduate levels in the natural and applied sciences with dutiful grace. Moore first provides a definitional context of natural sciences as well as applied sciences and then provides a rationale for various educational goals in these disciplines. The remainder of the chapter incorporates an overview of capstone experiences in natural sciences, engineering and computer sciences, agricultural sciences, and even medicine.

Chapter 13: Social Sciences

The final chapter, chapter thirteen, is devoted to the social sciences. Nikki DiGregorio, Amanda J. Rich, and Laura Evans begin by framing their suggestions around several educational frameworks including transformative learning, self-efficacy, and experiential learning. With these frameworks serving as the baseline foundation for their suggestions, the authors then move into a direct application of these theories as conduits for learning through culminating experiences. The authors bring the volume full circle by sharing insight into using critical reflection in social science projects and share suggestions for assessing culminating experiences in the social sciences.

Culminating student experiences can be valuable projects for students to both display and apply their knowledge. Resources like this one, which is instructor-centered, practical, and digestible, can help inexperienced instructors navigate the culminating experience for the first time and can be helpful for seasoned instructors to find unique ideas for in-depth instruction and assessment.

Section 1:
Culminating Experiences in Higher Education

Section 1 includes three chapters that all focus on culminating experiences in higher education. The section provides foundational information and a unifying baseline for culminating experiences. These first three chapters offer context for the rest of the volume by defining culminating experiences, discussing assessment, and offering a perspective on student reflection as a valuable and necessary component of these culminating experiences.

While we recognize there are unique circumstances that may alter one's view of what constitutes a culminating experience, the high-impact framework for defining culminating experiences, used by McCluskey in the first chapter, presents a unifying mantra for educators that reverberates throughout the entire volume. The second chapter about assessment, by Payette and Gupta, builds on the high-impact goal and presents a specific institutional example that is used to provide exemplar assessment resources that can be used to evaluate culminating experiences in multidisciplinary contexts. The third and final chapter in this section describes a student-centered approach to reflection. Hamilton and Wildermuth offer strategic and practical ideas for incorporating reflection into high-impact culminating experiences.

Taken together, these chapters offer a historical and philosophical foundation for educators to consider when incorporating culminating experiences into their multidisciplinary programs.

Chapter 1

Defining Culminating Experiences

Lindsay M. McCluskey

SUNY Oswego

Abstract: Culminating educational experiences are high-impact practices (HIPs) (Kuh, 2008) that vary across disciplines and in graduate versus undergraduate settings; however, their aim is generally the same: to help prepare students – future employees – for "what's next?" beyond the confines of their classrooms (both physical and virtual) and their college or university. It is imperative to examine and understand culminating experiences as "employers and the public increasingly feel that universities are not doing enough to prepare students for the workforce" (Kinzie & Akyuz, 2022). Furthermore, students face an evolving and competitive job market as we emerge out of the COVID-19 pandemic domestically and globally and look to an uncertain economic, political, technological, geopolitical, and social future.

This chapter sets the stage for the rest of this book by providing an overview and examines the state of culminating experiences and high-impact practices, why culminating experiences are important for students, and encourages educators and administrators to design, implement, and assess them with faculty and students in mind from the outset.

Keywords: capstone, culminating experiences, employers, high-impact practices.

***

Culminating educational experiences are high-impact practices (HIPs) (Kuh, 2008) that vary across disciplines and in graduate and undergraduate settings. Although their context may vary, their aim is generally the same: to help prepare students – future employees – for "what's next?" beyond the confines of their classrooms, both physical and virtual. It is imperative to examine and understand culminating experiences as "employers and the public increasingly feel that universities are not doing enough to prepare students for the workforce" (Kinzie & Akyuz, 2022, para. 1). This is especially true as students face an evolving and competitive job market and look to an uncertain economic, political, technological, geopolitical, and social future.

This chapter sets the stage for the rest of this book by providing an overview, examining the state of culminating experiences and high-impact practices, and why culminating experiences are important for students. It encourages educators and administrators to design, implement, and assess them with faculty and students in mind from the outset.

The State of Culminating Experiences and High-Impact Practices

Prevalence and Types of Culminating Experiences

Culminating experiences are also called capstone experiences. Many culminating experiences provide active, applied experiential learning opportunities with some key elements of experiential learning: experiencing, reflecting, thinking, and acting (Institute for Experiential Learning, n.d.; Rogers & Galle, 2015). The University of South Carolina's National Resource Center for the First-Year Experience and Students in Transition has conducted numerous national studies, in 1999, 2011, and 2016 on "senior-specific practices and characteristics of senior capstone experiences" (Young & Van Scoy, 2016, p.14). Their 2016 study included an online survey that invited 3,419 institutions to participate, with 383 institutions replying (11.2% response rate). More than 93% of those surveyed indicated they provided at least one capstone experience for students. This included more than 99% (n=297) of 4-year institutions and more than 61% (n=35) of 2-year colleges (Young & Van Scoy, 2016).

Capstone experiences were broadly defined in this study, with respondents reporting department or discipline-based capstone courses, comprehensive exams or exams leading to certification or professional licensure, art exhibitions, portfolios, integrative or applied learning projects, theses or independent research papers, service-learning or community-based learning projects, and supervised practice (e.g., internships, student teaching) as among the types of capstone experiences that were available to their students. Department- or discipline-based courses were the most common type of capstone among the following fields of study: Biological Sciences, Agricultural, and Natural Resources; Physical Sciences, Mathematics, and Computer Science; Social Sciences; Business; Communications, Media, and Public Relations; and Engineering. Exhibitions were most common in Arts and Humanities, while certifications or professional licensure exams were most common among Health Professions. Education (student teaching) and social service professions (internships) reported supervised practice as the most common types of capstone (Young & Van Scoy, 2016).

Similarly, the Center for Engaged Learning noted:

Even within a single university, the range of practice in capstones can be significant, and for good reason. Capstone experiences may occur as the culmination of a disciplinary major or mark the integration of multidisciplinary learning across a core curriculum. In either case, there is no universal way students might synthesize and apply their learning (Center for Engaged Learning, n.d.).

The University of South Carolina's 2016 study suggested a substantial growth in senior capstone experiences over time, with just 78% of 4-year institutions reporting that they had offered them in 1999 (Young & Van Scoy, 2016).

While there are numerous types of culminating experiences discussed briefly in this chapter, this book focuses on multidisciplinary approaches in Business, the Humanities, Natural and Applied Sciences, and Social Sciences and the following types of culminating experiences specifically: theses, dissertations, applied projects, comprehensive examinations, portfolios, and internships. Theses, dissertations, applied projects, and comprehensive examinations are generally traditional graduate-level culminating experiences while theses, portfolios, applied projects, and internships are often undergraduate opportunities for professional development.

Theses and dissertations are original and robust research projects often undertaken at the graduate level, although there is sometimes disagreement about what separates one from the other (Cone & Foster, 1993). Cone & Foster (1993) said:

> In universities in the United States, it has become common to distinguish between dissertations and theses by referring to the work done for a master's degree as a thesis and that done for a doctoral degree as a dissertation. This is not a universally accepted distinction by any means, and some schools…refer to dissertations as theses (p. 3).

Cone and Foster (1993) differentiated between theses and dissertations when looking at the scope of the work undertaken, the expected contribution of the work to the discipline and academy, the originality of the work, and the level of independence and supervision associated with the work, noting that they defined theses as master's level "empirical research" done on a smaller scale with extensive guidance and dissertations as doctoral level "empirical research" completed with more autonomy (Cone & Foster, 1993, pp. 3-4).

Some disciplines provide an opportunity for students to complete an individual or collaborative applied project as a culminating experience. This may involve conducting original research, service learning or community-based learning, working with a client, creating a specific product (e.g., manuals, multimedia, podcasts, websites, webinars), or crafting a presentation (American Association of Colleges and Universities, n.d.; Center for Engaged Learning, n.d.).

Comprehensive examinations, which require extensive preparation, can be oral and/or written demonstrations of knowledge and skills (Cassuto, 2012; Center for Engaged Learning, n.d). Cassuto (2012) advocated that they should "look forward as well as backward" in order to be most effective and valuable to students (Cassuto, 2012).

Portfolios, which today are frequently electronic portfolios in many disciplines, "enable students to electronically collect their work over time, reflect upon their personal and academic growth, and then share selected items with others, including professors, advisors, and potential employers" (American Association of Colleges and Universities, n.d.). Portfolios allow students to showcase exemplary and relevant coursework and projects, concrete work samples from internships, and example materials from freelance gigs in order to demonstrate their skills, knowledge, and proficiency to not only their faculty supervisors and advisers but also to potential employers.

The prevalence of internships, which can be paid and unpaid, has been trending upward among colleges and universities (American Association of Colleges and Universities, n.d.; Kuh, 2008). Internships, many of which are completed for college or university credits, "provide students with direct experience in a work setting—usually related to their career interests—and to give them the benefit of supervision and coaching from professionals in the field" (American Association of Colleges and Universities, n.d.). Internships can be virtual or in-person opportunities and the National Association of Colleges and Employers' (NACE) 2021 Internship & Co-op Survey Report (with data collected from December 9, 2020, through February 5, 2021) indicated that the average hourly compensation for interns was $20.76 among its 227 NACE member respondents and 39 nonmember respondents (Koc et al., 2021).

High-Impact Practices: Features and Types

George D. Kuh (2008) is generally recognized as one of the key figures in establishing and proliferating the use of the term high-impact practices (Berrett, 2019; Finley & McNair, 2013; Kuh & Kinzie, 2018; Kuh et al., 2017; Rogers & Galle, 2015). Kuh et al. (2017) positioned HIPs as a:

> powerful set of interventions to foster student success. By student success, we mean an undergraduate experience marked by academic achievement, engagement in educationally purposeful activities, satisfaction, persistence, attainment of educational objectives, and acquisition of desired learning outcomes that prepare one to live an economically self-sufficient, civically responsible, and rewarding life.

The rationale for making student success a national priority is clear and persuasive: insuring [sic] that America and its citizens thrive in the global future requires access to a postsecondary education that results in high levels of learning and personal development for students of all backgrounds (p. 9).

According to Kuh, O'Donnell, & Schneider (2017), *features* of HIPs include:

- "Performance expectations set at appropriately high levels"

- "Significant investment of concentrated effort by students over an extended period of time"

- "Interactions with faculty and peers about substantive matters"

- "Experiences with diversity, wherein students are exposed to and must context with people and circumstances that differ from those with which students are familiar"

- "Frequent, timely, and constructive feedback"

- "Opportunities to discover relevance of learning through real-world applications"

- "Public demonstration of competence"

- "Periodic, structured opportunities to reflect and integrate learning" (p. 11).

According to the American Association of Colleges and Universities (n.d.) and Kuh et al. (2017), specific *types* of HIPs include:

- Capstone Courses and Projects

- Collaborative Assignments and Projects

- Common Intellectual Experiences

- Diversity/Global Learning

- ePortfolios

- First-Year Seminars and Experiences

- Internships

- Learning Communities

- Service Learning, Community Based Learning

- Undergraduate Research

- Writing-Intensive Courses

Still, Kuh & Kinzie (2018) acknowledged that *how* HIPs are created and executed impacts their quality and efficacy, and Kuh et al. (2017) recognized that HIPs do not take a one-size-fits-all approach:

> HIPs can take different forms, depending on learner characteristics, institutional priorities and contexts. The positive influence of participating in a HIP is likely a function of multiple effective educational practices that are characteristic of a HIP done well. Thus, what makes a HIP developmentally powerful is that all of them induce high levels of student engagement in substantive tasks that in turn deepen learning (p. 11).

High-Impact Practices: Influence on Students, Including Underrepresented Populations

Kuh et al. (2017) asserted that "a HIP experience typically has *compensatory effects* for undergraduates who are first in their family to attend college, are less well prepared academically, and are members of historically underrepresented racial and ethnic groups," (p. 9) and "participating in multiple HIPs has cumulative, additive effects for learning and persistence" (p. 16). At the same time, they claimed "HIPs participation is inequitable, with first generation, transfer students and African-American and Latino students least likely to have such experiences" (p. 9).

Finley and McNair (2013) used National Survey of Student Engagement (NSSE) data from a sample of 25,336 students in California, Oregon, and Wisconsin to examine the role of high-impact practices generally and on underrepresented and underserved populations more specifically, with learning communities, service-learning courses, study abroad experiences, internships, capstone courses, and research with a faculty member as the six included types of practices. The researchers explored several key research questions, including "Across different student groups, how does participation in specific high-impact practices and in various numbers of these practices affect students' perceptions of their learning?" (Finley & McNair, 2013, p. 5).

Their results showed that students who engaged in a high-impact practice "perceived their learning significantly more positively" than those who did not have that same experience (Finley & McNair, 2013, p. 9). Students who engaged in individual practices self-reported a range of an average of 4.3 to 8.5 points higher on a standardized scale for "engagement in deep learning and perceived gains" than those students who did not, with those who participated in internships reporting a 5.2 point boost, those who had a senior capstone reporting a 6.1 point boost, and those who did student/faculty research reporting a 8.1 point boost on this measure. Furthermore, their study showed "a measurable, significant, and positive relationship between students' cumulative participation in multiple high-impact practices, on the one hand, and their perceived engagement in deep learning and their perceived gains in learning, on the other" (Finley & McNair, 2013, p. 9). Students with no HIPs reported a score of 51.0 on a standardized scale, students with 1-2 HIPs reported a score of 57.3, students with 3-4 HIPs reported a score of 63.8, and students with 5-6 HIPs reported a score of 70.8. Furthermore, students with no HIPs reported lower levels of gains in general education, practical competence, and personal and social development than those with varying numbers of HIPs (Finley & McNair, 2013).

Finley and McNair (2013) also asked "Within particular underserved groups, what is the effect of participation in multiple high-impact practices on students' perceptions of their own learning?" (Finley & McNair, 2013, p. 5). Their findings showed that first-generation students who engaged in high-impact practices reported between 11 percent higher (1-2 HIPs) and 35 percent higher (5-6 HIPs) engagement in deep learning than students of that same cohort who did not participate in HIPs. Transfer students who engaged in high-impact practices reported between 14 percent higher (1-2 HIPs) and 40 percent higher (5-6 HIPs) engagement in deep learning than students of that same cohort who did not participate in HIPs. The researchers also broke down the data by racial and ethnic categories. African American students reported between 11 percent higher (1-2 HIPs) and 27 percent higher (5-6 HIPs) boosts in deep learning, while Asian American students reported between 10 percent higher (1-2 HIPs) and 47 percent higher (5-6 HIPs) and Hispanic students reported between 10 percent higher (1-2 HIPs) and 26 percent higher (5-6 HIPs). White students reported between 12 percent (1-2 HIPs) and 37 percent higher (5-6 HIPs) boosts in deep learning (Finley & McNair, 2013).

Why Culminating Experiences are Important

Student Benefits: Career Preparation and Readiness

In addition to the aforementioned benefits associated with student learning, culminating experiences can play a key role in influencing students' career preparation and trajectory in the workforce. In a graduate setting, culminating experiences often help prepare students for careers in academia or research roles, while undergraduate culminating experiences often help prepare students for roles in professional industries (Ketcham, 2021).

The National Association of Colleges and Employers (NACE) put career readiness into perspective as "the new career currency":

> Career readiness is a foundation from which to demonstrate requisite core competencies that broadly prepare the college educated for success in the workplace and lifelong career management…Career readiness is the foundation upon which a successful career is launched. Career readiness is, quite simply, the new career currency…For employers, career readiness plays an important role in sourcing talent, providing a means of identifying key skills and abilities across all job functions; similarly, career readiness offers employers a framework for developing talent through internship and other experiential education programs (NACE, n.d.).

NACE has defined eight career readiness competencies: career and self-development, communication, critical thinking, equity and inclusion, leadership, professionalism, teamwork, and technology (NACE, n.d.). NACE's Job Outlook 2022 report found that employers identified critical thinking (98.5%), communication (98.5%), teamwork (97.7%), equity and inclusion (85.4%), and professionalism (86.9%) as the top five most important skills, scoring these skills as "very important" or "extremely important" for college graduates. At the same time, employers identified technology (79.8%), teamwork (77.5%), equity and inclusion (72.1%), critical thinking (55.8%), and communication (54.3%) as the areas in which recent college graduates were "very proficient" or extremely proficient (Gray, 2021).

Finley and McNair's (2013) focus groups of underserved students from nine campuses in California, Oregon, and Wisconsin also shed light on students' perceptions regarding workforce preparation and career readiness. Demographically, these groups included 40 transfer students, 46 low-income students, and 48 first-generation students. There were 28 self-identified as Hispanic, 24 African American, 14 multiracial, 11 Asian American, 9 White, and 1 Arab American.

In addition to identifying particular skills (e.g., oral and written communication skills, leadership skills, critical thinking skills, problem-solving skills) as central to the workforce and employability, "students often said that hands-on experience is necessary for employability" (Finley & McNair, 2013, p. 25). HIPs, as envisioned by Kuh (2008) and when executed effectively, target the development of many of these imperative skills and competencies as well as facilitate these experiences.

Designing Culminating Experiences with Faculty and Students in Mind

Understanding Generation Z

According to the Pew Research Center, Generation Z is "the most racially and ethnically diverse generation" and "are on track to become the most well-educated generation yet" (Fry & Parker, 2018). It is also important to consider that Gen Z's relationship to technology is distinctive:

> Technology, in particular the rapid evolution of how people communicate and interact, is another generation-shaping consideration. Baby Boomers grew up as television expanded dramatically, changing their lifestyles and connection to the world in fundamental ways. Generation X grew up as the computer revolution was taking hold, and Millennials came of age during the internet explosion.

> In this progression, what is unique for Generation Z is that all of the above have been part of their lives from the start. The iPhone launched in 2007, when the oldest Gen Zers were 10. By the time they were in their teens, the primary means by which young Americans connected with the web was through mobile devices, WiFi and high-bandwidth cellular service. Social media, constant connectivity and on-demand entertainment and communication are innovations Millennials adapted to as they came of age. For those born after 1996, these are largely assumed.

> The implications of growing up in an 'always on' technological environment are only now coming into focus. Recent research has shown dramatic shifts in youth behaviors, attitudes and lifestyles – both positive and concerning – for those who came of age in this era...(Dimock, 2019, para. 2).

The demographic and psychographic characteristics of Gen Z are redefining the workforce and the workplace in many respects and employers that are looking to attract and retain new, diverse talent are taking note of Gen Z's needs and demands. Deloitte's Global 2022 Gen Z and Millennial Survey, which included an initial survey (November 2021-January 2022) and follow-up qualitative interviews (April 2022), provided key insights into the employment habits and mindset of Gen Z while offering recommendations for employers based on their findings (Deloitte, 2022a; Deloitte, 2022b). For example, 40% of Gen Zers would like to leave their jobs within two years, while 35% of Gen Zers would leave their jobs without another job lined up. Furthermore, 75% of Gen Zers expressed a desire for hybrid or remote work practices and 33% of Gen Zers working remotely said that doing so helped them save money on various expenses (e.g., commuting). Good work/life balance (32%), learning and development opportunities (29%), high salary or other financial benefits (24%), positive workplace culture (23%), opportunities to progress/grow/take on a leadership role (23%), deriving a sense of meaning from work (21%), and flexible working models (20%) were among the key reasons Gen Z respondents gave for choosing to work for their current employer (Deloitte, 2022b).

Furthermore, Deloitte's report noted:

> While societal and environmental impact, along with a diverse and inclusive culture, are not always at the top of the priority list when choosing a job, these continue to be critical issues in terms of retention. Those who are satisfied with their employers' societal and environmental impact, and their efforts to create a diverse and inclusive environment are more likely to want to stay with their employer for more than five years (Deloitte, 2022b, para. 2).

Lastly, Deloitte offered five priority areas of focus for business and industry as they consider how to attract and retain Gen Z and millennial workers:

- "Support people struggling with economic uncertainty and financial stress"

- "Empower people to lead and drive change"

- "Implement hybrid work strategies"

- "Prioritize climate action, and empower people to help"

- "Support better workplace mental health" (Deloitte, 2022b, pp. 33-35).

Examining what early career Gen Zers are experiencing and demanding can help faculty, administrators, and HIP partners better design HIP experiences for those still attending colleges and universities to 1) use some of the same characteristics and techniques to attract students to these experiences and maintain their interest and involvement and 2) better mirror what they are likely to encounter and hope to encounter in the workplace.

Faculty and Student Support

It is critical that educators, administrators, and key partners (e.g., internship site supervisors, applied project clients, etc.) take these key trends and factors into consideration when designing, implementing, and assessing culminating experiences for the college and university students of today and tomorrow to create mutually beneficial relationships and maximize these opportunities for all involved. This requires institutional support in the form of time, faculty and staff resources, and funding to demonstrate the commitment to these experiences as a significant priority. Rogers and Galle (2015) and Kuh et al. (2017) noted that institutional values, systems, priorities, and practices as well as a lack of incentives for faculty can become barriers to successfully integrating HIPs into the fabric of departments and institutions.

Berrett (2019) warned that HIPs can be viewed as "onerous" by faculty. Halonen and Dunn (2018) noted that while HIPs have become the gold standard in higher education, with colleges and universities promoting and "brag[ging] about" their efforts in this area, there are real concerns about their impact on faculty. They cautioned that:

> High-impact practices can be exhausting. They are labor intensive — for students, yes, but especially for faculty members. Designing and managing these efforts can be all-consuming and energy-draining. You may need a manageable case of obsessive-compulsive disorder just to survive the experience (Halonen & Dunn, 2018, para. 1).

These scholars — a former dean and a department chair — also offered a list of helpful solutions to help faculty "avoid burnout" associated with HIPs (Halonen & Dunn, 2018):

- "Be realistic about the scope at the outset"

- "Grade selectively"

- "Use rubrics"

- "When you can, use digital shortcuts"

- "Tailor how you offer feedback"

- "Stagger deadlines"

- "Involve students in grading"

- "Ask students to reflect on the experience"

- "Play the HIP card with your department chair"

- "Make a case for additional grading support"

- "Lobby for the weighting of HIPs in personnel decisions."

In short, Halonen and Dunn (2018) encouraged institutions and administrators to "recognize and reward" the HIP efforts faculty undertake to deliver them.

Furthermore, future success for high-impact culminating experiences will require institutions to remove or at least minimize traditional barriers that can plague students and prevent their participation in and success in HIPs. These barriers, as presented by Chepp and Greenman (2021), can include time, transportation, and financial barriers, other commitments, and a lack of appropriate mentorship and advising. Similarly, Finley and McNair's (2013) focus group participants indicated they needed better advising and guidance to get information about HIPs and understand their relevance and associated outcomes. Those participants also cited "competing priorities" as barriers to engaging in HIPs.

If institutions want to continue to reap the benefits of "bragging" rights associated with HIPs, they must double-down on 1) recognizing these barriers, 2) identifying concrete steps, solutions, and resources to address them head-on, and 3) implementing change. This is particularly critical to the long-term health and success of HIPs at this juncture given that we are now seeing increasing post-peak pandemic signs of both students and faculty "quiet quitting" in an effort to prioritize other needs, interests, and commitments (Intelligent.com Higher Education Team, 2022; McClure & Fryar, 2022).

Supplemental Material:

End of Chapter Discussion Questions

1) What types of culminating experiences does your college or university offer undergraduate students?

2) What types of culminating experiences does your college or university offer graduate students?

3) What steps, if any, has your college or university taken to eliminate barriers to participation in and success in HIPs for students?

4) What steps, if any, has your college or university taken to support faculty in executing HIPs?

5) What realistic steps could be taken in the future at your college or university to incentivize students to participate in HIPs?

6) What realistic steps could be taken in the future at your college or university to incentivize and reward faculty to participate in HIPs?

References

American Association of Colleges and Universities. (n.d.). *Trending Topic: High-Impact Practices.* AACU. https://www.aacu.org/trending-topics/high-impact

Berrett, D. (2019, March 7). How to bring high-impact practices to your courses. *The Chronicle of Higher Education.* https://www.chronicle.com/newsletter/teaching/2019-03-07?cid=gen_sign_in

Cassuto, L. (2012, March 4). The comprehensive exam: Make it relevant. *The Chronicle of Higher Education.* https://www.chronicle.com/article/the-comprehensive-exam-make-it-relevant/?cid2=gen_login_refresh&cid=gen_sign_in#:~:text=comprehensive%20exams%20mark%20the%20barrier,on%20and%20write%20a%20thesis

Center for Engaged Learning. (n.d.). *Capstone Experiences.* Elon University Center for Engaged Learning. https://www.centerforengagedlearning.org/resources/capstone-experiences/

Chepp, V. & Greenman, S. (2021, October 26). *Implementing Equity-Minded High-Impact Educational Practices.* 2021 Assessment Institute. https://assessmentinstitute.iupui.edu/overview/institute-files/2021-institute/handouts-tuesday-2021/16I_greenman_handouts.pdf

Cone, J.D. & Foster, S.L. (1993). *Dissertations and Theses From Start to Finish: Psychology and Related Fields.* American Psychological Association. Washington, D.C.

Deloitte. (2022a). *The Deloitte Global 2022 Gen Z and Millennial Survey.* https://www2.deloitte.com/global/en/pages/about-deloitte/articles/genzmillennialsurvey.html?id=gx:2ps:3gl:mgzs22:5GC1000068:awa:cons:052322:millennials%20in%20the%20workplace:b:c&gclid=CjwKCAjwv-GUBhAzEiwASUMm4prWuPuUhdWbhcG-YxbxwgWezQjSwWRnQkd8rLvPwT8Hv0XtxB3bpBoCmjQQAvD_BwE

Deloitte. (2022b). *Striving for balance, advocating for change: The Deloitte Global 2022 Gen Z and Millennial Survey.* https://www2.deloitte.com/content/dam/Deloitte/global/Documents/deloitte-2022-genz-millennial-survey.pdf

Dimock, M. (2019, January 17). *Defining generations: Where Millennials end and Generation Z begins.* Pew Research Center. https://www.pewresearch.o rg/fact-tank/2019/01/17/where-millennials-end-and-generation-z-begins/

Finley, A. & McNair, T. (2013). *Assessing Underserved Students' Engagement in High-Impact Practices.* Association of American Colleges and Universities. https://files.eric.ed.gov/fulltext/ED582014.pdf

Fry, R. & Parker, K. (2018, November 15). *Early Benchmarks Show 'Post-Millennials' on Track to Be Most Diverse, Best-Educated Generation Yet.* Pew Research Center. https://www.pewresearch.org/social-trends/2018/11/15/e arly-benchmarks-show-post-millennials-on-track-to-be-most-diverse-best-e ducated-generation-yet/

Gray, K. (2021, December 23). *Competencies: Employers Weigh Importance Versus New Grad Proficiency.* Naceweb. https://www.naceweb.org/career-readiness/competencies/competencies-employers-weigh-importance-versu s-new-grad-proficiency/

Halonen, J.S. & Dunn, D.S. (2018, November 27). Does high-impact teaching cause high-impact fatigue? *The Chronicle of Higher Education.* https://www.c hronicle.com/article/does-high-impact-teaching-cause-high-impact-fatigue/

Institute for Experiential Learning. (n.d). *What is Experiential Learning?* Experiential Learning Institute. https://experientiallearninginstitute.org/res ources/what-is-experiential-learning/

Intelligent.com Higher Education Team (2022, September 13). https://www.int elligent.com/one-third-of-college-students-quiet-quitting-to-preserve-men tal-health

Ketcham, C.J. (2021, October 6). *Inclusive Capstone Experiences, Pathways, and Pipelines.* Elon University Center for Engaged Learning. https://www.centerf orengagedlearning.org/inclusive-capstone-experiences-pathways-and-pipeline

Kinzie, J. & Akyuz, F. (2022, May 15). *Exploring the Influence of Course-Based Career Experiences and Faculty on Students' Career Preparation.* Naceweb. https://www.naceweb.org/career-readiness/trends-and-predictions/explori ng-the-influence-of-course-based-career-experiences-and-faculty-on-stude nts-career-preparation/

Koc, E.W., Kahn, J., Koncz, A., Galbraith, A., & Longenberger, A. (2021, April). *2021 Internship & Co-op Survey Report: Executive Summary.* Naceweb. https://www.naceweb.org/uploadedfiles/files/2021/publication/executive-summary/2021-nace-internship-and-co-op-survey-executive-summary.pdf

Kuh, G. D. (2008). *High-Impact Educational Practices: What They Are, Who Has Access to Them, and Why They Matter.* Association of American Colleges and Universities. https://provost.tufts.edu/celt/files/High-Impact-Ed-Practices1

Kuh, G. D. & Kinzie, J. (2018, May 1). What really makes a 'high-impact' practice high impact. *Inside Higher Ed.* https://www.insidehighered.com /views/201 8/05/01/kuh-and-kinzie-respond-essay-questioning-high-impact-practices -opinion

Kuh, G., O'Donnell, K., & Schneider C. (2017). HIPs at ten. *Change: The Magazine of Higher Learning, 49*(5), 8-16. http://doi.org/10.1080/00091383. 2017.1366805https://www.colorado.edu/odece/sites/default/files/attached -files/ku h_et_al_hips_at_10_change_2017.pdf

Rogers, S. & Galle, J. (2015). *How to be a "HIP" College Campus: Maximizing Learning in Undergraduate Education.* Rowman & Littlefield.

McClure, K. R. & Fryar, A. H. (2022, January 19). The great faculty disengagement. *The Chronicle of Higher Education.* https://www.chronicle.com/article/the-great-faculty-disengagement?cid2=gen_login_refresh&cid=gen_sign_in

National Association of Colleges and Employers (n.d.). *What is Career Readiness?* Naceweb. https://www.naceweb.org/career-readiness/competencies/career-readiness-defined/

Young, D.G. & Van Scoy, I. (2016, October 17). Senior capstones: National perspectives and one capstone journey. Presented at National Conference on Students in Transition, New Orleans, LA. University of South Carolina National Resource Center. https://sc.edu/nrc/system/pub_files/15324434 36 _0 .pdf

Chapter 2

Assessing Culminating Experiences: Balancing Rigor and Flexibility in the Design and Delivery of a Capstone Experience

Patricia R. Payette
University of Louisville

Nisha Gupta
Centre College

Abstract: This chapter describes the design, implementation, and assessment protocol development for the new Culminating Undergraduate Experience (CUE) at the University of Louisville (UofL). The authors contextualize their CUE efforts within the larger capstone trends in higher education and share the approach they took to engaging colleagues across their campus in the creation and piloting of a new critical thinking and culminating experiences requirement for all undergraduate programs. The chapter includes a discussion of their multi-year organizational change strategy steeped in a commitment to lasting change and scholarly rigor that is balanced by flexibility which allowed for meaningful assessment within diverse disciplinary contexts. The authors explain the importance of scaffolding change up over time, engaging stakeholders, and building the work on best practices, as well as assessing their progress every step of the way. Their discussion includes an explanation of faculty development and organization change strategies, assessment instruments, practical resources, and lessons learned for introducing and implementing similar curricular projects.

Keywords: Assessment, Learning community, Culminating experiences, Organizational change, Critical thinking, Collaboration, Faculty development

***

The Rise of the Culminating Experience

Capstone courses and capstone projects have long been a staple of undergraduate curricula. For a capstone opportunity, sometimes known as a culminating experience, students are asked to integrate and apply the disparate skills, disciplinary knowledge, and dispositions they have cultivated during the preceding years in college. These experiences have traditionally taken the form of research papers, recitals, performances, and portfolios, but have also included public demonstrations of students' competencies and private forms, such as group presentations, comprehensive exams, or an actual test (Zilvinski 2019). While students may commonly consider their capstone as a perfunctory hoop to jump through on the way to graduation, faculty and administrators value capstones as a final chance to have students demonstrate the skills and knowledge they expect of their graduates and to engage them in meaningful reflection, integrating their thinking across several domains of experiences (Rowles et al., 2004). Capstones add a much-needed layer of assessment of student learning (Rhodes & Agre-Kippenhan, 2011).

Capstones have long been a feature of certain degree programs, such as those in nursing, engineering and communication. However, when capstone experiences were included in George Kuh's 2008 much-heralded list of effective High Impact Practices (HIPs) in undergraduate education their popularity really took off. Kuh's (2008) HIPs include undergraduate research, first-year seminars, learning communities and capstones, among others, that have been shown to have significant and lasting benefits for learners (Roach & Alvey, 2021; Zilvinskis, 2019). In recognition of the remarkable benefits of capstones as HIPs, institutions across the spectrum have been integrating them into all types of majors and for all types of students. The intention is for students to be able to demonstrate in their final year their best work—the result of focused, intense, meaningful, and integrative intellectual activity. An ungirding assumption of these senior-level projects is that they help prepare students to transition into new roles as employees, as citizens, and lifelong learners (Ferren & Paris, 2013; Rowles et al., 2004).

When capstones are framed as culminating experiences, it places them in relationship to the overarching learning goals of an institution. As a requirement of a concentration or major, they invite students to "demonstrate proficiency and facility with key learning objectives articulated at the level of the concentration as well as the broader general education goals of their institution" (Brown, 2018, pp. 3-4). Therefore, the "culminating experience" moniker of applied learning practices positions a capstone experience as the apex of a student's intellectual and developmental undergraduate journey that "allows students to demonstrate a range of abilities" (Murray, 2008, p. 198). For many institutions, the assumption behind the embrace of this high-impact practice is that culminating senior experiences are an important bridge for learners between their academic careers and the world of work (Ferren & Paris 2013; Rowles et al., 2004). Successful culminating experiences have the following features: meaningful, structured reflections about themselves as learners; integration of learning from personal, academic and professional contexts; and potential pathways for life after college (Brown, 2018). The popularity and significance of culminating experiences invite us to consider conceptually how to structure and integrate these features into these assignments thoughtfully, how best to promote support, and how to assess these assignments at the departmental and institution level.

The Importance of Assessment

At its core, the culminating senior experience provides an important quality check for assessing program-level outcomes by asking: "What does the student know? What can the student do?" (Rowles et al, 2004). We can only answer these questions if our assessment of culminating experiences is thoughtfully designed and consistently carried out. Assessment efforts can be further challenged by the very nature of culminating projects in which we are interested in the final product and the learning process itself, both of which can be context-specific and multi-dimensional (Rhodes & Agre-Kippenham, 2004).

The key to success can be found in providing best practices and flexible structures for success for programs and faculty to use or adapt to their own disciplinary context. This was an effective approach for us at the University of Louisville as we introduced and institutionalized a new culminating experience across our campus. The University of Louisville is a large, metropolitan research university located in Louisville, Kentucky. The authors of this paper were hired as part of the Quality Enhancement Program (QEP) staff team to lead the project; Patricia served as the executive director and Nisha was the specialist for culminating undergraduate experiences. We describe our journey below and emphasize the deliberate approach we took to create, pilot, and disseminate relevant assessment practices that fit our faculty and our five-year initiative. We convey our experience within our specific institutional context while emphasizing the principles and guidelines that came out of our journey so that other institutions can build upon our work. We take to heart Rowles et al's (2004) reminder that "Capstone assessment is messy, with many fits and starts, and lengthy, with each successive plan drawing on the other before it." (p. 12). This chapter traces our own circuitous, lesson-filled path and provides guidance for others about to embark on their assessment journeys.

For some institutions, the motivation for a hard look and deep dive into culminating experiences comes after reviewing students' capstone artifacts and realizing the lack of alignment among the curriculum, learning activities, and the capstone performance. In some cases, the culminating experience is championed as "as a quality assessment tool to satisfy the standard of accreditation" (Catchings, 2004, pp. 6-7).

Honoring Our Institutional Context

Here at the University of Louisville, we jumped on the culminating experiences bandwagon when we introduced a new capstone requirement that was part of our institution's 2007 quality enhancement plan (QEP), a required component of institutional accreditation set in place by the Southern Association of Colleges and Schools Commission on Colleges (SACSCOC). The QEP is an innovative project proposed by each SACSCOC institution in order to address a self-identified student learning and/or student success gap. The QEP is launched at the time of an institution's re-accreditation process with SASCOC and is to be implemented over the course of five years with an impact report to follow.

In 2007, the University of Louisville launched its first QEP called Ideas to Action, or i2a. This wide-reaching QEP had two central goals: 1) students will be able to think critically; and 2) students will demonstrate their ability to integrate critical thinking skills with disciplinary knowledge in a culminating undergraduate experience (CUE), such as a thesis, serving learning project, internship or other capstone experience. Although completion of a capstone experience had already been a hallmark aspect of some of the existing undergraduate programs on our campus, such as engineering, nursing, and business, the launch of the QEP meant that all undergraduate programs needed to institute a CUE project for students prior to graduation.

Shortly after the accreditation evaluation team came for its on-campus visit in 2007 and gave our QEP proposal the green light, we shifted our focus first to defining critical thinking. The QEP staff team knew our campus "needed a common conception of what critical thinking actually entailed, a shared vocabulary that allowed for articulating and measuring learning goals and assessment methodologies across a wide array of disciplinary learning contexts." (Payette & Ross, 2016, p. 100). After vetting a number of critical thinking approaches, and conferring with our campus advisory board, known as the i2a Task Group, we chose the Paul-Elder (2014) framework. More information about our creation and use of our Task Group is discussed later in this article. This integrated, holistic critical thinking model provided our campus with a robust and flexible theory of thinking that other approaches lacked. Additionally, this approach centered around a set of thinking elements and intellectual standards that could be used across disciplines, course activities and assignments. See Table 2.1 for a list of the framework's components. The Paul-Elder framework was created by philosopher Richard Paul and educational psychologist Linda Elder in order to encapsulate the essence of critical thinking concepts using everyday language. They intended the discipline-neutral framework to be employed by faculty to design instruction, assignments, and tests and for students to employ when learning in any subject area. Paul and Elder created the Foundation for Critical Thinking (criticalthinking.org) as an educational and research organization to make available this framework and its corresponding tools and workshops.

The Paul-Elder framework provided an intellectual foundation that lent itself well to scaffolding learning across a program's curriculum and was the springboard for high-level thinking activities at the senior culminating experience. It was clearly aligned with the existing language and outcomes in our General Education curriculum. The intentional alignment across the curriculum set our campus up well for the corresponding scaffolding of assessment processes.

Table 2.1. Scaffolded Assessment Example

Elements of Thought

Purposes

Questions

Information

Inferences

Concepts

Assumptions

Implications

Points of View

Intellectual Standards

Clarity

Accuracy

Precision

Relevance

Depth

Breadth

Logicalness

Fairness

Significance

Completeness

Intellectual Traits

Intellectual Humility

Intellectual Courage

Intellectual Empathy

Intellectual Autonomy

Intellectual Integrity

Intellectual Perseverance

Confidence in Reason

Fairmindedness

A Common Conceptual Definition of a CUE

While our faculty could—with some faculty development support provided by our staff team—learn to overlay the common Paul-Elder vocabulary critical thinking on their teaching practices quite readily, the conceptualization of a common culminating undergraduate experience (CUE) requirement meant we were starting this conversation from scratch. We knew that having a shared understanding of what we mean by the skills involved with "critical thinking" was vital so we also had to make explicit our understanding of what makes an effective culminating experience. Without a shared concept of what constitutes a "culminating experience," we would not be able to implement an integrated assessment approach across schools and colleges. We worked with our Task Group to set up a subcommittee of interested faculty to exclusively focus on defining the CUE. This preliminary work of the CUE subcommittee, led by the specialist for CUEs, involved reviewing the literature to identify existing best practices, research and scholarship on capstone projects, and current models for defining culminating experiences.

Right away, the subcommittee realized that it was not practical or realistic to introduce a new CUE assignment format that every program must adhere to. Instead, we had to identify a common set of curricular features and assignment criteria for the CUE requirement that would "fit" across the over 100 undergraduate degree programs across 11 schools and colleges. The literature from *experiential education theory* (National Society for Experiential Education; Eyler, 2009) together with *integrative/applied learning* (see for example: Huber et al., 2007) provided the subcommittee with enough information to craft a set of common criteria that both described the nature of the experience and routes to assessment of the experience. We called these the CUE "Defining Features" and it meant regardless of the discipline – across engineering, English, music, finance, or nursing, etc. – students' CUEs would include these CUE Defining Features, or components:

1.   Is undertaken after sufficient academic preparation, e.g., after completion of at least 90 credits of coursework or key prerequisite courses.

2.   Is part or all of an approved or accepted:
     § credit-bearing course in the major, or;
     § experience in the discipline/major(e.g., honors project or independent study).
     The unit/department has the responsibility for designing the culminating undergraduate experience.

3. Provides the opportunity for demonstration of the student's mastery of content, reflection on accumulated content and experiences, and the integration and application of critical thinking skills.

4. Addresses an "authentic" issue. Authenticity includes meaningful, real-world issues, problems, or concerns that are relevant to the learner and the discipline and are shaped by practical constraints of time, space, or resources.

5. Incorporates ongoing, comprehensive feedback from students, faculty, or others involved with the experience (which may include midterm or final student evaluation, periodic review by department faculty, feedback from internship/practicum sites, or other assessment measures).

6. Results in output that can be assessed by internal or external reviewers using evaluation criteria favored by the discipline. Examples of outputs include a paper, portfolio, or performance.

This approach allowed us to provide necessary guidance and structure for faculty in order to emphasize the need for rigor and consistency in capstone experiences, while avoiding a prescriptive approach on a programmatically diverse campus (Rowles et al., 2004). The Defining Features approach also meant existing capstone experiences could be adapted to meet the new CUE criteria. Solidifying the Features was an important leap for our CUE development journey, proposing a shared, foundational understanding of what—as its essence–constitutes a CUE on our campus.

Attempting to create a common set of expectations for a learning experience as dynamic and diverse as a capstone and culminating experience is tricky. This set of expectations must be aligned with the realities of the campus and must be reflective of scholarly best practices. This shared construct will pay dividends by giving colleagues a shared vocabulary for this work and by simplifying the assessment process. When we have a shared concept of what "culminating experiences" actually entail at our institution, then we are able to align and share our assessment practices, even if our disciplinary contexts or specificity of those activities are quite diverse (Forest & Keith, 2004). The process of identifying the components that would become the Defining Features slowed down our ambitious timeline, but it ensured that we thoroughly understood best practices and could then engage our campus colleagues in vetting an approach that fit our faculty and their students.

Piloting our Defining Features

To introduce effectively a shared conception of what constitutes a "culminating undergraduate experience," we first had to ask our faculty colleagues to "test drive" this approach in their own teaching. We asked a group of faculty to pilot how the features "overlaid" on their existing culminating assignments and courses. We adapted the Faculty Learning Community (FLC) approach for this pilot. FLCs bring together a group of cross-disciplinary faculty together for ongoing learning around a teaching and learning topic. Typically FLCs create a small collaborative community for faculty to act as learners, coming together over the course of a year to benefit from a facilitated curriculum focused on enhancing teaching and learning, the scholarship of teaching, and community building. (Cox, 2004). We had earlier success in using the FLC model to bring together diverse faculty in order to teach and support them in incorporating the Paul-Elder critical thinking framework into their teaching.

Based on this prior experience, we felt using FLC would be ideal for introducing and helping faculty to launch the Defining Features in their respective culminating experiences. To do this, we assembled a group of 24 faculty to pilot an adoption of the Defining Features. Through a process of both strategically identifying and tapping faculty teaching existing senior-level courses and asking unit heads to put forth the names of their capstone faculty, the Faculty Learning Community on Culminating Undergraduate Experiences (FLC-CUE) was launched. This FLC was facilitated by our culminating experiences specialist and required participating faculty to read and discuss relevant scholarly articles, engage in a series of short formative activities to reflect on and shape their culminating assignment and assessment practices, and have ongoing, intensive discussions about taking the Defining Features from theory to practice. FLC-CUE participants were asked to identify an assignment or assessment that they could adapt or create to meet authentically the CUE Defining Features and submit that artifact as their "product" of this program.

Several participants identified existing assignments, such as a final project that they modified to include key elements, while others designed or redesigned the entire course to incorporate more fully these new, common Defining Features. For example, the Spanish Languages Capstone course content was redesigned around students' *demonstration of proficiency in real world settings* while the Computer Sciences Security Senior Seminar shifted the final assignment from a *case study model to a community-identified problem-solving exercise with formal report.* Teacher Education used its existing student-teacher practicum course to develop a series of *reflection entries and process-oriented assignments.*

The piloting of the CUE Defining Features led to the refinement and finalization of the common features but also allowed us to begin assessing the effectiveness of the CUE. Assessing the CUE has been a central part of our process. Assessment is used for individual student's learning, course improvement, and academic program development.

Our Assessment Principles & Practices

Using Assessment to Spark Intentional Design at the Course Level

All of our conversations with faculty, recommendations for assessment, and the tools we developed were based on best practices as well as teaching and learning scholarship. This meant we were slowing down to consult campus and external experts—and the literature—to inform our work. We consistently modeled the principle of "closing the loop" with our findings as part of the piloting and discovery process. The "closing the loop" principle in assessment practices promotes a feedback loop by organizing information learned from an experience, taking it back to inform goals, completing conversations, and discussing results with stakeholders who are vested in the exploratory or investigative process. Closing the loop "stimulates improvements in teaching, learning, and student services such as advising" (Banta & Blaich, 2010, p. 22).

Our "loop" included circling back to the Task Group about the results of the FLC-CUE to make our case for extending our piloting timeline because we needed more data from diverse disciplinary faculty. We also conducted information sessions to raise awareness across our campus that a well-designed CUE would provide invaluable information about what our students have learned. This allowed us to disabuse faculty of the notion that revising their culminating assignments was a hoop to jump through for accreditors and help them embrace the core question at the heart of assessing senior culminating experiences: "When we claim to be graduating students with specific skills or competencies, do we have evidence of our claims?" (Walvoord, 2004, p. 5).

We also used the CUE development opportunity to teach our faculty about the principles of "backward design" in which curricular and assignment planning begin with the end in mind. In backward design, educators clarify their goals and priorities as they answer a series of questions–what should students be able to demonstrate they know or do? What evidence would be acceptable? How do we plan learning experiences and instruction to achieve this? (Wiggins & McTighe, 2005). Some institutions find this backward design orientation beneficial after their annual review of their students' performance on capstone assignments is disappointing. Backward design prompts them to identify and grapple with the incongruity of curriculum goals, assignments, and teaching practices (Catchings, 2004).

Using an intentional, backward design approach (Wiggins, Wiggins & McTighe, 2005) with our faculty and program leaders, married with the CUE

Defining Features as guideposts, we were able to gain traction by shifting the focus of our work from "doing this because SACSCOC says so" to "we want to support your work so that your graduating seniors are able to achieve your goals for them." Along the way, our backward design conversations are attuned to creating assessment strategies that are aligned with our learning objectives and the teaching and learning strategies and "can be used to inform future revisions of either or both." (Ash & Clayton, 2009, p. 28).

With our common critical thinking skills across programs--and the defining features of a CUE--in place, we were able to develop companion assessment tools. We needed an approach to assessment that worked at the micro level, measuring student learning and the effectiveness of a course while also serving at the macro level, informing us how well a program is reaching its desired student learning goals (Murray et al., 2008). We consistently modeled—and emphasized—assessment as an iterative cycle of learning and the implicitly practical value it held for departments, programs, faculty, and for a view of learning at the institutional level.

Assessment with Direct Measures

We knew that our CUE assessment plan needed to include direct measures of learning. "Direct evidence of student learning is tangible, visible, self-explanatory, and compelling evidence of exactly what students have and have not learned." (Suskie, 2009, p. 21). Our CUE direct measures took the form of rubrics. Rubrics assist the instructor in making explicit, objective, and consistent the criteria for performance which otherwise is implicit when a letter grade is used as an indicator of performance. Clear criteria provide instructor-to-student communication about expectations for an assignment while giving consistent means to measure and collect evidence of student learning for program and course development. (Little, 2006).

Our CUE Student Reflection Rubric (Appendix A) works across institutional dimensions. This means the rubric could provide instructors with a common set of standards to inform assignment formats and to assess directly the resulting student artifacts. By aligning this rubric with our CUE Defining Features, academic programs could also use the rubric results in the aggregate to assess and provide data about how well students are able to demonstrate mastery of program-level outcomes. At the institutional level, it provides a framework for viewing graduating students' learning performance.

We crafted this CUE Rubric using language from our Paul-Elder critical thinking framework. Given that our QEP focused on *fostering students 'critical thinking* throughout General Education courses, asking students to apply these critical thinking skills in disciplinary-specific contexts through the CUE, we needed a strong alignment between the critical thinking scaffolded learning activities and the senior-level capstone experience (see CUE Defining Feature #3 on page 4). Hence the learning domains within the rubric included "critical thinking, "content application" and "reflection. Our shared Paul-Elder critical thinking framework also provided a common language for standards and elements that we used to draft the "cells" of this rubric. Teaching and learning models for rubric design provided much-needed guidance in the construction of the rubric. Little (2006) and Suskie (2009) were two resources that helped us define the categories and dimensions of the CUE Rubric.

As faculty and programs began to implement their CUE courses and assess student learning, feedback showed that the dimensions of the CUE Rubric were more *descriptive than evaluative*. We needed another way to evaluate how well students were demonstrating their ability to apply their learning to real-world contexts. The CUE rubric dimension of "content application" was certainly informative about student performance, but we found that we needed to expand the criteria and better perceive their ways of thinking and doing. To accomplish this, we developed a second rubric to allow for measuring students' ability with more depth complexity in relation to *application of one's thinking and one's learning.*

Our CUE subcommittee with representatives from all the undergraduate units convened to review the literature, examine meanings within discipline-specific contexts, and meet for over six months to come to a consensus on a concise set of dimensions. It drew specifically upon engagement research and the integrative learning and critical thinking literature. The American Association of Colleges and Universities (AACU) Value Rubrics project was emerging as a promising resource at the same time (Finley, 2011).

This work resulted in the Addressing Community Issues (ACI) Rubric which evaluates "the ability to bring to bear the culmination of one's learning across the program of study and apply to issues of the community of one's discipline or profession." (ACI definition). ACI has been described as a state of mind, a disposition, an ability, an efficacy, or a capacity in which one is serving others in the community; understanding and applying information; appreciation without discrimination of diversity; integrating ideas across content, disciplines, and experiences; engaging with real-world issues and questions; and critical thinking. (c.f., Axelson & Flick 2001; Colby et al., 2003; Kuh, 2008). We adopted this definition to inform and assist our writing of this rubric: ACI is the process of making connections among ideas and experiences, synthesizing and transferring learning to new, complex situations, with a deeper understanding in order to distinguish valuable knowledge, manage complexity, tolerate ambiguity, and consider different points of views.

The ACI Rubric (Appendix B) provides rich data about how students' thinking changes over time while also providing four categories of learning that inform the design of CUE courses and assignments. These categories include discipline-specific literature review, application of discipline-specific literature, discipline-based methodology, and critical discussion. Since capstone courses and assignments vary depending on the program of study, we advise faculty and programs to consider the purpose of their assessment to determine whether to use the CUE Rubric or the ACI Rubric. The former works well if *content analysis* is a learning objective and the latter is more suitable for *application of one's learning.*

Assessment with Indirect Measures

Indirect forms of assessment also are part of the CUE assessment effort. Indirect measures rely on "proxy signs" that students are learning and commonly take the form of students' self-reports of their perceptions of their own learning experiences on surveys, rating forms, and reflection instruments (Suskie, 2009, pp. 20-21). We developed two indirect instruments–CUE Student Evaluation (Appendix C) and CUE Student Reflection (Appendix D)–for instructors to fill in the picture of student learning that performance measures, like rubrics, cannot. These two surveys illuminate students' *experience* and help us better understand why students are successful or not, how we might improve the learning process, and highlight their attitudes and dispositions (Suskie, 2009).

The CUE Evaluation instrument asks students to report on their experience and how their skills were enhanced, while the CUE Reflection instrument asks students to report on the growth and development they gained as a result of their experience. The CUE Reflection provides a common set of questions that many instructors use to measure changes in students' thinking, administering the tool at the start of the course and again at the end. We once again employed the Paul-Elder critical thinking framework to give both context and structure to the instruments and continuity of learning concepts. One faculty member used the CUE Reflection pre- and post-course to demonstrate growth that supported Computer Engineering Capstone course learning outcomes as well as the existing engineering accreditation standards through the Accreditation Board for Engineering and Technology (ABET).

These assessment tools were developed to support faculty who were designing assignments and courses for the CUE and to provide avenues for assessing student learning. In the pilot phase, and over time, as faculty began teaching CUEs, we saw a key issue emerge: students need to be able to demonstrate their ability to apply their learning to real-world contexts. Only in practice with faculty, did we begin to appreciate the importance of including intentional reflection as part of the assessment process and the value of these rubrics. Building in a reflection process requires thoughtful, intentional prompts purposefully planned into one's pedagogy.

Building Capacity at Program Level: Introducing Requirements and Resources

The CUE development process discussed above—from adopting common components for our new required capstone experience to the development and piloting of indirect and direct assessments---required us to engage individual faculty and cohorts of select faculty in the research, development, and piloting process. Working closely with willing faculty on this process not only enabled buy-in to the CUE and QEP goals, but it also allowed us to be nimble in the research and development phase of the QEP before releasing CUE expectations to the wider campus.

New CUE Requirement and Reporting Structures

In order to support the next step, introducing the CUE to a wider campus audience to support the gradual adoption of the new CUE program requirement, we began to consider how to engage and support units in embracing the CUE at the program level. Because the CUE was a new curricular requirement related to our QEP and was a mandatory aspect of institutional accreditation, it permitted us to leverage accreditation as the reason for their compliance with this change. However, we had to balance this conversation about compliance with our desire to earn faculty commitment to the CUE because of its potential to enhance student learning through a well-designed capstone experience.

One essential leverage point was to use our accreditation requirement and five-year timeline to create a deadline by which units and departments were required to put their CUE assignments and courses in place. Faculty had to ensure that the Defining Features were reflected in an existing capstone assignment or activity or they had to create a new assignment for the capstone course that met the Defining Features. The QEP Task Group, with input from the QEP staff team, agreed that departments would have two years to put the CUE in place for at least 50% of their programs. Progress at the department and program level was tracked through the existing Student Learning Outcomes (SLO) Annual report. This report requires programs to submit annually a narrative that includes their program mission; program goals; student learning outcomes for each goal; measures and targets; insights from the prior academic year; and an action plan based on those findings. The CUE SLO became one of three SLO categories that each program reported on. When it came to reporting on the CUE "measures and targets" for these institutional reports, many programs found the existing CUE Rubric and ACI Rubric helpful tools to recommend completing their reports.

By requiring programs to document their CUE plans or progress on the SLO Annual Report that they already had completed and submitted to our Office of Academic Planning and Accountability (OAPA), we were able to integrate seamlessly CUE planning into existing program-level protocols. And, by allowing them to "scaffold up" their CUE progress over two academic years, we were able to give them the flexibility to introduce, develop, and report on this new requirement in a way that made sense for their own program and departmental planning processes. These reporting expectations, created by our OAPA institutional effectiveness colleagues, that required units to document the continuous improvement of student achievement at the program level were just getting established as the CUE was being implemented, allowing us to align our QEP-related requirements to new reporting structures.

Data-based CUE Conversations and the role of the CUE Toolkit

The second important leverage point to bolster CUE adoption at the program level came from the wealth of pilot program findings we had assembled. We had sample assignments and valuable feedback from the faculty who had piloted the CUE assessment documents and who had developed or revised courses that fit both CUE Defining Features and specific academic program requirements. These pilot experiences provided excellent examples for other faculty colleagues to model additional CUE courses, assignments, and learning outcomes.

To help empower programs and units to adopt the CUE at the program level, or adapt existing capstones, and to help faculty design assignments and courses that meet the common Defining Features, we created and launched a set of online resources of curricular and pedagogical tools to help faculty Our CUE Toolkit provides faculty and programs with best practices, sample assignments and syllabi language, and literature and further readings for each of the CUE Defining Features (https://louisville.edu/ideastoaction/about/cue/curriculartoolkit). Each CUE Defining Feature is "unpacked" through sample language, examples of CUE courses, and further scholarly reading. As the number of CUEs grew, our second phase of the toolkit included supportive teaching practices, sample assignments, standardized assessment instruments, and a growing body of successful course design models. This toolkit can be viewed at: (https://louisville.edu/ideastoaction/about/cue/cue-resources-for-course-design-assignments-and-teaching-practices)

It is clear that the capstone opportunity is often a vital and highly visible component of an academic program. Program leaders and faculty often value this program component for their students because of a capstone's potential to "foster deep learning, build significant relationships with faculty, and develop academic and professional skills." (Brown University, 2018, p. 3). However, the potential of these high-profile curricular activities as a springboard for engagement in assessment –and as a rich source of data–at the course, program and institutional level is sometimes overlooked.

Our scaffolded change strategy discussed above was deliberate. We assembled and shared practical curricular tools, developed and piloted homegrown rubrics that aligned with our lower-division general education outcome vocabulary, piloted new structures with instructors who were early adopters, and aimed to piggyback on existing program reporting structures. This multi-year approach to introducing and ramping up this CUE requirement shows our appreciation for our campus context and how we were attuned to helping colleagues embrace the CUE requirement as an opportunity to improve existing practices and not demand that they completely rethink their capstone experience.

Using the Institutional Lens to Deepen and Strengthen Practices Employing a Campus Advisory Committee.

Introducing new curricular goals, supporting disparate disciplinary-based colleagues in making these changes meaningful, and then assessing learning and tracking results can be a daunting process. At a large, research-intensive university like our own, it sometimes felt like an uphill battle. An invaluable foundation to this process is a university-wide advisory board for the steering committee. While many universities establish an advisory board to develop and implement at QEP, they are sometimes underutilized or launched without a clear charge and purpose and can flounder.

Our QEP Task Group was a lynchpin to our success because of how we organized and tapped them as advocates for our change process and as disciplinary experts. The QEP Task Group, chaired by our QEP executive director, was made up of faculty representatives from each of the academic units and included a student representative and the other members of our QEP staff team. Their written charge—created by the QEP staff team but handed down from the provost on official letterhead—made it clear that they were to be active agents in making the QEP project a reality on campus and in their respective units. Subcommittees were established to take a deep dive into key components of the QEP, including the CUE, and make recommendations to the larger Task Group body for input before releasing information and requirements to the campus at large. The CUE subcommittee members were Task Group faculty who helped our Specialist for CUE staff members engage at every level of the CUE development and assessment process.

One vital component to our QEP and CUE success was our ability to equip members of our Task Group to be ambassadors with their disciplinary-based colleagues when it came to introducing new critical thinking and capstone expectations. This collaborative planning process, which often involved Task Group members co-creating and co-delivering presentations about the QEP to departmental colleagues or other faculty meetings on campus, allowed us to put the focus on unpacking new expectations using discipline-specific language, norms, and opportunities instead of taking on these changes because our accreditors are forcing us too. We discovered that it was far more productive to engage faculty in dialogue about our QEP- or CUE-related goals when we started by asking them about *their* critical thinking and capstone-related goals for students, and then introduced our rubrics, curricular tools and outcomes as helpful strategies to accomplish or elevate the work they were already doing. Beginning with a view of assessment and curricular practices at the local level, before widening the conversation and framing them within the context of the institution and its change agenda, went a long way to winning the hearts and minds of our colleagues rather than starting with a set of required hoops they or their program must jump through.

An advisory group or campus committee should be made up of faculty and staff from the "front lines" of the assessment or curricular change work who can give new ideas and approaches a reality check and become strategic allies through every stage of the change process. A well-run advisory board provides an essential, cross-section of institutional perspective and assists with "strategic thinking, peer advisory and management of the natural ebb and flow" of your change initiative (Payette & Shaw, 2010).

Plugging into University Structures and Standards

Aligning our CUE activities with existing university structures and programs was another strategic move to ensure that we could weave this new curricular component into the fabric of our culture. The nature of the new CUE requirement and its connection to a mandatory aspect of reaccreditation justified making the CUE part of the President's Scorecard. The Scorecard was a public-facing accountability report in which our institution shared goals and metrics drawn from its strategic plan and updated its annual progress toward those goals. Ensuring that our CUE-related (and critical thinking-related) goals for our institution were represented and updated annually on the Scorecard provided our QEP change agents with the "stick" to induce units and programs to make progress on CUE integration and report on that progress and provided a "carrot" by ensuring that these same units and programs were called out by name as QEP adopters when sharing information with our institution leaders.

Change agents can lean into common sources of institutional data to assist with making the case for student success or new curricular programs. We used our current campus NSSE data to help tell the story of our students' experiences with critical thinking and CUE-related activities and make the case for our QEP. We used NSSE items related to critical thinking and those related to a) *culminating senior experiences* and b) *the institution contributing to students' solving complex real-world problems* as rich sources to measure impact by comparing NSSE results pre-QEP and post-QEP. An important piece of any assessment puzzle is considering the institutional learning assessment instruments that have been in use—or could be employed—to fill the picture of what students are, or not gaining, through capstone experiences or other pedagogical practices.

In order to ensure that our emerging assessment work was not relegated to a "QEP silo" required that we partner with other offices on campus whose mission overlapped with CUE goals. This included collaborating with our student affairs colleagues to employ some of our critical thinking and reflection to define learning outcomes and assessment practices with student activities and programs outside of the classroom. One collaboration that was particularly fruitful involved working with the Office of the Vice President for Community Engagement as part of our CUE programs and efforts. Natural areas for cross-pollination across our programs included inviting one of their representatives to connect conversations around community engagement with the work our faculty were doing in our FLC-CUE, sharing our CUE Student Reflection with their staff to capture the impact of community engagement work, and working on campus-wide projects together such as the Carnegie Community Engagement Classification application and showcase events in which students presented their research or capstone projects, including CUEs.

Building trust and cooperation across campus programs takes time and effort, but this can be considered an investment in the meaningful success of a change initiative. Given that curricular decisions on our campus were largely decentralized, we needed to foster what Kezar and Eckel (2002) described as a "collegial culture" in which progress is made through dialogue and conversation, not top-down fiats. We learned to lead collegial conversations with the needs of learners and faculty at the center, making the accreditation requirement merely the frame within which we were committed to making positive change.

Conclusion, Recommendations & Resources

Proposing, implementing and assessing the new CUE requirement on our campus was a complicated project that taught us important lessons about fostering change and innovation with diverse stakeholders. We learned the importance of scaffolding change over time, engaging stakeholders, building on the work on best practices, and assessing our progress every step of the way. We found that centering our assessment conversations with colleagues around learning goals/outcomes and capstone assignments, the need to make progress toward those goals visible was more fruitful than framing assessment activities as about accreditation or institutional reporting. Based on this experience, we offer the following recommendations for implementing similar projects.

Start Small, Do it Well, then Expand

Starting small, doing it well, then expanding is a helpful philosophy when beginning large-scale change initiatives. "Conducting small-scale pilot programs with early adopters creates a low-risk, learning atmosphere that helps everyone forge new ground together and figure out what is working and what is not" (Detmering & Payette, 2021, p. 960). When concerns arise about the feasibility of new pedagogical or assessment tools, change agents can advocate for assessing those concerns through a pilot program so that progress does not get stalled before all the questions are answered. Gathering information—the good, the bad, and the ugly—during a pilot, and then feeding it back into planning, is a helpful way to build trust across stakeholders and model a commitment to the assessment cycle. We learned not to be afraid to extend or repeat our CUE pilot program and gather additional data because this added valuable depth and breadth to our strategy for scaling up our introduction of innovation and assessment approaches, even when they slowed down a predetermined timeline.

Frame Assessment as Commitment to Learning, not Compliance

Working on a QEP—and the CUE requirement—taught us the value of framing the assessment of student learning as a benefit to everyone involved. It is natural to expect faculty and staff to filter assessment work or curricular change through the lens of "What's in it for me?" (Suskie, 2004). We established structures and opportunities for input, such as the CUE subcommittee, and then involved faculty in the process of leveraging their own lived experience as instructors—and brought their disciplinary or departmental lenses to the fore–as we created, piloted, and shared new assessment tools and protocols. In this way, our QEP staff team served as liaisons who assisted faculty and program leaders in making larger institutional priorities meaningful, relevant, and accessible.

Balance Rigor with Flexibility

Throughout our years of working on the CUE requirement, we found numerous ways to ensure we were intentional and scholarly with our work, while at the same time affording flexibility and choice along the way. We ensured that our definitions, recommendations, and assessment practices had a solid scholarly foundation. This meant an investment of the QEP staff team's time—especially the Specialist for CUEs--in a rigorous review of the literature on capstones, strategies for pedagogy and reflection, and applied learning practices. Knowing the principles and best practices of culminating experiences and how to assess them provided a bedrock of knowledge upon which we could then teach faculty to apply them in diverse disciplinary contexts. This allowed us to achieve a balance of rigor and flexibility in our work with individual faculty in helping us reach our wider goals of the QEP. We demonstrated this principle in the ways in which the Defining Features provided guidance to faculty on what to include in a CUE, while allowing a wide range of choices in how they met those guidelines. We also created rubrics and reflection tools that were scholarly which our colleagues could choose to use or adapt for their needs. Our commitment to piloting the CUE components within the QEP itself modeled for colleagues how to be rigorous and thoughtful in our launch of new tools or curricular structures while assessing those approaches and being flexible to make changes based on what we learned along the way.

Supplemental Resources

1. U of L Resources for Developing & Assessing Culminating Experiences

The appendices of this chapter include the CUE rubrics that were developed and implemented as part of our QEP and can be adapted or used by other individuals or organizations with proper attribution to the University of Louisville.

The CUE Curricular Toolkit is a publicly accessible website that provides support and resources for others who are developing, implementing, and assessing culminating undergraduate experiences.

https://louisville.edu/ideastoaction/about/cue/curriculartoolkit

2. Rubric Resources

Rubistar is an interactive website and repository for instructors looking for support in creating rubrics or accessing existing rubrics in their field:

http://rubistar.4teachers.org/index.php

These references provide an explanation and design of grading rubrics:

Little, D. (2006). Grading with rubrics: Developing a fair and efficient assessment tool. https://ira.virginia.edu/sites/ias.virginia.edu/files/trc_gradingrubric.pdf

Georgetown University Assessment: https://assessment.georgetown.edu/home/course-level-assessment/interpreting-evidence-of-learning/rubrics/

3. Additional Readings on Experiential Learning that might be useful for *appli*.

Simons, L., Fehr, L., Blank, N., Connell, H., Georganas, D., Fernandez, D., & Peterson, V. (2012). Lessons learned from experiential learning: what do students learn from a practicum/internship? *International Journal of Teaching and Learning in Higher Education, 24*(3), 325-334.*ed learning courses, assignment, and assessment design.*

Felten, P., Gardner, J. N., Schroeder, C. C., Lambert, L. M., Barefoot, B. O., & Hrabowski, F. A. (2016). *The undergraduate experience: Focusing institutions on what matters most.* John Wiley & Sons.

National Society for Experiential Education from https://www.nsee.org/

References

Ash, S. L., & Clayton, P. H. (2009). Generating, deepening, and documenting learning: The power of critical reflection in applied learning. *Journal of Applied Learning in Higher Education, 1,* 25–48.

Axelson, R. D., & Flick, A. (2011). Defining student engagement. *Change: The Magazine of Higher Learning, 43*(1), 38–43. https://doi.org/10.1080/00091383 .2011.533096

Banta, T.W. & Blaich, C. (2010). Closing the assessment loop, *Change: The Magazine of Higher Learning, 43(1),* 22-27. http://doi.org/10.1080/00091383.2011.538642

Banta, T. W., & Palomba, C. A. (2014). *Assessment essentials: Planning, implementing, and improving assessment in higher education.* John Wiley & Sons.

Bean, J. C. (2011). *Engaging ideas: The professor's guide to integrating writing, critical thinking, and active learning in the classroom.* John Wiley & Sons.

Brown University. (2018). Crafting meaningful culminating experiences: Best practices for capstones in the concentration. Brown University academics. https://www.brown.edu/academics/college/support/faculty/sites/brown.e du.academics.college.support.faculty/files/uploads/Capstone%20Report_R evised%20with%20Ex%20Sum.pdf

Catchings, B. (2004). Capstones and quality: The culminating experience as assessment. *Assessment Update, 16*(1), 6-7. https://doi.org/10.1002/au.161

Colby, A., Ehrlich, T., Beaumont, E., & Stephens, J. (2003). Educating undergraduates for responsible citizenship. *Change: The Magazine of Higher Learning,* 35(6), 40-48. https://doi.org/10.1080/00091380309604127

Cox, M. D. (2004). Introduction to faculty learning communities. *New directions for teaching and learning, 2004*(97), 5-23. https://doi.org/10.1002/tl.129

Darling-Hammond, L., & Snyder, J. (2000). Authentic assessment of teaching in context. *Teaching and teacher education, 16*(5-6), 523-545. https://doi.org/10 .1016/s0742-051x(00)00015-9

Detmering, R., & Payette, P. (2021). Finding a new fit for student success: Librarians as agents of teaching innovation and institutional change. *Journal of Library Administration, 61*(8), 947-963. https://doi.org/10.1080/01930826.2021.1984138

Eyler, J. (2009). The power of experiential education. *Liberal education,* 95(4), 24-31. https://files.eric.ed.gov/fulltext/EJ871318.pdf

Ferren, A., & Paris, D. (2013). How students, faculty, and institutions can fulfill the promise of capstones. *Peer Review, 15*(4), 4.

Finley, A. P. (2011). How reliable are the VALUE rubrics? *Peer Review, 13*(4/1), 31.

Forest, J. J., & Keith, B. (2004). Assessing students' moral awareness. *Assessment Update, 15*(6), 10-12. https://doi.org/10.1002/au.161

Green, K., & Hutchings, P. (2018). Faculty engagement with integrative assignment design: Connecting teaching and assessment. *New Directions for Teaching and Learning,* 155, 39-46. https://doi.org/10.1002/tl.20301

Huber, M. T., Hutchings, P., Gale, R., Miller, R., & Breen, M. (2007). Leading initiatives for integrative learning. *Liberal Education,* 93(2), 46-51. https://files. eric.ed.gov/fulltext/EJ775636.pdf

Huber, M. & Hutchings, P. (2004). *Integrative learning: Mapping the terrain.* Association of American Colleges and Universities.

Kezar, A. & Eckel, P. (2002). The effect of institutional culture on change strategies in higher education, *The Journal of Higher Education, 73*(4), 435-460. https://doi.org/10.1353/jhe.2002.0038

Kuh, G. D. (2003). What we're learning about student engagement from NSSE: Benchmarks for effective educational practices. *Change: The Magazine of Higher Learning,* 35(2), 24-32. https://doi.org/10.1080/00091380309604090

Kuh, G. D. (2008). *High-impact educational practices.* Association of American Colleges and Universities.

Little, D. (2006). Grading with rubrics: Developing a fair and efficient assessment tool. *Teaching Concerns,* 1-3. https://ira.virginia.edu/sites/ias.virginia.edu/files/trc_gradingrubric.pdf

Murray, M. C., Perez, J., & Guimaraes, M. (2008). A model for using a capstone experience as one method of assessment of an information systems degree program. *Journal of Information Systems Education, 19*(2), 197. https://digitalcommons.kennesaw.edu/cgi/viewcontent.cgi?article=2379&context=facpubs

National Society for Experiential Education (n.d.) https://www.nsee.org/

Paul, R. & Elder, L. (2014). The miniature guide to critical thinking: concepts and tools. (7th Ed.). Foundation for Critical Thinking.

Payette, P., & Ross, E. (2016). Making a campus-wide commitment to critical thinking: Insights and promising practices utilizing the Paul-Elder approach at the University of Louisville. *Inquiry: Critical Thinking Across the Disciplines, 31*(1), 98-110. https://doi.org/10.5840/inquiryct20163118

Payette, P., & Shaw, A. (2010). Establishing, maximizing, and refining your advisory board. *Academic Briefing.* https://www.academicbriefing.com/administration/establishing-maximizing-and-refining-your-advisory-board

Roach, S. & Alvey, J. (2021, February 4). Fostering integrative learning and reflection through "signature assignments." *AAC&U Liberal Education.* https://www.aacu.org/article/fostering-integrative-learning-and-reflection-through-signature-assignments

Rhodes, T. L. (2011). Emerging evidence on using rubrics. *Peer Review, 13*(4/1), 4.

Rhodes, T. L., & Agre-Kippenhan, S. (2004). A multiplicity of learning: Capstones at Portland State University. *Assessment Update, 16*(1), 4-5. https://doi.org/10.1002/au.161

Rowles, C. J., Koch, D. C., Hundley, S. P., & Hamilton, S. J. (2004). Toward a model for capstone experiences: Mountaintops, magnets, and mandates. *Assessment Update, 16*(1), 1. https://doi.org/10.1002/au.30239

Stevens, D. & Levi, A. (2005) *Introduction to Rubrics: An assessment tool to save grading time, convey effective feedback, and promote student learning.* Stylus.

Suskie, L. (2009). *Assessing student learning: A common sense guide.* Jossey-Bass.

Walvoord, B. (2004). *Assessment clear and simple: A practical guide for institution, departments and general education.* Jossey-Bass.

Wiggins, G., Wiggins, G. P., & McTighe, J. (2005). *Understanding by design.* ASCD.

Zilvinskis, J. (2019). Measuring quality in high-impact practices. Higher Education, 78(4), 687-709. http://dx.doi.org.ezproxy.centre.edu/10.1007/s10734-019-0036

Appendix:

University of Louisville. Ideas to Action. CUE Student Reflection Rubric.

	4-Exemplary	3-Proficient	2-Developing	1-Beginning
Content Application	Comprehensive (Depth and Breadth) connections made among knowledge gained in the academic program and *culminating experience.*	Thorough (Depth) discussion of the connections among some content with the *culminating experience.*	Superficial connections are made among some knowledge gained in the academic program and *culminating experience.*	Few, if any attempts are made to connect knowledge gained in the academic program with *the culminating experience.*
Critical Thinking	Clearly identifies the relevant issue, topic or situation for the experience.	Clearly identifies a topic or situation for the experience.	Formulates an identifiable issue, topic or situation.	Unclear identification of the issue, topic or situation for the experience.
	Accurately interprets relevant information.	Accurate interpretation of limited relevant information.	Either inaccurate interpretations or irrelevant information are present.	Inaccurate interpretation and irrelevant information are present.
	Develops well-reasoned conclusions.	Develops limited well reasoned conclusions.	Develops superficial conclusions.	Attempts to draw conclusions but they are undeveloped
	Consistently considers assumptions, implications and consequences of alternative points of view.	Usually considers assumptions, implications and consequences of alternative points of view.	Attempts to consider assumptions, implications and consequences of alternative points of view.	Single focus of assumptions, implications and consequences.
Reflection (If included as a component of the graded project)	Clear, comprehensive discussion about how participating in the *culminating experience* changed or enhanced their ability to address either a real-world or disciplinary issue, topic, or situation.	Clear, thorough discussion about how participating in the *culminating experience* changed or enhanced their ability to address either a real-world or disciplinary issue, topic, or situation.	Superficial discussion about how participating in the *culminating experience* changed or enhanced their ability to address either a real-world or disciplinary issue, topic, or situation.	Unclear discussion about how participating in the *culminating experience* changed or enhanced their ability to address either a real-world or disciplinary issue, topic, or situation.

Comments:

*Adapted from the Foundation for Critical Thinking's Critical Thinking Grid (www.criticalthinking.org)and the National Service Learning Clearinghouse's Using Rubrics to Assess Learning through Service in Maine (http://www.winona.edu/AIR /documents/Guide3.pdf)

Critical Thinking Applied Rubric.

For use with CUE and experiential learning contexts.

DESCRIPTOR	EXCEPTIONAL (4)	ACCEPTABLE (3)	DEVELOPING (2)	BEGINNING (1)
Discipline Specific Literature Review Demonstrate the ability to examine, organize and evaluate "valuable" knowledge by comparing and contrasting knowledge in at least one field of study	Comprehensive (Depth and Breadth) connections made among knowledge gained	Thorough (Depth) discussion of the connections among some content	Superficial connections made among knowledge/content gained in the academic program	Few, if any attempts to make connections among knowledge/content gained
Grounded in Discipline Appropriate Literature Integrate alternate, divergent or contradictory perspectives or ideas	Situates claim or argument in a larger context and clearly demonstrates awareness of inter-relationships among self, the discipline, society, and culture	Situates claim or argument in a larger context and demonstrates some awareness of inter-relationships among self, the discipline, society and culture	Situates claim or argument with some defined context and demonstrates little awareness of inter-relationships among self, the discipline, society, and culture	Does not situate claim or argument in a larger context and does not yet demonstrate awareness of inter-relationships among self, the discipline, society, and culture
Discipline-based Methodology Demonstrate the ability to transfer and apply knowledge using a discipline-based approach(-es)	Clearly and reflectively applies relevant argumentation and methodology of the discipline	Applies relevant argumentation and methodology of the discipline	Attempts relevant argumentation and methodology of the discipline	Does not incorporate appropriate argumentation and methodology of the discipline
Critical Discussion Show discipline-based appropriate understanding of diversity of options/thought processes	Examines conclusions, uses reasonable judgment, discriminates rationally, synthesizes data, views information critically	Formulates conclusions, recognizes arguments, notices differences, evaluates data, seeks out information	Identifies some conclusions, sees some arguments, identifies some differences, paraphrases data, assumes information valid	Fails to draw conclusions, sees no arguments, overlooks differences, repeats data, omits research

University of Louisville. Ideas to Action.

Culminating Undergraduate Experience (CUE) Student Reflection*

Course: _____

CUE: _____

Please respond to the following questions about your CUE:

1. Content Application

   a. What specific skills and knowledge from previous courses did you use when completing the CUE?

   b. What new skills and knowledge did you gain from completing the CUE?

   c. How did participating in the CUE help you either relate your classroom work to the real world or contribute to knowledge in the discipline?

2. Critical Thinking

   How did completing the CUE help you:

   a. Clearly identify the key issue, topic, or situation for the experience

   b. Accurately interpret relevant information

   c. Develop wellf reasoned, specific conclusions and problems

   d. Consider assumptions, implications and consequences of alternative points of view

   e. Precisely communicate the experience to others

3. Self Development

   a. What difference has participating in the CUE made in your intellectual, personal, ethical, and/or spiritual development?

   b. Why was the CUE valuable to you as a learner?

   c. How has your work in the CUE been relevant, practical or applicable for you and your career goals?

4. Please include any additional reflection about the CUE that you feel is relevant and important.

*Adapted from Paul, R. & Elder, L. (2008). The miniature guide to critical thinking: Concepts and tools. Dillon Beach, CA: Foundation for Critical Thinking and Zubizaretta, J. (2009). The learning portfolio: Reflective practice for improving student learning. San Francisco, CA: Jossey-Bass.

University of Louisville. Ideas to Action.
Culminating Undergraduate Experience Student Evaluation*

Course: _____

Culminating Undergraduate Experience: _____

Please indicate the extent of your agreement with each of the following statements about your culminating undergraduate experience:

	Strongly Disagree	Disagree		Agree	Strongly Agree
1. The culminating undergraduate experience helped me either connect what I learned to real life situations or contribute to knowledge in the discipline.	1	2	3	4	5
2. The culminating undergraduate experience provided me an opportunity to apply skills and knowledge I have gained from my major courses.	1	2	3	4	5
3. The culminating undergraduate experience helped me to see how critical thinking can be used in everyday life.	1	2	3	4	5
4. The culminating undergraduate experience helped me to better understand other course materials and activities.	1	2	3	4	5
5. The culminating undergraduate experience helped me become more aware of the issues in my major or discipline.	1	2	3	4	5
6. The culminating undergraduate experience helped me address an authentic issue, topic or situation in my major of discipline.	1	2	3	4	5
7. The culminating undergraduate experience clarified my choice of a major.	1	2	3	4	5
8. The culminating undergraduate experience improved my ability to analyze ideas and multiple points of view.	1	2	3	4	5
9. The culminating undergraduate experience enhanced my ability to communicate my ideas in a real world or disciplinary context.	1	2	3	4	5

10. Additional comments you would like to share about any aspect of the culminating undergraduate experience:

*Adapted from Gelmon, S.B., Holland, B.A., Driscoll, A., Spring, A., Kerrigan, S. (2001). Assessing service-learning and civic engagement: Principles and techniques. Providence, RI: Campus Compact and Portland State's Capstone Student Survey.

Chapter 3

Student Reflection

Andrea Hamilton

Department of Defense at Wright-Patterson AFB

Susan Wildermuth

University of Wisconsin-Whitewater

Abstract: Individuals across all walks of life naturally engage in self-reflection as a way to process behavior. In our society, there is a well-established social belief that taking time to "think about what we've done" is an effective way to learn and grow from an experience. Not surprisingly then, the use of high-quality critical reflection as a way to promote student learning is a popular teaching strategy supported across multiple education levels and disciplines (Veine, et al., 2019). Reflection is an essential learning tool in many higher education classrooms because educators see reflection as a tool to help students develop the life-long skills necessary to look at aspects of their professional practice, make accurate judgments about what happened and why, and improve future outcomes (Weimer, 2012). However, engaging effectively in the type of high-quality reflection that leads to learning is not an easy skill for students to acquire, and guidance, instruction, and support from faculty are essential to its development. The goal of this chapter is to discuss reflection as a means of enabling deep learning before, during, and after culminating experiences. After defining critical reflection and its impact on learning, we discuss various key aspects of reflection assignments and how to best assess them for maximum student learning.

Keywords: Reflection, learning, engagement, application, transformation, intentional, scaffolded, assignments, assessment

***

From a parent's exasperated cry of "What were you thinking?!" when a child has done something foolish, to the anguished "Why do I keep putting myself through this?" self-questioning after a difficult workday, individuals across all walks of life naturally engage in reflection as a way to process behavior. In our society, there is a well-established social belief that taking time to "think about what we've done" is an effective way to learn and grow from an experience. Not surprisingly then, the use of high-quality critical reflection to promote student learning is a popular teaching strategy supported across multiple education levels and disciplines (Veine et al., 2019). Reflection is an essential learning tool in many higher education classrooms because educators see it as a strategy to help students develop the life-long skills necessary to look at aspects of their professional practice, make accurate judgments about what happened and why, and improve future outcomes (Weimer, 2012). Educators support Dewey's (1933) claim that we do not learn from experience, we learn from reflecting on experience. However, engaging effectively in the type of high-quality reflection that leads to learning is not an easy skill for students to acquire, and guidance from faculty is essential to its development. The goal of this chapter is to discuss reflection as a means of enabling deep learning before, during, and after culminating experiences. After defining critical reflection and its impact on learning, we discuss various key aspects of reflection assignments and how best to assess them for maximum student learning.

Definition and Models of Reflection

While reflection as an assessment of student learning is extremely common and continues to grow in popularity (Veine et. al., 2019), a clear and unified definition of what constitutes reflection is difficult to find in the literature. The concept of reflection is complex and has been defined in myriad ways with debate about reflection's various components and about how reflection actually occurs (Ixer, 1999). In this chapter, we define reflection as engaging in metacognition about an experience, thought, or feeling for the express purpose of deeper understanding and personal growth (Gursansky et al., 2010). By this definition, the process of reflection involves thinking about one's own role and contemplating why one took certain actions, thought certain thoughts, or felt certain feelings (Gursansky et al., 2010). Reflection involves drawing on past experience, reflecting on that experience in the present, and using the conclusions you reach to inform future actions. High-quality critical reflection can be very powerful as it can lead to new perspectives, changes in beliefs and thought patterns, and changes in behavior and outcomes (Kember et al., 2008).

According to Dyment and O'Connell (2011), several scholars have attempted to clarify the reflective process with conceptual frameworks or models. These seek to organize reflection into clearly defined stages to illuminate its transformative process better. While these models may have differing numbers of steps or labels for various steps, a comparison of the most popular models demonstrates clear agreement among scholars regarding elements of the reflection process most essential for effective learning.

One of the simplest models of reflection is the Driscoll model (2007). The Driscoll model is based on three questions: 1. What?, 2. So What?, and 3. Now What? Driscoll connected these questions to three stages of a learning cycle and then added trigger questions to each step that he believed should be answered.

Under Step 1 (the "What?" question), Driscoll encourages learners to describe the experience/situation/incident they are reflecting on.

-   What happened, what did the learner do, who else was involved, and was the experience good/bad/a mix?

Under Step 2 (the "So What?" question), Driscoll encourages learners to think about why the situation or experience was important or significant.

-   What feelings was the learner experiencing when the situation happened, how did the learner and others react in the situation and why, and what past experiences might have influenced how they felt about the situation?

During Step 3 (the "Now what" question), Driscoll argued that learners should think about possible actions that could be taken in the future should a similar or related situation arise.

-   Should behavior be changed?

-   Why or why not, and in what way?

-   What can the learner do to better prepare themselves for future experiences?

A slightly different approach was developed by Atkins and Murphy (1994). They proposed that when learners have a new experience, especially one that gives rise to uncomfortable feelings or thoughts and they are prompted to engage in reflection about that experience, the first step is *awareness* that the experience requires thinking about. The second step in the reflection process is *description* in which learners should describe the situation in detail. In this step, learners should identify the thoughts and feelings during the experience, summarize salient events, and describe key features of the experience in as much detail as possible. The third step is *analysis* during which learners should analyze feelings about their experience and critique their knowledge relevant to the situation. Learners should challenge their own assumptions and explore multiple possible understandings of the facts. The fourth and final step is *planning*. This involves identifying any learning that occurred, evaluating the relevance of the new knowledge, and developing a plan to use that new knowledge effectively in the future.

Gibbs' model of reflection (1988) provided a slightly more detailed model of reflection with six steps:

Step 1 is description.

- Gibbs argues that learners should start the reflection process by engaging in a description of the experience or event to remind themselves of details, the scene, and the context.

Step 2 is *feelings.*

- Learners should consider and define how they felt before, during, and after the experience.

Step 3 is *evaluation.*

- Learners should look objectively at both the positive and negative aspects of the experience. What went well? What did not go so well?

Step 4 is *analysis.*

- Learners should explore why the various elements of the experience were positive or negative and identify the relevant factors that led to those outcomes (previous experiences, the people with them, their own and other relevant people's skill sets and expertise, etc).

Step 5 is drawing conclusions.

- Learners should focus on what they learned. Were there any new skills developed or new knowledge gained as a result of the experience? Are there areas of knowledge or particular skills that still need to be developed?

Finally, Step 6 is *making an action plan.*

- Learners should ask: what specific actions should be taken to build on existing knowledge or skills?

The most complex of the models we will discuss in this chapter is Mezirow's (1981) reflection model. He organized the reflection process into seven levels:

Level 1: *Reflectivity.* At this first level, learners become aware of a specific perception, meaning, or behavior. This may be a one-time event that comes to their awareness as something to be examined further (e.g., "That fight with Colin in the car was really nasty, what happened?"), or they may perceive it to be part of a pattern (e.g. "It seems like whenever I ride with Colin, we fight. What is going on?"). This stage helps learners identify and become aware of ingrained habits of perceiving, thinking, or acting.

Level 2: *Affective Reflectivity.* At this second level, learners become aware of the feelings they have about certain thoughts, meanings, or behaviors, and how they feel about habitual perceptions, thoughts, or actions. At this level, they start to label emotions and feelings that they may not have examined before.

Level 3: *Discriminant Reflectivity.* At this level, learners assess the usefulness and effectiveness of those perceptions, thoughts, actions, and habits of doing things and identify how those perceptions, thoughts, actions, and habits have come into being. For example, learners might find that lived experience or upbringing are the root causes of their perceptions.

Level 4: *Judgmental Reflectivity.* At this stage, learners become aware of the broader value judgments about the world and about how the world works that are inherent in their perceptions, thoughts, actions, or habits.

Level 5: *Conceptual Reflectivity.* This is the level where the underlying assumptions of the problem are questioned. At this level, learners ask "Why is this even important to me? Why do I care about this issue in the first place? What concepts, schemas, or scripts have I internalized?"

Level 6: *Psychic Reflectivity.* At this level, learners recognize that interests and anticipations influence how they perceive, think, or act. They become aware of the tendency to make precipitant judgments based on limited information and cultural or psychological assumptions.

Level 7: *Theoretical Reflectivity.* At this level, learners strive to recognize and explore other perspectives that may offer more functional alternative criteria for perceiving, thinking, and acting.

Regardless of the proposed levels of complexity, each model strives to help learners use reflection as a structured learning process to gain awareness of why they think, feel, or act the way that they do, and then critique that awareness. These models make it evident that critical reflection is about helping learners construct and deconstruct their own meaning-making process, question "universal truths," and broaden their established frames of reference. The models agree that awareness, description, analysis, and future planning are all essential components.

Benefits of Reflection

A comparison of these models of reflection illustrates agreement in the key elements of the reflection process and that reflection is complex, difficult, and potentially unnerving. Examining one's key assumptions about how the world works and why one thinks in a particular way can be very scary as previously held beliefs may be questioned and found wanting. Given this, why do educators ask students to engage in work that can be so upsetting and difficult? It is because a great many benefits come from engaging in high-quality reflection with learning as the single largest benefit (Kolb, 1984; Lungren & Poell, 2016). Dewey (1933) is credited with first articulating that reflection is an important component of learning. He theorized that reflection's role in the learning process aids learners in incorporating new information and experiences into their existing frame of knowledge. He suggested that it is not sufficient simply to have an experience in order to learn. Without reflecting upon an experience, the knowledge gained from that experience may quickly be forgotten, or its learning potential lost. It is from active engagement with the experience through the process of reflection that learning occurs (Biggs, 2012; Dewey, 1933; Gibbs, 1988). Reflection is an active and dynamic process that engages the mind, requiring time and focus. Learners make connections, draw on lived experiences, and think critically. These elements enhance learning and improve the understanding, retention, and application of knowledge (Dunlosky et al., 2013).

A second benefit to reflection is that reflection does not stop at the analysis or knowledge acquisition stage., but instead applies the gained knowledge to future contexts. Dewey (1933) stated that the meaning-making component of the reflection process was valuable because it gave the learner deeper knowledge about a topic *and* it gave the learner the tools to apply new knowledge to inform future action. He referred to reflection as the link between thinking and doing (Dewey, 1933).

The final benefit of reflection to be discussed here is that reflection has the potential to be transformative. Gibbs (1988) argued that without reflection, experience alone might cause us to "reinforce stereotypes…, offer simplistic solutions to complex problems and generalize inaccurately based on limited data" (Ash & Clayton, 2009, p.26). Engaging in critical reflection, however, helps us "articulate questions, confront bias, examine causality, contrast theory with practice and identify systemic issues all of which help foster critical evaluation and knowledge transfer" (Ash & Clayton, 2009, p. 27). Reflective thinking can change learners' understanding of an experience, allowing them to analyze an issue from different perspectives, gain a greater understanding of a situation, and examine previously unexplored perspectives, biases, and assumptions about the world (Kitchenham, 2008).

Reflection Best Practices

While the process of reflection has many benefits for learners, it is also labor intensive for both student and teacher. Thus, before using reflection as a class assignment, it is important that educators think carefully about a number of variables that could impact its effectiveness.

- Instructors need to be intentional about their use of reflection.

  It is essential that instructors are intentional about their use of reflection. Reflection should not be used as a classroom assessment without careful thought about its application and expected outcomes. Things to consider include:

  o What classroom learning outcomes would the use of reflection directly address?

  o Is a reflection assignment the best way to assess those learning outcomes?

  o Do the students and instructors involved have the time / energy for this type of intensive learning exercise?

If teachers give students opportunities to reflect, they also must assess how well students are reflecting and provide feedback that deepens the students' skills. If learning from reflection is to be effective, instructors need to build in the personal time and commitment necessary to give detailed feedback to that reflection. They need to dedicate classroom time for discussions about the reflection process and about what the students are learning as the process goes on. Faculty may need to allow time for one-on-one meetings with students and facilitate other opportunities for discourse and student self-development that place reflection and feedback at the heart of the educational experience. Good quality feedback on a student's reflection must be accurate, timely, comprehensive, and appropriate, but also accessible to the learner, have value, and inspire confidence and hope (Quinton & Smallbone, 2010). Using reflection is a significant commitment on the part of both the instructor and the student, so careful consideration of logistical factors, goals, and student/faculty bandwidth is essential.

- Scaffolding should be provided.

The capacity to reflect critically is indicative of excellent critical and higher-level skills and higher-level thinking. Many students are not able to engage in this type of abstract thinking without training and support. However, while critical reflection may come more easily for some students than others, it is a skill that can be learned through practice and high-quality constructive feedback (Dewey, 1933, Rodgers, 2002). Thus, when developing reflection assignments, faculty need to scaffold the expectations for the assignments to students' current skills. Learners should be supported in the reflection process through structured development activities that progressively increase their abilities and agency while reducing teacher-led direction (Vygotsky, 1978). It is important to keep in mind that reflection is not something that students engage in automatically and they need help and support in order for it to be an effective learning strategy (Wedelin & Adawi, 2014).

- Students need to see the value.

Academic literature and popular media report on the power of journaling and other forms of reflection to reduce depression, anxiety, hostility, and stress. Additionally, popular media coverage has promoted reflection as an authentic life-long learning tool (Chan & Horneffer, 2006). However, even students who find keeping a personal journal valuable may not see the same value in educational or workplace reflection. As with all measures of learning, students need to see the value if they are to be motivated to complete a reflection exercise to the best of their ability and gain its maximum effect. If they feel a reflection activity is "busy work," they are unlikely to gain from the exercise. Many instructors ask for reflection through discussion boards, short papers, and journaling. Unfortunately, such assignments can be perceived by students as work that is not tied directly to assessing their understanding of course material. Thus, educators must think carefully about how they frame reflection for their students and how often reflections are required and turned in for grading. Reflection can be very effective when students have been taught the value of the reflection process, where non-graded reflection opportunities are consistently embedded in the course through in-class exercises, activities, and class discussions, and where assessed reflection opportunities are used strategically with prompts or examples connected to course content and followed up with quality feedback

- Students should share their reflections with others.

Reflection assignments should be accompanied by opportunities for students to engage in activities with their peers to consolidate their learning and validate their experiences (Gursansky et al., 2010). While meaning is individualistic and found inside the learner, rather than prescribed by external influences, that meaning often only becomes significant to the learner through critical discourse with others (Kitchenham, 2008).

- The medium of reflection should be carefully considered.

Assignments that call for reflection are most often written-response assignments such as reflective journals, judgments on case studies, short reflection papers, and contributions to online discussions (Kember et al., 2008). Students often do not know the best way to write reflective responses or have challenges with writing skills in general (Tanner, 2012). Poor writing skills may hamper students' ability to display accurately their high-quality reflection skills. Additionally, even students with strong writing skills may not be familiar with reflective writing if it was not a type of writing they were required to previously learn and thus, they may tend to be superficial and merely descriptive in their reflections (Hatton & Smith, 1995). Certain student groups may be unduly disadvantaged by the use of written-response-type reflection assignments. Faculty should be sure that such writing tasks do not unduly advantage or disadvantage any particular student. One way to address this concern is to allow for reflection responses in multiple formats. For example, video journaling, creative writing, public performance, storytelling, and visual artwork are all appropriate ways for students to demonstrate a reflective process.

- Subject matter and timing must be considered.

Reflection commonly involves reviewing past thoughts, feelings, or experiences. The reflection's topic could be something that happened years ago or something that occurred just a few moments before one engages in the reflection. The ideal academic subject matter for reflection depends on the assignment's learning outcome goals and typically focuses on experiences directly related to course content and/or professional practice (Kember et al., 2008). Instructors need to consider the best timing for student reflection assignments. Instructors will often use a combination of forward-looking, "in-the-moment," and backward-looking reflection. Forward-looking reflection involves asking learners at the beginning of a course, project, or assignment, to think about their expectations and goals for the future, what they believe will be challenging, what they feel confident about, and their reasons for their thoughts. Reflection may be required at designated times or framed as journaling that takes place throughout the entire experience. "In-the-moment" reflection is designed so that when learners are having a particular learning experience and immersed in that experience, they reflect on it right then. Backward-looking reflection is a good way for students to take stock at the end of an experience. Learners might be asked to review their previous reflections and discuss their growth or learning over time and whether they have met their original goals.

Assessing Reflection

Validity is a prominent issue involved in the assessment of reflection (Creme, 2005; Guransky et al., 2010). When asking students to reveal their inner thoughts, embedded in an educational system where only "correct" answers are rewarded, the act of deep and meaningful reflection is inherently disadvantaged (Creme, 2005). Students, with a mindset focused on higher grades and greater scores, are often reluctant to engage with the essence of reflection – to share weaknesses and challenges openly and to learn to manage negative emotions associated with the learning process (Dyment & O'Connell, 2010). Social desirability effects can severely limit the willingness of students to take on the opportunity to reflect on learning as a social process shared with peers or the instructor (Boud, 2001). Students may simply lie, or put their best "face" forward in their reflections in pursuit of a higher grade or other social pressures (Gursansky et al., 2010).

However, the entire purpose of reflection-based coursework is to consider the messy internal work that goes into learning. By assigning reflections, rather than essays or exams, instructors generally want to see the growth and development of students over time, which students may be unwilling or unable to provide within the context of the typical grading and assessment processes. So, as assessors of student work, how do we determine whether students' reflections illustrate their "truth," rather than the version of truth they wish to share with us? As educators, how do we encourage students to be authentic in their reflective process, so they are best able to benefit from engaging in reflection?

The following sections will outline tips for assessing reflective work so that the effort is both meaningful and inclusive for students and manageable for instructors.

Ethical Considerations

As with most pedagogical decisions, assessment of reflection touches on poignant ethical questions that instructors need to wrestle with before assigning such work to students. One of the first questions in this process is whether reflections should even be assessed at all. Students are keenly aware of this tension – as evidenced by common questions they ask in regard to the grading standards for evaluation of reflection: "How can you grade based on what I feel?" or "How are you able to judge my personal experiences and reactions to those?" It is truly a challenge for an outside observer to cast judgment on the internal thoughts of someone else (Creme, 2005; Varner & Peck, 2003) without engaging in subjective evaluations. Even with a strong rubric in place to guide assessment, several cognitive biases are triggered when beginning the process of evaluating student reflective work (Varner & Peck, 2003). While recognizing these biases is an important step to engage in ethical and equitable grading of student reflection, overcoming them is complex and challenging.

Assessing this type of student work, with these potential errors, begs questions about the inclusivity of grading reflections. Certain students may be new to reflective work, find it challenging, and value it differently, disadvantaging them in relation to their peers (Dyment & O'Connell, 2011; Varner & Peck, 2003). Students with unique cultural or ethnic backgrounds or those who reflect in their non-native language may also find themselves disadvantaged by the evaluation of their reflection (Clarkeburn & Kettula, 2012). This creates a pedagogical tension that instructors must address. Where is the balancing point between developing and strengthening reflective and other academic performance indicators? To answer this question, instructors must return to the learning objectives of the course and reaffirm whether reflective assignments are still the best for seeing and evaluating student learning. If the answer is still reflection, instructors must be prepared to support student growth in their reflection skills.

Overcoming these critical ethical challenges is possible, but solutions must be built into the assignment prompt and feedback and evaluation that occur afterwards. The following tips will help guide instructors through the process of creating a framework for assigning and evaluating reflection so that students are best able to make their learning effort clear.

Reflective Assignment Guidelines

As for all student work, the clearer instructors are about guidelines, the better students are able to meet those expectations. Providing students with a reflective assignment with a detailed and specific rubric will facilitate their performance and ensure students are reflecting on the factors that are most important for any learning objective (Grossman, 2009). Sharing such criteria with students can also help support reflection that is a valid indicator of students' actual internal states (Ash et al., 2005; McKeachie, 1986). Instructors can create meaningful reflective assignments using reflective models such as those described above as frameworks for assignment guidelines.

Using a reflective model as a reflection assignment framework alleviates some of the concerns about authenticity in reflection as students are active in the identification, application, and analysis of specific situations for the assignment. Furthermore, the criteria in most reflective models are broad, allowing for a wide range of interpretations and student creativity, but also specific enough to ensure student reflection meets instructor expectations. Whichever reflective model is used as the structure of a student assignment, providing clear expectations about what students should reflect on and how to meet various assignment guidelines is critical to successful student reflection-as-assignments. Integrating these components into a rubric also makes it easier for instructors to provide valid and fair feedback to all students, regardless of cognitive biases and students' unique characteristics and style differences (Varner & Peck, 2003).

One of the most common tools to promote reflection in education are reflection journals, also referred to as reflective diaries or learning logs (Moon, 2004). Students are asked to write down events they have experienced, their meaning, and what they might have learned from it. The journals provide students with a framework to structure and remember their thoughts and reflections. The level of structure can be prompted by specific themes or questions to reflect upon or unprompted, where students reflect on topics they consider important (Wallin & Adawi, 2018a, 2018b).

Assessing versus Grading

Discussion of assessment is often commingled with guidelines on how to grade student work. However, especially when it comes to reflection, isolating the two can help instructors clarify the evaluation process. While assessment is focused on reviewing work, providing feedback, and taking the pulse of where students are in their learning of course content and their reflective skills, grading is assigning quantitative value to submitted work. Students are often primarily fixated on grades, whereas instructors often wish they were more focused on learning.

One of the key barriers to this open exchange of learning, trying and failing, is inherent within our grading systems. By moving to alternatives, such as competency-based grading, pass/fail evaluation of student work, increased opportunities for feedback on drafts, and the ability to revise work for an improved score, instructors can more meaningfully support the enterprise of learning without students' fear of failure. Work in this area suggests that low-stakes reflection assignments are better able to promote the type of learning and achievement that reflection is designed to support: student-driven course outcome mastery (Cohn & Stewart, 2016). Instructors adopting a low-stakes model, however, need to be aware of the tension between student perceptions of "busy work" and reduce the pressure to create reflective products that are socially desirable (Boud, 2001).

Another way to move students farther from grade- to learning-focused is to evaluate reflection-based work holistically, rather than based on more incremental rubric categories. This enables both streamlining the grading process for instructors and avoiding inconsistencies in grading (Kember et al., 2008). Clarkeburn and Kettula (2012) found it challenging for independent coders to agree on evaluations of student work when, for example, one section of a paper demonstrated high-quality reflection, while another was lacking in key ways. To resolve this issue, they called for a broader evaluation of reflection assignments.

Assessment of Repetitive Reflection

When students are asked to engage in reflection at several points throughout a course, in the form of a learning journal, repeated evaluation of their performance over time, or other designs where students engage in reflective work multiple times, additional assessment questions remain. Instructors must also determine how often in a course student reflection will be submitted for feedback and evaluation. As with most skills or performance indicators, repetition coupled with timely feedback best supports student growth in critical reflection on course content and metacognitive perspective (Guransky et al., 2010). However, evaluating these reflections creates a significant workload for instructors and grading support, leading some to burn out and remove reflective work from a course (Varner & Peck, 2003).

Much of the literature agrees that final assessments, with no prior drafts or practice, lead to the poorest reflection quality. Students who are given multiple opportunities to exercise and refine their reflective practice generally perform at higher levels at the end of a course (Jensen & Joy, 2005). Instructor feedback guides students to meet assignment criteria and allows them to demonstrate their learning and mastery of course outcomes more effectively (Grossman, 2009). These improvements, however, must be weighed carefully with the time and effort required to evaluate these reflections. Instructors must also be authentic about the emotional burden that can stem from reading students' internal dialogue and thoughts. Additionally, they must realistically evaluate how much time providing adequate feedback on reflection assignments will take and whether it is even possible to do all that they wish to provide students as they develop their reflective skills. Prior work suggests that detailed feedback early in the semester will boost student skills efficiently, leading to reduced time demands on later evaluations (Phipps, 2005) while still giving students the tools they need to improve their reflective craft. Others suggest that requiring students to engage meaningfully with instructor feedback to revise and improve one particular reflective assignment can lead to measurable and notable improvements in performance (Ash et al., 2005). Assignment design also ensures that the time dedicated to providing feedback does not end up neglected and ignored (Quniton & Smallbone, 2010).

Supporting Student Reflection Skills

Just creating a detailed study guide and reviewing it prior to an exam, providing a culture conducive to authentic reflection and metacognition will allow students to be more successful. Reflection is a skill that, similar to the practice of mindfulness, needs direct instruction, regular support, and timely feedback (Guransky et al., 2010; Jensen & Joy, 2005; Varner & Peck, 2003). Students simply asked to reflect with little support will often, understandably, fail to live up to expectations. By integrating support for reflective practice instead, instructors can encourage high-quality reflection among students and help cultivate their reflective practice beyond a specific course, which has shown to be beneficial for mental health (Smyth et al., 2018), their career (Bolles, 2022), and their personal relationships (Thieme et al., 2011).

Although our ultimate goal might be for students to become better at reflecting on concepts and their own thoughts, behaviors, and attitudes, specifically grading students on the extent to which they achieve these aims can be detrimental. As discussed earlier, in this environment students are more likely to reflect in socially desirable ways rather than authentic ones. Uncoupling the quality of the reflection from the assessment of whether students were *transformed* as a result of engaging in reflection can help guide us to provide better and more meaningful feedback to students. Whereas it might not be possible for students to determine the answers to the question *"Now what?,"* it is well within their capacity to improve their responses to the questions that comprise any reflective model. Shifting our assessment focus can help us better identify our students' strengths and weaknesses in reflective practice and support their growth and development.

Furthermore, providing some resources to make the goals of reflection transparent and defined can shift students from perceiving reflection as busy work that requires little time or effort. In a course where students are asked to reflect regularly, it is helpful to demonstrate why such reflective practice is beneficial for their learning and achievement of course outcomes. Furthermore, clarity of the required components of any reflective model is often useful for students. For example, sharing an overview of the specific reflective model used in an assignment can give students a better perspective on how to engage with the assignment prompt successfully.

Lastly, building rapport with students can be an essential ingredient to encourage authentic self-disclosure in reflective work (Dyment & O'Connell, 2011). Much like working with a therapist, when students are asked to confide their inner thoughts, incomplete opinions, and non-linear learning processes to instructors, they are vulnerable. Researchers speculate that when students and instructors have developed strong rapport, their reflections are higher quality and less prone to social desirability effects (Dyment & O'Connell, 2011). Rapport-building among students and faculty should be an important component of any class, but is essential to promote the level of self-disclosure often required by reflection and individual growth and development (Derlega & Chaikin, 1977).

Reflecting on Culminating Experiences

Culminating education experiences have been increasingly incorporated into the curriculum as a means of supporting students in the synthesis, reflection on, and demonstration of their educational experiences (Kenzie, 2013). Taking a variety of forms – study abroad, service learning, internships, independent research projects, capstone courses, and more – these concluding and "high impact" educational experiences are ripe opportunities for the level of self-growth and development instructors might wish their students to undergo (Kuh, 2008). Given these desired and embedded learning outcomes, reflection is a meaningful fit between what we hope students draw out of culminating experiences and how we can evaluate their progress toward these goals. Reflection over the term of these experiences can help illuminate the internal processes that students are navigating as they engage in these complex, challenging, and often frustrating educational moments (Wallman et al., 2008). Importantly, reflective products can support students in the connection between their existing and shifting values and what they have learned or experienced throughout their experience (Hatcher et al., 2004), opening up pathways for the types of insight and transformation reflection best allows (Mezirow, 1981).

Conclusion

Integrating reflection into the curriculum can be a rewarding and beneficial experience for students and faculty. Instructors must provide the appropriate structure when crafting these learning experiences for students. Instructors looking to jumpstart reflective practices among their students should begin by aligning the reflective goals with existing course learning outcomes and look for key opportunities for students to share their learning in a reflective voice. Once opportunities for reflection are identified, selecting an appropriate reflective model can help guide the development of the framework for such reflective tasks and reduce the need to "reinvent the wheel" when it comes to organizing reflection. Once assigned, instructors must answer further questions about how to ethically and effectively assess and evaluate student reflection.

Supplemental Materials

To support the use of reflection as an assessment tool in your courses, we've developed a set of supplemental materials for use in a wide variety of courses.

Discussion Questions

1. How do we "know" whether student reflection is authentic? What clues do students give us in their work that help us form these opinions of their work?

2.   How might the development of authentic reflection skills help students in their future careers? In their personal and professional relationships?

3.   What pitfalls might students encounter when reflecting objectively on their emotions and in-the-minute decisions and actions? How can instructors support quality and meaningful reflection on these states and actions given these challenges?

4.   What other ethical considerations must instructors contemplate as they assign, evaluate, and provide feedback on a student's reflective work? How can instructors respond to these ethical dilemmas in an appropriate and student-centered way?

5.   Discuss the pros and cons of using one of the various reflection models discussed above. What are the limitations of each model, and what are the benefits? Under what conditions or circumstances might instructors want to use a more complex model over a simpler one? When might they want to use a less complicated model and why?

Sample Reflection Assignments

1.   At the mid-term of the course, ask students to write a reflection that comments on where they are in the course of the semester thus far, what remaining questions or difficulties are they having in the course, and what they would like to accomplish before the end. Consider also asking students to write this letter as a reflection addressed to the instructor, rather than in an essay format.

2.   Before a major assignment, ask students to outline SMART goals for their upcoming project. Smart goals are: Specific, Measurable, Achievable, Relevant, and Timely. After the major assignment, ask them to reflect on their work as a function of the goals they set for themselves at the beginning of the project.

3.   Ask students to create a KWL Chart related to a particular unit or module in the course. In a KWL Chart, students reflect on what they already Know about a topic, Want to Know, and Learned in a particular section of a course. Create a template for students to use, ask them to divide a paper into three columns for an in-class exercise, or request they form a table in a Word document to organize their thoughts and ideas.

References

Ash, S., Clayton, P. & Atkinson, M. (2005). Integrating reflection and assessment to capture and improve student learning. *Michigan Journal of Community Service Learning, 11*(2), 49 - 60. https://quod.lib.umich.edu/m/mjcsl/3239521.0011.204/1

Ash, S. L., & Clayton, P. H. (2009). Generating, deepening, and documenting learning: The power of critical reflection in applied learning. *Journal of Applied Learning in Higher Education, 1(1),* 25-48: https://scholarworks.iupui.edu/bitstream/handle/1805/4579/ash-2009-generating.pdf?sequence=1&isAllowed=y

Atkins, S. and Murphy, K. (1994) Reflective practice. *Nursing Standard, 8*(39), pp.49-56, http://doi.org/10.7748/ns.8.39.48.s64

Biggs, J. (2012). What the student does: Teaching for enhanced learning. *Higher Education Research & Development,* 31(1), 39–55. http://doi.org/10.1080/07294360.2012.642839

Bolles, R. N. (2022). *What color is your parachute? A practical manual for job-hunters and career-changers.* Ten Speed Press.

Boud, D. (2001). Using journal writing to enhance reflective practice. *New Directions for Adult and Continuing Education, 90*(9), 9 – 18 http://doi.org/10.1002/ace.16

Chan, K.M, & Horneffer, W.K. (2006). Emotional Expression and psychological symptoms: A comparison of writing and drawing. *The Arts in Psychotherapy, 33(1),* 26-36, http://doi.org/10.1016/j.aip.2005.06.001

Clarkeburn, H. & Kettula, K. (2012). Fairness and using reflective journals in assessment. *Teaching in Higher Education, 17*(4), 439 – 452. http://doi.org/10.1080/13562517.2011.641000

Cohn, J., & Stewart, M. (2016). Promoting metacognitive thought through response to low-stakes reflective writing. *Journal of Response to Writing, 2*(1), 58-74. http://www.journalrw.org/index.php/jrw/article/view/51

Coulson, D., & Harvey, M. (2013). Experience-based learning: A framework. *Teaching in Higher Education, 18*(4), 401-413. http://doi.org/10.1080/13562517.2012.752726

Creme, P. (2005). Should student learning journals be assessed? Assessment & *Evaluation in Higher Education, 30*(3), 287-296. http://doi.org/10.1080/02602930500063850

Derlega, V. & Chaikin, A. (1977). Privacy and self-disclosure in social relationships. *Journal of Social Issues, 33*(3), 102 – 115. http://doi.org/10.1111/j.1540-4560.1977.tb01885.x

Dewey, J. (1933). *How we think: A restatement of the relation of reflective thinking to the educative process.* Heath & Co Publishers.

Driscoll, J. (2007). *Practicing clinical supervision: A reflective approach.* Bailliere Tindall.

Dunlosky, J., Rawson, K. A., Marsh, E. J., Nathan, M. J., & Willingham, D. T. (2013). Improving students' learning with effective learning techniques: Promising directions from cognitive and educational psychology. *Psychological Science in the Public Interest, 14,* 4–58. http://doi.org/10.1177/1529100612453266

Dyment, J. & O'Connell, T. (2010). The quality of reflection in student journals: A review of limiting and enabling factors. *Innovative Higher Education, 35*(3) 233 – 244. http://doi.org/10.1007/s10755-010-9143-y

Dyment, J., & O'Connell, T. (2011, February). Assessing the quality of reflection in student journals: A review of the research. *Teaching in Higher Education, 16(1),* 81-97. http://doi.org/10.1080/13562517.2010.507308

Gibbs, G. (1988). *Learning by doing: A guide to teaching and learning methods.* Oxford.

Grossman, R. (2009). Structures for facilitating student reflection. *College Teaching, 57*(1), 15-22. http://doi.org/10.3200/CTCH.57.1.15-22

Gursansky, D., Quinn, D., & Le Sueur, E. (2010). Authenticity in reflection: Building reflective skills for social work. *Social Work Education, 29(7),* 778-791. http://doi.org/10.1080/02615471003650062

Hatcher, J. A., Bringle, R. G., & Muthiah, R. (2004). Designing effective reflection: What matters to service-learning? *Michigan Journal of Community Service Learning, 11*(1), 38–46

Ixer, G. (1999). There's no such thing as reflection. *The British Journal of Social Work, 29*(4), 513-527. https://www.jstor.org/stable/23714983

Jensen, S. & Joy, C. (2005, March 01). Exploring a module to evaluate Levels of reflection in baccalaureate nursing students' journals. *Journal of Nursing Education, 44(3).* http://doi.org/10.3928/01484834-20050301-08

Kembera, J., McKay, J., Sinclair, K., & Wong, K. (2008). A four-category scheme for coding and assessing the level of reflection in written work. *Assessment & Evaluation in Higher Education, 33(4),* 369–379. http://doi.org/10.1080/0260 2930701293355

Kinzie, J. (2013). Taking stock of capstones and integrative learning. *Peer Review, 15*(4), 27.

Kitchenham, A. (2008). The evolution of John Mezirow's transformative learning theory. *Journal of Transformative Education, 6,* 104-123. http://doi.org/10.117 7/1541344608322678

Kuh, G. D., & Schneider, C. G. (2008). *High-impact educational practices: what they are, who has access to them, and why they matter.* Association of American Colleges and Universities. https://www.aacu.org/publication/high -impact-educational-practices-what-they-are-who-has-access-to-them-and -why-they-matter

Lungren, H., & Poell, R. (2016). Integrative literature review on critical reflection: A review of Mezirow's theory and its operationalizations. *Human Resource Development Review, 15(1),* 3–28. http://doi.org/10.1177/1534484315622735

McKeachie, W. (1986). *Teaching tips: A guidebook for the beginning college teacher.* Heath.

Mezirow, J. (1981). A critical theory of adult learning and education. *Adult Education Quarterly, 32,* 3-24. http://doi.org/10.1177/074171368103200101

Phipps, J. J. (2005) E-journaling: Achieving interactive education online. *Educause Quarterly, 28*(1) https://er.educause.edu/articles/2005/1/ejournali ng-achieving-interactive-education-online.

Quinton, S., & Smallbone, T. (2010). Feeding forward: Using feedback to promote student reflection and learning – a teaching model. *Innovations in*

Education and Teaching International, 47(1), 125-135. http://doi.org/10.1 080/14703290903525911

Rodgers, C. (2002). Defining reflection: Another look at John Dewey and reflective thinking. *The Teachers College Record, 104*(4), 842-866

Smyth, J. M., Johnson, J. A., Auer, B. J., Lehman, E., Talamo, G., & Sciamanna, C. N. (2018). Online positive affect journaling in the improvement of mental distress and well-being in general medical patients with elevated anxiety symptoms: A preliminary randomized controlled trial. *JMIR Mental Health, 5*(4). http://doi.org/10.2196/11290

Tanner, K. D. (2012). Promoting student metacognition. *CBE Life Sciences Education,* 11(2), 113–120.

Thieme, A., Wallace, J., Thomas, J., Chen. K., Kramer, N & Oliver, P. (2011). Lover's box: Designing for reflection within romantic relationships. *International Journal of Human-Computer Studies, 69*(5), 283 – 297. http://doi.org/10.1016/j.ijhcs.2010.12.006.

Varner, D. & Peck, S. (2003). Learning from learning journals: The benefits and challenges of using learning journal assignments. *Journal of Management Education, 27*(1), 52 – 77. http://doi.org/10.1177/1052562902239248

Veine, S., Anderson, M., Andersen, N., Espenes, T., Soyland, T., & Wallin, P. (2019). Reflection as a core student learning activity in higher education-Insights from nearly two decades of academic development. *International Journal for Academic Development, 25,* 125-135. http://doi.org/_10.1080/1360144X.2019.1659797

Vygotsky, L. S. 1978. *Mind and Society: The Development of Higher Psychological Processes.* Cambridge, MA: Harvard University Press.

Wallman, A., Lindblad, A. K., Hall, S., Lundmark, A., & Ring, L. (2008). A categorization scheme for assessing pharmacy students' levels of reflection during internships. *American Journal of Pharmaceutical Education, 72*(1), 05. https://doi.org/10.5688/aj720105

Wedelin, D., & Adawi, T. (2014). Teaching mathematical modeling and problem-solving - A cognitive apprenticeship approach to mathematics and engineering education. *International Journal of Engineering Pedagogy* (IJEP), 4(5), 49–55.

Weimer, M. (2012, June 26). Four levels of student reflection. *Faculty Focus.* https://www.facultyfocus.com/articles/teaching-and-learning/four-levels-of-student-reflection/

Section 2:
Examples of Culminating Activities

After reading Section 1, it is clear why culminating experiences are important for student development.

The chapters in Section 2 describe in detail examples of culminating activities including theses, dissertations, applied projects, comprehensive exams, portfolios, and internships. The authors of these chapters provide great advice for those designing such experiences, with questions to ask, rubrics, guidelines for providing feedback to students, specifics about assignments to consider, guidelines for success, and warnings of pitfalls.

A common theme in this section is how the activity is completed should be determined by the goals for the project. It is not enough just to say that a student should complete a culminating experience and then scramble to put something together. The academic department and institution need to have a sense of what the student should get out of the process and then how to support that process. Thus, a large part of the work that must be done prior to developing requirements for students is to articulate the objectives, asking what exactly the goals are and how to achieve them within the academic and institutional context. The chapters in this section illuminate the steps along the way in this process.

Chapter 4

Thesis

Amanda R. Martinez

Davidson College

Abstract: Chapter 4 describes what an undergraduate thesis is, why students might pursue this type of culminating research experience for their major field of study, and various considerations that oftentimes factor into the decision to conduct thesis research such as a desire to gain research experience from start to finish, including research question development, literature reviewing, study design, data collection, and analysis. The following topics are explored in sequence: effective thesis writing, navigating the advisor and advisee work relationship, process logistics, and working within typical timeline constraints of the academic year. The chapter concludes with supplemental resources for thesis advisors to implement with their advisees at various stages of the thesis process. Though academic disciplines or fields may vary on the specific expectations, time frames, logistical and intellectual rigors surrounding the undergraduate thesis as a culminating experience option, the chapter takes a broad approach in exploring the general social science, humanities, and STEM orientations to undergraduate thesis research.

Keywords: undergraduate thesis, independent research, advising.

***

For many undergraduate college students, the individual culminating experience for their major often depends upon the conventions of the specific department and its supporting faculty, the type and size of the institution, and the routines and expectations within the discipline more broadly influenced by the national and international contexts. Future work opportunities, whether academic or industry, and advanced schooling opportunities that graduates may pursue as they look ahead to post-undergraduate life often factor into the path students choose for their culminating experience. The work environments that students enter in their post-undergraduate years vary tremendously, although likely "research skills will be necessary in all workplace experiences" (Ford et al., 2009, p. 435).

These have been an option in undergraduate academic settings for many years, although they are typically one of a few options available to culminate a degree. Many majors require a capstone project or a senior seminar which often includes a significant paper that engages existing research with an analytical, applied, or creative component. In the social sciences especially, empirical research is a prized goal for the senior thesis, however, there are certainly other types of analytical, intellectual work deemed appropriate for thesis projects. For example, some theses may include creative writing or a creative product and an accompanying analysis. Theses in STEM fields may include a large component of findings showcased through charts and tables with a brief write-up of the results. It is worth noting that most of the peer-reviewed scholarship about the undergraduate thesis as a culminating experience focuses on elements pertaining to process rather than content. Perhaps this dearth of scholarship reflects the wide variety of thesis types and structures across undergraduate degree-granting institutions. It is likely common that general thesis expectations include a review of relevant research that informs the area of inquiry and some original analysis or contributing depth work where the voice of the thesis writer shines through clearly. In this chapter, empirical research is the primary focus.

Harrington (2009) asserts, "undergraduate theses are important because such papers are often gateways to graduate study and research and may serve as writing samples in graduate school applications" (p. 398). The undergraduate thesis "requires students to find relevant literature, process complex information, use scientific reasoning, think critically and work individually" (Haagsman et al., 2021, p. 1270). These are different from seminar papers insofar as they require many steps before the refined topic of study takes shape, including taking methodology coursework, designing research instruments such as surveys or experiments, securing grant funding, and traveling to a data collection site, to name a few common examples. Students benefit from developing research skills since the thesis process requires that students demonstrate the capability to develop a research plan, review literature, derive a conceptual theoretical framework, define the aim of the study, and pose research questions (Agricola et al., 2021). Academic departments vary in their approach to the thesis process, sometimes relegating its pursuit available only to those students with a high GPA threshold and a well-articulated thesis prospectus. Some departments permit any interested student to pursue thesis research and impose few, if any, gatekeeping mechanisms.

Thesis research usually extends over more than one semester, through focused independent study with an advisor (or co-advisors) and a committee of professors whose expertise guides the thesis student in incremental progress in the study design. In a two-semester thesis model, a due date for the end of the first semester may include the development of the thesis proposal that describes: "'the students' intended area of research for the senior thesis and includes an outline, literature review, discussion of methodology, and tentative work schedule" (Ford et al., 2009, p. 439). Thesis research typically takes shape outside of the context of regular classroom meetings, presenting challenges for students in terms of consistent dedicated time and energy. Intellectual curiosity and ongoing thirst for knowledge are often the primary driving forces behind student thesis research which requires devoting a significant commitment of time and effort (Harrington, 2009). For many students, the idea of being intellectually in control of the project's development is an exciting challenge (Henttonen et al., 2021), and for others considering a thesis, this reality can be intimidating and dissuasive. Sachs (2002) found that "students using a deep approach [i.e., wanting to integrate learning into what they know and what is yet to be discovered] to learning tend to have a more positive academic experience, and both these variables have a positive impact on attitude to writing a thesis" (p.106). Theses tend to be less collaborative in a traditional sense; "theses are generally single-author works with a sole authorial voice attempting to offer new analysis and interpretation" (Harrington, 2009, p. 398).

In this chapter, a description of what a thesis is, including its general uses and rationale as a culminating experience for undergraduates, unfolds. The topics of effective thesis writing and advising will be covered, including suggestions for process logistics with best practices and timeline increments. Additionally, recommendations to enhance interpersonal relationship dynamics that can facilitate a productive working relationship based on feedback loops and mutual accountability will be provided. The chapter concludes with a set of supplemental resources including discussion questions, reflection prompts, and activities for thesis advisors to use in guiding their advisees in various stages of the thesis research process.

What is a Thesis? General Uses & Rationale

A thesis is an undergraduate independent research project guided by a set of research questions or hypotheses on a topic of interest to the individual student informed by coursework taken within the major. The thesis topic engages existing scholarly literature as a key foundation to inform the research question(s) and/or hypotheses that guide the study design. Thesis researchers often search for topic and design inspiration based on the knowledge they have of theory, method, and topics derived from their major coursework. The overarching idea is to bring together the major curriculum through the thesis as the culminating experience. While these often include a formulaic set of sections and sequence of information, there remains flexibility depending on the nature of the study and the interest area of the researcher. Typical thesis sections include a title page, acknowledgments, table of contents, introduction, literature review, research question(s) and/or hypotheses, method (including sample and procedure), results, discussion, theoretical and practical implications, limitations, and directions for future research, and conclusion, most of which conform to standard peer-reviewed article structure. The reference list and any appendices, such as Institutional Research Board (IRB) documents, consent forms, interview question protocols, surveys, experiment stimuli, screenshots of visual data, images, and transcripts, belong at the end of the thesis. While students may "discover the appropriate genre by reading research articles," they should keep close in mind the reality that, in many disciplines, "genres are not static and there is always a danger that through identifying, naming and teaching them very explicitly, they may become reified and frozen" (Paxton, 2011, p. 62). Flexibility in format is key as academic fields experience shifts and changes to common practices in thesis and independent research writing.

Students find thesis research desirable to gain experience with research design, data collection, and analysis, as well as having an opportunity to contribute to a scholarly conversation by filling an identified gap in existing scholarship. The skillset students apply and refine through their thesis research experience provides a good foundation far beyond the thesis, such as developing research questions, problem-solving, enhancing analytical and intellectual growth, and presenting findings regarding their study's practical and theoretical implications. The undergraduate thesis represents an academic challenge that carries prestige through its requisite long-term intellectual investment and perseverance. It may ultimately conclude with a defense presentation given to the thesis committee and other audience members including peers, professors, and members of the broader community, including family, friends, and practitioners. The thesis serves as an elaborate portfolio piece used as a concrete focal point for demonstrating the researcher's tangible skills and rigorous intellectual capabilities. These kinds of skills as evidenced through the polished thesis readily show relevance to post-graduate academic and non-academic work.

The undergraduate thesis as a culminating experience option for a student in senior year endures as a highly challenging and gratifying endeavor for both the thesis writer and the advising committee lending support and guidance throughout the process. Next, a discussion about what constitutes effective thesis writing and how to make this determination at various stages of the process ensues.

Effective Thesis Writing

Harrington (2009) stated, "thesis work requires that students use several different sets of skills, including critical-thinking, research, time management, organizational, and writing skills" (p. 398). After committing to the thesis, the student must assemble a committee that will be the guiding support system from topic refinement to thesis defense and final revisions. The thesis student should work very closely with the thesis advisor to get help with important decisions as the topic is refined to a research question or hypothesis set that develops from gaining command of a scholarly conversation demonstrated by the literature review. Often topics start out quite broad and ambitious but as the student begins to articulate what is most intriguing in the topic, clarity evolves.

Thesis writers should begin by understanding how the introduction and literature review are distinct but connected parts that build upon one another meaningfully. The introduction material may include scholarly sources alongside a wide range of other types of sources, including popular culture, mainstream press, current events, and community level to worldwide phenomena. The goal is a creative introduction that serves the purpose of explaining to both expert and lay audiences what is involved in and relevant to the topic. Framing the introduction as the broad scope, baseline information provides a deductive organizational structure that leads well into the scholarly review of the literature. Of course, it is possible that a specific discipline or multidisciplinary field has different expectations about what constitutes appropriate genre writing for the introduction and literature review. Paxton (2011) asserts, "genre knowledge is not just knowledge of formal conventions but knowledge of structure, appropriate topics and relevant details" (p. 58). For example, differences in expectations between a non-honors versus an honors thesis project are delineated at many institutions by a set of standards.

The overarching purpose of the literature review is for the thesis student to demonstrate command of the scholarly literature before arriving at the research questions that drive the focus of the study's design. A section devoted entirely to exploring the theoretical framework employed accentuates the importance of theory as a guiding lens to anticipate patterns in the data.

The literature review expands upon the research that has already been done on the topic or relevant subtopics with attention to peer-reviewed scholarly publications, such as books and journal articles, and top publication outlets in the field (Wilson, 2012). A quick search in an academic library database yields several detailed sources that articulate the organizational strategies and steps to reviewing scholarly literature. For instance, Jesson et al.'s (2011) book gives an overview of traditional reviews, writing the review, and appropriate styles of referencing and avoiding plagiarism. Thesis students should ask themselves: *What has already been done? What do we know and understand about the topic? What research gaps are there? What might my contribution be to this scholarly conversation?* To answer these questions, students must also consider where the scholarly conversation can be found. Does the topic exist in heavily discipline-specific spaces or is it widely multidisciplinary? To what extent might engaging interdisciplinarity be acceptable for the purposes of the thesis as a major culminating experience? Writing a thorough review of relevant literature requires that the student be versed in and demonstrate command of the existing scholarly work.

An annotated bibliography provides a structured method of organizing the research and determining how to present it cohesively in the review. First, skimming and scanning through research article abstracts and then reading full articles gives the thesis student a sense of what each study contributes to the broader scholarly conversation (Lajom & Magno, 2010). Research shows that the more a student maintains a positive attitude towards reading, "the more likely they are to employ better reading strategies and the less likely they are to exhibit information avoidance" and "they are less likely to experience information overload" (Fuertes et al., 2020, p. 694; 707). Perhaps among the most important writing strategies that sometimes feel like two distinct mental and analytical modes for students are reading and writing about the research findings and then moving towards integration and pronouncement of the researcher's voice. Simply summarizing the research does not suffice for the review; instead, the thesis writer should guide readers through an interpretation of the research by highlighting how each research piece intertwines with the others. For example, a thesis writer may highlight points of strong consensus or well-documented relationships or correlations in the data trends as well as controversies, competing explanations and arguments, and how other phenomena may potentially impact the scholarly conversation.

At the end of the thorough literature review, a clear transitional moment should come when a student writes, "based on the preceding literature review, I posit the following research question(s) and/or hypothesis/es" before moving into the method section. Lajom and Magno (2010) state that "the need to study a question is indicated by three important things extracted from several studies: gaps, contradictions, and concepts that need further explanations" (p. 30). Viable empirical research question(s) demonstrate "enough basis for relating a set of variables and enough basis for looking into the effect of an independent variable to a dependent variable" (Lajom & Magno, 2010, p. 30).

Importantly, the research questions and hypotheses, where appropriate, should be finalized before committing to the most appropriate methodological approach to conduct the study. Careful examination of the kind of understanding and knowledge should primarily inform the best method approach to conduct the study. In the method section, the thesis writer articulates in detail each decision and its accompanying rationale when designing the study, including procedures for data collection and analysis, sampling strategies, and mode of access to the data population, where appropriate. Reminding students that researchers have an ethical, social, and scientific obligation to describe their method approach in elaborate detail helps them to think carefully and critically about what they are doing through the thesis, and why and how they will do so in conducting their research. Replicability is a methodological principle that remains widely accepted and expected which requires transparency in the description of the method. As with the literature review, clarity in writing enhances the method section for the purposes of comprehensibility and a demonstration of the thesis student's thorough understanding of employing this method in research.

Encouraging students to think about the writing process at this midway section of the thesis as non-linear encourages an open-mindedness that best captures the realities inherent to conducting original research. Perhaps a shift in methodological approach must take shape because of an unanticipated access barrier to data or participants. Sometimes new information presents itself that the thesis writer did not foresee, anticipate, or consider but that is relevant and inspirational to the dynamic trajectory of the research process. Going back to earlier parts of the thesis to integrate new information, changes, or shifts should be embraced rather than seen as backward momentum that stalls progress. Strengthening earlier parts of the thesis through additions or elaboration enhances the overall thesis project. Ford et al. (2009) state that thesis writers "need to be told that research is messy, that it is o.k. to have slipped a little off their schedule, and that the best thing is to start throwing ideas down on paper about the connections they see in the messiness" (p. 447).

When conducting empirical research, following successful data collection and analysis, the presentation of results and discussion of the findings comes next in the thesis sequence. The thesis writer should learn that this section occupies the heart of the thesis because it is their unique, original contribution to the broader scholarly conversation. Whether to include one subheading for a combination approach to the "Results and Discussion" or to separate them into two subheadings, "Results" and "Discussion," may be determined by methodological conventions. For example, in quantitative research, the results section distinguishes itself from the discussion section with its relatively direct, straightforward reporting of the results in their numerical, descriptive, and statistical form; in the discussion, the interpretation of the results follows in meaningful depth that puts the findings in conversation with the existing literature covered in the literature review. In contrast, a typical strategy in qualitative research highlights the results alongside the interpretations of them together for a sort of "show, then tell" rhythmic organization pattern. The idea in either approach remains the same: showcase the findings in detail by linking them back to the research questions and hypotheses, write about how they add to our understanding, and provide answers to the questions motivating the study in the first place. The "show, then tell" approach may be kept at the forefront of the thesis student's mind as a key practice in ensuring that the data and findings take center stage. Show what the data reveal and how they contribute to the analytical observation to corroborate the results, and then tell how and why the findings reveal their meaning.

In empirical and non-empirical studies, the discussion requires intellectual labor beyond analytical writing and into the realm of crafting and asserting key arguments derived from the data analysis. Weaving one's voice into the literature review to highlight patterns of consensus and divergent thought, the thesis writer uses the discussion section to unpack the findings for readers.

Lastly, the thesis includes the expected elaboration upon the limitations and directions for future research. Thesis writers should understand that no study answers all questions about a given topic and every study has its shortcomings or limitations. One particularly effective strategy in developing this section asks thesis students to imagine if they were privileged enough to have unlimited time, energy, and resources to conduct this research and then remind them that most people do not have such a privilege with research. Framing the limitations in relation to the future directions for research gives a positive and forward-thinking tone to what the thesis did not accomplish and lends authority to the thesis student's voice in communicating about what they envision as the next steps to the research.

The last part of the written thesis body, the conclusion, serves as a reiteration of what has been accomplished in the thesis research. It is a brief, concise recap of what was undertaken, what was revealed, and why it matters in terms of its specific explanatory power about the topic subject matter and about the theoretical and practical implications beyond the scope of the thesis project specifically on related phenomena. An effective conclusion leaves a lasting impression and stops short of introducing new information.

The thesis is a largely independent research process that demands a great deal of intellectual thought and self-motivation and an effective thesis advising professional relationships. The role of the advisor in this relationship is described in the next section.

Effective Thesis Advising

The magnitude of a thesis research project requires tremendous attention and investment from the thesis student and so having a strong student-advisor relationship is crucial. As Ford et al. (2009) point out, "students have never spent two semesters thinking through an extended assignment, so they need prodding, encouragement, and reassurance along the way" (p. 447). Thesis students' expectations include the following generic categories: "gaining professional knowledge and competency, planning and organizing the work, and taking stock of personal resources" (Henttonen et al., 2021, p. 1). Lajom and Magno (2010) affirm that "self-regulation in doing a thesis involves planning or goal-setting, organizing, self-consequencing, seeking help and information, and environmental structuring" (p. 28). Additionally, overarching task orientation includes conceptualization, monitoring, and persistence (Sachs, 2002). The advisor and thesis writer assumes a shared initiative for organizing, scheduling, and setting the agenda for the meetings but students should take the lead on this as they make incremental progress and as various needs arise (Strebel et al., 2021). Thesis students' feelings and thoughts will likely fluctuate in intensity and nature of sentiment during the different stages of the thesis process, so being attentive to these tendencies is necessary for a proactive advising relationship (Wu et al., 2017). Some predictable overarching issues may arise, such as time management (Henttonen et al., 2021), "organizing the stages of the research process, and building in enough time for researching, writing, and editing a draft over an extended period" (Harrington, 2009, p. 398). Thesis students thrive with plenty of structure to both the workflow process and routines and the feedback loops and guidance provided by the advisor. Of course, "proactive measures can be taken to identify students who might feel less than confident in their ability to write a thesis" (Sachs, 2002, p. 106). In their research on factors that influence undergraduate thesis performance, informed by the student engagement framework, Cahyadi et al. (2021) found that thesis writers were more driven towards progress by external factors such as deadlines, expectations of them from others (e.g., thesis advisor) than by internal factors such as lack of knowledge and skills, or doing other activities.

Among the most important initial phases of the thesis process is for the thesis student and the advisor to develop collaboratively a syllabus for the thesis progress with incremental due dates. This syllabus would go beyond the mere "psychological contract" of reciprocal give-and-take investment in the thesis process toward tangibility in concrete workflow expectations (Bordia et al., 2010, p. 2361). Many institutions allocate thesis credit through an independent study course designation and so it is very reasonable to treat the thesis as a course, albeit with some flexibility to account for the dynamic nature of research processes. Developing a thesis syllabus signals meaningfully that there is a contract or commitment to the thesis work agreed upon between the advisor and student. Accountability benefits both the advisor and thesis student in their mutual responsibility towards one another, for the student to make progress on a weekly basis, and for the advisor to provide guidance and specific feedback based on the student's progress. The openness and accessibility of an advisor create a strong start to an effective advisor-thesis writer relationship.

Many departments have a thesis syllabus template that can be modified with details for the specific thesis. It is best not to assume that students come to the thesis process well-versed in what is expected of them and the structure of the timeline. The advisor might begin the thesis syllabus with a set of baseline expectations that the student can add details to for incremental progress, meetings, draft due dates, and other committee member or resource consultations. The more detailed this document is, the better because then the advisor and thesis writer are both clear about what they have agreed to and how those workflows will be prioritized over the course of the thesis timeframe. Logistical scenarios can be included, such as what to do if a meeting is missed or needs to be changed, or how to send drafts and receive feedback (e.g., do you prefer to use a shared Google Drive folder with dated files? Or emailed drafts? Google Documents for a living file that can be modified asynchronously and updated with saves in real time?). A candid discussion before thesis work begins and as the syllabus is being finalized should center on expected and preferred interpersonal modes of communication, such as meeting places, times, length of meetings, and when due dates for progress should be for the advisor to have time to review and return feedback. Furthermore, "issues such as supervision style, work values, learning style, theoretical orientation, work experiences, project goals, and responsibilities should be openly discussed so that both the advisor and the student have a shared understanding of issues that will impact the supervision relationship" (Bordia et al., 2020, p. 2379).

Students and advisors often come together for thesis research based on mutual interest, areas of expertise, and coursework taken with the professor. However, no matter the depth of interpersonal familiarity that exists prior to the thesis process, a vow to prioritize clear, open, constructive, and candid conversations throughout helps cultivate an amicable working relationship (Bordia et al., 2020). If a circumstance arises that requires a hard conversation or intervention, a foundation of clear and open communication will serve both the advisor and the student well. As a best practice, both individuals should feel comfortable expressing candid feedback and concerns so that supportive interventions may ensue promptly (Strebel et al., 2021). Developing a classroom community dynamic, instructor, and student rapport as well as a sense of connectedness enhances student participation overall which positively impacts behavioral and learning outcomes (Frisby & Martin, 2010). Feedback loops implemented as a routine in the thesis process empower the student to share ideas and progress with the intention of gaining perspectives that can fuel forward momentum.

Though the thesis is widely framed as an independent process, the thesis might be better framed as a collaboration because students "depend on their advisor for relevant information, appropriate direction, inspiration, and motivation necessary for successful thesis completion" (Bordia et al., 2010, p. 2362). Of course, leveraging the surrounding campus resources or collegial community certainly benefits the thesis writer in this journey. For example, aside from routine meetings with the thesis advisor, office hours appointments might be easily scheduled with other professors in the department or related fields for specific consultations on aspects of the research as needed. Checking in routinely with peers, fellow majors, and especially fellow senior thesis writers serves the broader purpose of accountability and creating a sense of solidarity among students. Having the opportunity to think about others' projects also can shed light on new or different ways for students to think about their own work. To enrich the camaraderie among a cohort of thesis writers, an advisor could suggest the formation of peer thesis writing groups to enrich the sense of community around the thesis process and to build in additional accountability, even if thesis writers are just sitting together in the library as they devote time to their projects. For students working on immersive, long-term research projects especially, the power of building and sustaining "a regular writing practice among their campus community of writers" leads to well-documented benefits, such as maintaining motivation and limiting distractions, and an overall sense of positive peer pressure (Quynn & Stewart, 2021, p. 1). Thesis advisors, solo or together with other departmental faculty, could take a more hands-on approach to group meetings at strategic incremental milestone points in the research process by hosting, for example, a group advising session to help students overcome problems like writer's block (Henttonen et al., 2021). The value of peer review sessions where thesis writers exchange rough drafts of their theses provides another layer of feedback through comments that may prompt deeper thought on various thesis research elements for the thesis writer (Ford et al., 2009). Positive sources of social support, including feedback, guidance, and encouragement affect the thesis writer emotionally and empower them with motivation (Cahyadi et al., 2021).

The balance between allowing a thesis student to figure things out alone and providing supportive intervention and guidance often relies upon the advisor's early assessment of the advisee's research skills (Agricola et al., 2018). Creating short-term progress plans with thesis students and monitoring progress regularly enables the advisor to assess progress and research skills that may require further development (Cahyadi et al., 2021). To avoid confusion and "faulty assumptions about students' familiarity with the library research process" (Wilson, 2012, p. 47), advisors must introduce advisees to discipline specifics and lend guidance about types of sources, where to find them, and how to assess timeliness. For example, when referring to an article, the advisor should clarify that "article" in thesis research refers to a "peer-reviewed" scholarly journal article (Wilson, 2012). Helping students ascertain the distinction between a scholarly journal article with empirical peer-reviewed research and the broader category of articles, such as popular press, mainstream news, or other types of web sources with articles demonstrates information literacy in practice that thesis researchers must follow. Recent research has found that library databases are widely perceived by thesis writers as "the most helpful information source in the thesis-writing process" and this attitudinal tendency remains consistent spanning the entire thesis process (Wu et al., 2017, p. 268). Beyond the gathering of sources that inform the innovative data collection and analysis process, advisors must provide writing and format expectations. Paxton (2011) found that research advisors "indicate that they do not regard writing as central to the real work of research, in fact, they seem to separate writing from the act of researching" (p. 57) which implies consequences for students in assessment of their final work. In other words, advisees benefit from the advisor treating the write-up of the research with substantial importance, just as they do the design, collection, and analysis of it. Strebel et al. (2021) found that thesis supervision measurably impacts the thesis outcome when the focused guidance occurs "at the beginning of the thesis, when the aims of the bachelor thesis are defined" and pertaining to methodological support (p. 881).

Thesis advisors keeping attentive to the thesis student's range of needs in the process may decide how to ask questions to support their advisee based on Agricola et al.'s (2021) decision distinctions: 1) affective, and 2) cognitive student-centered decisions, such as attention to students' social needs and empowering students to self-advocate and develop their research arguments, and checking for understanding, in addition to 3) cognitive thesis advisor-centered decisions, including information gathering and what to focus on pertaining to the student's needs. Student autonomy to arrive at newfound knowledge or ideas underlies the question-asking strategy because "when the supervisors used the supervising action of asking questions, the students had several positive perceptions of receiving student control, personal attention, or a stimulus to think for themselves" (Agricola et al., 2021, p. 892).

Effective thesis advising includes ensuring that thesis students know about existing resources on campus that they can leverage to support their research, such as the research librarians who often hold appointments for consultations, the student-run writing and speaking centers, the data science lab on campus, digital learning team, or media consultants. Sometimes, stigma can influence whether a student seeks out the guidance of campus resources, so a thesis advisor aware of this unspoken tendency should encourage the thesis student to use such sources as an additional mechanism of feedback on their work. Perhaps collaboration between advisors and librarians (Wilson, 2012), other experts, or web-based support services readily accessible on campus (Harrington, 2009) removes a barrier to support source reliance for thesis writers. Requiring a minimum of one consultation with each of the following enhances the quality of thesis research and gives students additional reassurance that they are on the right track: research librarian, writing center, and speaking center (as preparation for the thesis defense presentation). The nature of the advisor-advisee working relationship emphasizes the subject matter expertise of the advisor and the research topic of the student. However, the professional working relationship of providing support, guidance, and feedback deserves careful and thoughtful attention to enhance the overall thesis research and writing process, and attention to this dynamic development should assume priority.

These often conclude with a thesis defense oral presentation and a question-and-answer session after the presentation so that they may engage in a scholarly conversation with the audience about their thesis research. Pending a final round of revisions post-defense, the thesis enters an archive, either maintained by the department and/or the institution's library. As Exline (2016) noted, "the repository provides students ongoing access to projects after graduation and helps foster an enduring connection to their undergraduate institution" (p. 26). The final grading of the thesis typically factors in the two major components: the written thesis, and the oral defense presentation (Ford et al., 2009). Haagsman et al. (2021) found that scientific quality and structure arise as the best predictors for the thesis final grade over other factors such as professional attitude, which combines the workflows of responding to feedback, showing enthusiasm and commitment, and fulfilling agreements and deadlines. More specifically, scientific quality includes the ability to compare results of multiple studies together, alongside "2) demonstration of a high level of knowledge, 3) adequate discussion of the results, 4) well explained and supported arguments, and 5) clear distinction of facts and hypotheses" as main assessment criteria (Haagsman et al., 2021, p. 1280). Typically, after the thesis defense presentation, the thesis advisor and institution provide information pertaining to due dates and graduation deadlines imposed by administrative offices such as the registrar's office.

Conclusion

In conclusion, this chapter describes how the undergraduate thesis research project may take on a wide range of topics and the content may unfold in depth to relevant subareas that lend to a better understanding of the central focus. Though many programs expect students to make empirical research contributions, these assume many styles of writing and content expectations that vary by institution, department, and discipline, among other possibilities. The overview of the purpose and rationale for the undergraduate thesis as the culminating experience explains the reasons students elect to undertake independent research and how they may go about preparing for the experience. Furthermore, effective thesis writing best practices and timeline considerations help guide both the student in how to approach their workflows and the advisor to attend to the evolving needs of the thesis writers. Indeed, building a professional, amicable interpersonal relationship can positively impact thesis work-related dynamics through a foundation of routine feedback loops and mutual accountability. Finally, a set of supplemental resources that advisors may use with their thesis advisees, including discussion questions, reflection prompts, and activities follows this chapter to empower thesis students and advisors to implement some of the suggested strategies mentioned in this chapter.

Supplemental Resources

Discussion Questions

- #### The "So What?" Question

What is the "so what?" question at the core of the elements involved in this thesis topic? Why does this matter? How do you know? What are the implications of this research beyond your refined focus for pursuing a greater understanding of it? What lessons do we learn from this research that may be more generally applicable to how we think about this topic phenomena? *If students continually ask themselves the very pointed "so what?" question each step of the way, they are prompted to continually assert the reasons their thesis research matters and what it contributes to our greater bodies of knowledge.

- #### Facing Data Barriers

Whether a student is conducting research that includes recruiting people as participants or curating existing and publicly available information, the possibility of encountering access (or other un/expected) barriers to data collection may arise. Use the following discussion questions to imagine possibilities if the first plan for data collection presents hindrances: 1) How will you attempt to work around data collection barriers you may encounter with the first plan? 2) How much time are you willing to spend on new strategies for data collection to maintain the first plan for the thesis? 3) What is a second plan of action for data collection in light of unanticipated or rigid barriers that hinder data collection? 4) How will you gain access? 5) What kind of support might you require for dealing with to hopefully overcome data collection access issues?

Reflection Prompts

- #### Thesis Workflows

Thesis research demands a significant independent study motivation driven by a thirst for knowledge. It is important that thesis students understand the workflow expectations early on. Ask the student to take some time to do a self-reflection exercise on the following topics: time management, drive and motivation, dealing with procrastination, overcoming barriers to the work, organization skills, incremental progress markers, self-accountability, meeting due dates, and writing and revising. For each topic, ask yourself: How will I face each of these possibilities when they arise? What specific actions can I take to ensure that I keep moving forward with the thesis, despite the inevitable challenges that may arise as my thesis proceeds?

- **Identifying Research Gaps**

What are some connections that you suspect might be or that you notice are at present missing from existing scholarly conversations in published research? Identify the gaps that a) researchers in peer-reviewed scholarly articles on your topic area articulate as the motivation for their work, and b) generate a list of possible gaps you perceive after a thorough review of the existing scholarly literature. Which gap(s) spark your interest the most? Why? What might be the value in your aim to fill an existing gap? Write a concise few sentences in which you state the gap and how the thesis will attempt to fill this knowledge gap and add to our understanding.

Activities

- **Keywords & Brainstorming**

What are some keywords that describe your topic of interest? Think about your keywords as an intertwined set of ideas. What else matters to this constellation of keywords? How are they connected, and potentially of influence to one another?

  o Here are some approaches to brainstorm topics, guided by the preceding questions: 1) Mindmap on paper or via an online mindmapping platform using bubbles and color coding to show connections and relationships among elements pertaining to the topic. 2) Write brainstormed lists either free flowing based on whatever comes to mind or thematically organized by topic.

- **Annotated Bibliography**

After a thorough keyword search is completed, collect and organize relevant sources and generate a bibliography. Next, develop annotations that capture the essence of each source. Annotations may include the following about the source content: 1) what the researchers did, 2) why they conducted the study they did, 3) theory and method they used, 4) what they found, and 5) why it matters or adds to our understanding of this topic. Annotations may also include the following that assist the thesis writer in piecing together the literature review: 1) what subtheme of the broader scholarly conversation or topic this contributes to, 2) what other sources in the list does this seem to be in conversation with specifically, 3) how much elaboration does this source deserve in the literature review due to its salience, novel findings, and relevance to the thesis as a foundational piece of scholarship that precedes the thesis research design, 4) any critiques the thesis student has about the source and why those critiques arise. The citation style guides have online resources that describe how and why to develop an annotated bibliography. I recommend also advising students to include "notes to self" in the annotations. This practice of communicating with yourself through the synthesized annotations gives the thesis student a firm grasp of how the literature goes together and why they decide to organize it together in a particular sequence and thematic flow. The goal is to help students put the scholarship in conversation with one another and avoid the tendency to simply summarize each source in separate successive paragraphs.

- **3-Minute Elevator Pitch**

How would you describe your topic in a 3-minute elevator pitch that includes both expert and lay audience members? *One of the best ways to demonstrate command of a given research topic is to be versed in it so that explaining it to any mixed audience is a feasible exercise. Whether in higher education fellow expert contexts or ones with laypeople and in diverse job settings, being mindful of the strong possibility of an audience with mixed knowledge on the topic prepares a researcher well for any pitch level of discussion.

- **Research Findings: Show, Then Tell**

When the time comes to present and write about the research findings and discussion, ask the thesis student to enact the "show, then tell" strategy. Show the data first and really let it shine through and demonstrate its salience, then tell readers what is important/interesting/significant about the data. The goal in thesis research findings and discussion sections is to center the data first, and then unpack its power with analytical explanation to guide readers through an understanding of its meaning in the context of itself and in relation to existing scholarship, or what we already know, about the topic.

References

Agricola, B. T., Prins, F. J., van der Schaaf, M. F., & van Tartwijk, J. (2018). Teachers' diagnosis of students' research skills during the mentoring of the undergraduate thesis. *Mentoring & Tutoring: Partnership in Learning, 26*(5), 542-562. https://doi.org/10.1080/13611267.2018.1561015

Agricola, B. T., Prins, F. J., van der Schaaf, M. F., & van Tartwijk, J. (2021). Supervisor and student perspectives on undergraduate thesis supervision in higher education. *Scandinavian Journal of Educational Research, 65*(5), 877-897. https://doi.org/10.1080/00313831.2020.1775115

Bordia, S., Hobman, E. V., Restubog, S. L. D., & Bordia, P. (2010). Advisor–student relationship in business education project collaborations: A psychological contract perspective. *Journal of Applied Social Psychology, 40*(9), 2360-2386. https://doi.org/10.1111/j.1559-1816.2010.00662.x

Cahyadi, S., Wedyaswari, M., Susiati, E., & Yuanita, R. A. (2021). Why am I doing my thesis? An explorative study on factors of undergraduate thesis performance in Indonesia. *Journal of Educational, Health and Community Psychology, 10*(2), 351. https://doi.org/10.12928/jehcp.v10i2.19912

Exline, E. (2016). Extending the institutional repository to include undergraduate research. *College & Undergraduate Libraries, 23*(1), 16-27. https://doi.org/10.1080/10691316.2014.950782

Ford, J. D., Bracken, J. L., & Wilson, G. D. (2009). The two-semester thesis model: Emphasizing research in undergraduate technical communication curricula. *Journal of Technical Writing and Communication, 39*(4), 433-453. https://doi.org/10.2190/TW.39.4.f

Frisby, B. N., & Martin, M. M. (2010). Instructor–student and student–student rapport in the classroom. *Communication Education, 59*(2), 146-164. https://doi.org/10.1080/03634520903564362

Fuertes, M. C. M., Jose, B. M. D., Nem Singh, M. A. A., Rubio, P. E. P., & De Guzman, A. B. (2020). The moderating effects of information overload and academic procrastination on the information avoidance behavior among Filipino undergraduate thesis writers. *Journal of Librarianship and Information Science, 52*(3), 694-712. https://doi.org/10.1177/0961000619871608

Haagsman, M., Snoek, B., Peeters, A., Scager, K., Prins, F., & van Zanten, M. (2021). Examiners' use of rubric criteria for grading bachelor theses. *Assessment & Evaluation in Higher Education, 46*(8), 1269-1284. https://doi.org/10.1080/026 02938.2020.1864287

Harrington, S. (2009). Librarians and undergraduate thesis support: An annotated bibliography. *The Reference Librarian, 50*(4), 397-412. https://doi.o rg/10.1080/02763870903107448

Henttonen, A., Fossum, B., Scheja, M., Teräs, M., & Westerbotn, M. (2021). Nursing students' expectations of the process of writing a bachelor's thesis in Sweden: a qualitative study. *Nurse Education in Practice, 54*, 103095. https://doi.org/10.1016/j.nepr.2021.103095

Jesson, J., Matheson, L., & Lacey, F. M. (2011). Doing your literature review: Traditional and systematic techniques. SAGE.

Lajom, J. A., & Magno, C. (2010). Writing your winning thesis. *International Journal of Research & Review, 4*. https://doi.org/10.2139/ssrn.1429357

Paxton, M. (2011). How do we play the genre game in preparing students at the advanced undergraduate level for research writing? *Teaching in Higher Education, 16*(1), 53-64. https://doi.org/10.1080/13562517.2011.530755

Quynn, K., & Stewart, C. (2021). Sustainable writing for graduate students: Writing retreats offer vital support. *Journal of Further and Higher Education, 45*(10), 1385-1397. https://doi.org/10.1080/0309877X.2021.1875200

Sachs, J. (2002). A path model for students' attitude to writing a thesis. *Scandinavian Journal of Educational Research, 46*(1), 99-108. https://doi.org/10.1080/00313830120115633

Strebel, F., Gürtler, S., Hulliger, B., & Lindeque, J. (2021). Laissez-faire or guidance? Effective supervision of bachelor theses. *Studies in Higher Education, 46*(4), 866-884. https://doi.org/10.1080/03075079.2019.1659762

Wilson, E. K. (2012). Citation analysis of undergraduate honors theses. *The Southeastern Librarian, 60*(1), 7.

Wu, D., Dang, W., He, D., & Bi, R. (2017). Undergraduate information behaviors in thesis writing: A study using the Information Search Process model. *Journal of Librarianship and Information Science, 49*(3), 256-268. https://doi.org/10.1177/0961000616654960

Chapter 5

Dissertation

Karen Head
Missouri University of Science & Technology

Kevin Dvorak
Nova Southeastern University

Shirley O'Brien
Eastern Kentucky University

Russell Carpenter
Eastern Kentucky University

Abstract: Doctoral students expect applied experiences that prepare them for the next step in their journey. For some, this next step is professional; they will, once they graduate, step into an industry or professional career. For others, there is a focus on entering the academy, either as faculty or staff. To help doctoral students transition out of the university setting into the next step of their career, faculty must develop effective dissertation processes as culminating experiences. The dissertation, as a culminating experience, can take many forms across different disciplines. This chapter, as an interdisciplinary resource focused on dissertations, will help professionals prepare doctoral students for both professional/industry-focused or academic careers by focusing on designing transformative culminating experiences in the dissertation process.

Keywords: dissertation, writing, research, mentor

***

As they prepare for graduation, doctoral students expect applied experiences that train them for the next step in their professional pathway. For some students, this next step is professional. Once they graduate, they plan to advance into industry or professional careers. For other graduates, however, the focus is on entering the academy, either as faculty or staff, often with a focus on educating students and research.

To help students transition out of the university setting into the next step of their career, faculty must develop effective culminating experiences at the graduate level. The most common applied experience for doctoral students is the dissertation, which can take many forms across different disciplines.

This chapter offers a multidisciplinary resource focused on dissertations, designed to help professionals prepare students for both corporate/industry-focused and academic careers. By focusing on designing transformative culminating experiences in the dissertation process, educators ensure that students both learn and advance through the process. The dissertation provides opportunities for learning, skills development, and professional growth. This usually involves a substantial, original, and significant research-oriented written piece that allows the author to examine a specified and pre-defined topic in great detail, answer research questions, examine a hypothesis, or provide an innovative approach to discovery in an academic field.

Dissertation researchers might dedicate a year or longer to the writing process, with research often spanning a longer duration even before the writing process begins. In addition, the dissertation process might involve developing a prospectus, which is a proposal focused on the dissertation research, design, and process, and a defense, which is an oral presentation with visual aids to committee members and members of the institutional community. Details and timelines can vary from program to program.

The dissertation process is an exciting area of exploration and examination given its status as a culminating experience and the significance of both the process and product (the dissertation itself). However, much remains to be understood in the ways we design dissertation processes as culminating experiences that transform learning and knowledge and transfer to professional experiences. Graduates, upon successful completion of the dissertation, are often asked to rely on or refer to knowledge gained during the research and writing process. Thus, this process is a high-stakes commitment.

In this chapter, we examine the dissertation process through the lens of academic culture in graduate studies where both students and faculty navigate a complex set of goals, outcomes, and constraints. To do this, we examine student success practices in the dissertation process while aligning perspectives that span complex considerations inherent in both planning and writing. We see the dissertation as a transformative culminating experience (compared to a performative experience) that involves careful planning as both capstone and experiential learning. The authors recognize different types of doctorates, their intended outcomes (e.g., Ph.D., Psy.D., Ed.D., OTD), and practical experiences, and consider that other programs also require students to demonstrate evidence of learning through published articles in portfolios. We make the case that dissertation work should align with doctoral curricula and that the support and design mechanisms that educate students should scaffold the dissertation process.

What is the Dissertation?

In the most basic terms, a dissertation is the capstone experience for a graduate student pursuing a doctoral degree. Traditionally, a dissertation has been a comprehensive scholarly exploration of a topic relevant to the student's area of focus. That document, which varies in length depending on the discipline, is the written chronicle of a research project or a collection of scholarly articles related to a specific research agenda. For example, in a field like history, the dissertation is likely a book-length monograph in which much of the work is previously unpublished. In a field like industrial engineering, the dissertation would be a collection of peer-reviewed and published articles with introductory and concluding chapters that comment on and link together the body of research presented in the individual articles. Generally, the work is meant to contribute novel ideas to the given field, with the preponderance of the research and writing completed by the doctoral student with the focus on the dissertation as the final product.

As the expectations in some fields have evolved, a traditional dissertation has made way for a project or case study that is more focused on praxis. In these cases, the textual portion of the dissertation may be shorter and function more as a summary of the work completed with the primary focus of the dissertation as the practicum work.

Each dissertation-writing doctoral student has an advisory committee. Often there is one advisor who takes on a principal role, but that is not always the case. The rest of the committee comprises readers who have expertise in the primary field of the dissertation or related areas. Additionally, many programs require an external committee member, who is often a faculty member from another discipline or institution or an external researcher, practicing professional, or practitioner with expertise in the area–who acts in the interest of the field as a whole. Students work with their committee members to outline the scope of their dissertation, and, when the project is nearing completion, they will be expected to present an oral defense of their project to the committee.

Because dissertations are scholarly and discipline-specific, there is no single way of approaching the task. Consequently, the most important first task for any doctoral student is to gain a clear understanding of the expectations of their dissertation, not only of their field of study and its discourse standards but also for the expectations of the local committee members, noting that these two sets of expectations may not always align.

What Purpose(s) Does a Dissertation Serve?

For many doctoral students, the dissertation marks the transition from classroom-based learning as a traditional student to scholarly work. This is a complex move for both the student and their mentors and committees and should be done carefully. Dissertations serve several important purposes:

- Assess learning at deep levels;

- Communicate learning across complex topics;

- Demonstrate research competency in a field;

- Provide new, innovative ideas with merit.

Each purpose complements and extends the next. Mentors can also guide students by making the process transparent with a clear and intentional focus on the purpose, task, and criteria for success (Winkelmes et al., 2019) and carefully designing moments of intentional and deep reflection at key times in the process. While the students are learning disciplinary conventions of the process, they also realize and have opportunities for growth in other areas as well. While after graduation some will move into academic fields, they can transfer their newly honed skills into research and other professional environments where they can use their leadership and expertise.

Types of Dissertations

We identify and offer three different ways students can complete a dissertation, depending on programmatic and institutional requirements and guidelines, outlined in Table 5.1.

1) Traditional

This is a pathway for direct-admit doctoral or master's degree students. It involves the completion of a dissertation.

2) Applied doctoral dissertation project

This pathway allows students to focus their dissertation work on an applied area. The form of this dissertation pathway often culminates in a project.

3) Project-based or product development doctoral dissertation

Project-based or product development doctoral dissertations focus on problem-based research of value to corporate or research fields. This type of dissertation might be appropriate for those planning to enter areas of industry, corporate environments, or research.

Table 5.1. Dissertation Pathways

I. Traditional Academic Pathway Direct Admit Doctoral or Master's Degree Admission	II. Applied Doctoral Dissertation Project	III. Project-based or Product Development Doctoral Dissertation
1. Hold Bachelor's degree with major in specialty you plan to pursue	1. Hold Master's degree with focus in specialty or closely associated field	1. Hold Master's degree with focus in specialty or closely associated field
2. Doctoral courses that include Master's degree level work (If you hold a Master's degree, you will have fewer required courses)	2. Doctoral course work	2. Doctoroal course work
3. Qualifying Exam	3. Research Projects (usually 3-5)	3. Problem research
4. Dissertation Proposal	4. Publishable quality papers written (some programs require at least one paper be published)	4. Project/Product Development
5. Dissertation Research & Writing	5. Comprehensive Introduction & Conclusion written for portfolio	5. Comprehensive Report (including reviews of project/product)
6. Dissertation Defense · Possible Dissertation Revisions · Resubmission	6. Dissertation Defense · Possible Dissertation Revisions · Resubmission	6. Dissertation Defense · Possible Dissertation Revisions · Resubmission
7. Doctoral Degree Granted	7. Doctoral Degree Granted	7. Doctoral Degree Granted

What Types of Learning Do Dissertations Exhibit?

The Revised Bloom's Taxonomy offers an important perspective on the learning and learning process involved in dissertations. Anderson and Krathwohl (2001) argued that objectives "help us focus our attention and our efforts; they indicate what we want to accomplish" (p. 3). A similar focus on objectives and learning outcomes can be applied to dissertation processes, allowing for a focus on learning and learners (the dissertation writers themselves).

Transferable employability skills (see National Association of Colleges and Employers, 2021; Carpenter & Dvorak, 2022a, 2022b, 2022c) factor heavily in the dissertation process, from both the student and mentor perspectives. Table 5.2. indicates the employability skills from the dissertation process identified by the National Association of Colleges and Employers (NACE). The developed skills might 1) inform dissertation writer development, 2) be taught in the curriculum and writing process, 3) offer guidance for writing professional development and support. In addition, consider the ways the following skills impact or influence dissertation writing and writers.

Table 5.2. NACE Transferable Employability Skills

Career- and Self-Development

Proactively develop oneself and one's career through continual personal and professional learning, awareness of one's strengths and weaknesses, navigation of career opportunities, and networking to build relationships within and without one's organization.

Communication

Clearly and effectively exchange information, ideas, facts, and perspectives with persons inside and outside of an organization.

Critical Thinking

Identify and respond to needs based upon an understanding of situational context and logical analysis of relevant information.

Equity & Inclusion

Demonstrate the awareness. Attitude, knowledge, and skills required to equitably engage and include people from different local and global cultures. Engage in anti-racist practices that actively challenge the systems, structures, and policies of racism.

Leadership

Recognize and capitalize on personal and team strengths to achieve organizational goals.

Professionalism

Knowing work environments differ greatly, understand and demonstrate effective work habits, and act in the interest of the larger community and workplace.

Teamwork

Build and maintain collaborative relationships to work effectively toward common goals, while appreciating diverse viewpoints and shared responsibilities.

Technology

Understand and leverage technologies ethically to enhance efficiencies, complete tasks, and accomplish goals.

Scaffolding the Dissertation

Dissertation writers have likely never written a dissertation before–and they have quite possibly not even read a dissertation–so they have likely not been exposed to the genre at a level that would make them comfortable writing one. Therefore, skills that are necessary to complete the dissertation should be built into and scaffolded throughout the program. Scaffolding dissertation processes can be beneficial for both faculty and students. Intentionally scaling valuable and transferable writing skills into the curriculum at specific times ensures that skills necessary for a successful dissertation are incorporated into the program and are transparent to faculty and students. It can be frustrating for dissertation writers and advisors to learn during the dissertation writing process that a student lacks experience synthesizing sources, writing literature reviews, or designing research methods they need to complete their projects. If such skills are incorporated into specific points of the program–for example, a second-semester course including an extended literature review about a relevant topic–faculty can assess student development throughout the program and provide additional assistance necessary to move on to the next level. The following skills can transform dissertation experiences on both sides when built into the program:

1. Reading and Writing as a Researcher

    a. Students should be introduced to high-level, discipline - specific academic writing. They should be able to read, comprehend, summarize, and synthesize material, as well as recognize conventions within the discipline's genres (e.g., journal articles, books, reports).

2. Reviewing the Literature

    a. Students should be able to evaluate resources, synthesize, and write reviews that incorporate a range of literature relevant to a specific topic.

    b. These can be individual assignments, ranging from 8-20 pages. They can even begin (scaffolded) by starting with an annotated bibliography that is developed (revised) into a literature review.

3. Designing Research Questions

    a. While students are developing a deep understanding of the field, they should be introduced to ways of designing research questions that are relevant to the field. This can include locating gaps in research.

4. Developing Methodology and Methods

    a. While students are preparing their dissertation plans, they design the study according to appropriate research processes and methodologies. This process allows students to apply the impactful protocol to their systematic analysis of the research questions or data collected.

To ensure that these skills are developed prior to the dissertation process, academic program faculty should determine the skills needed by doctoral students to prepare for and manage dissertation work. Then these faculty should analyze the courses in the doctoral program, considering the intended outcomes of the program and working backward to ensure that students have the opportunity to: 1) gain the needed skills, 2) practice the needed skills, and 3) receive learner-centered feedback on the skills. The faculty should map where these opportunities are situated within the program curriculum.

Table 5.3. Sample Dissertation Skill Curriculum Map

	Year 1		Year 2		Year 3* * Prospectus		Year 4	
	Semester 1	Semester 2	Semester 3	Semester 4	Semester 5	Semester 6	Semester 7	Semester 8
Reading and Writing as a Researcher	X	X	X	X	X	X		
Literature Reviews	X	X	X		X			
Designing Research Questions			X	X	X			
Developing Methodology and Methods			X	X	X	X		

In the prospectus stage, students demonstrate skills gained through the curriculum with each previous skill preparing them for the next learning-oriented task. The prospectus, as shown in Table 5.3, then provides students with the opportunity to integrate the skills previously developed in isolation before moving to the next stage of the dissertation process.

The curriculum design offered here, along with carefully designed support, ensures an intentional process built into the program. In addition, this creates collaborative opportunities for faculty mentors along with dissertation students. Faculty mentoring a dissertation writer for the first time can benefit from this experience as well. Such design can ensure that the dissertation processes are designed as student-centered while also articulating clear faculty and student roles and the process as one that is both rigorous and carefully scaffolded.

Effective Dissertation Writing

Preparing for the Dissertation Writing Process

The dissertation writing process usually involves five phases, outlined in Figure 5.1.

Figure 5.1. The Dissertation Writing Process

Vision and Planning

This phase of the process involves assessing the landscape of available previous research within the scholarly area or discipline. In addition, it includes a careful and systematic scan of the literature in this area, collected often through a citation management platform or annotated bibliography. Both can serve as useful and productive approaches to review the literature. This process involves working closely with the research questions designed for the study.

In addition, importantly, dissertation writers will often identify issues, opportunities, or gaps in the existing body of research. Thus, the goal of the dissertation is to address this gap or the need for additional research. The dissertation writer clearly identifies this gap, the urgency or significance of addressing related research in this area, and the value added to the field or discipline by conducting the study in this area. In some cases, carefully aligned goals—for project-based dissertations—can guide the process in comparable ways.

Proposal

The path forward builds from this point, building on carefully composed questions to identify the dissertation's place within the larger scholarly conversation. In the proposal stage, the writer should clarify the vision for the dissertation which includes the data collection process, organization, overall structure, and how the work will be carried out. The proposal phase is an important opportunity to invite feedback from committee members. It is, in many ways, an initial version of the dissertation, providing an overview and showing proof of concept before the entire work is carried out in full.

The proposal often requires adherence to a certain page length and other established and transparent parameters. This process ensures a reasonable focus on the dissertation topic and clear articulation of the purpose of the dissertation, research questions, research process, and potential impact on the field.

During the proposal phase, the research may be reviewed for innovation or novelty and for its potential for publishability. An important consideration in the proposal process is whether the research and dissertation will have merit and add value to the field. At this time, the committee has the opportunity to ask questions that can assist the author in moving forward, refining research questions, or honing the dissertation writing plan.

Drafting

The drafting process usually spans multiple semesters, depending on the type of dissertation. While many processes depend on the alignment of the program, drafting might take place on a chapter-by-chapter basis, with feedback coming at the conclusion of the drafting process for each chapter.

The drafting process involves working within a predetermined structure of chapters—for example, Introduction, Literature Review, Research, Analysis, and Implications (or Discussion). Although the format can vary by program, these components are common. The dissertation can develop and take shape around these larger structural guides.

Revision

Revision in the dissertation process is often ongoing. The revision process can begin with higher-order concerns, focused on conceptual issues that are broad in scope, then move to lower-order concerns, such as those that affect issues at the sentence level. These often involve grammar, punctuation, and wording that must be addressed.

Incorporating Feedback

Feedback might come from the dissertation advisor, committee members, and external reviewers It is critical that dissertation writers pay close attention to feedback and incorporate it into the written product. Writers might need to address an additional round of feedback based on the defense or final presentation.

Effective Dissertation Advising

Writing the dissertation is an experience involving developing writing, learning transfer, and metacognitive skills in addition to a credentialing moment that positions students as leaders in their respective areas. Building relationship-rich opportunities is vital in the dissertation advising process. Dissertation advising encompasses a blend of mentoring, academic advising, and knowledge and skill in the research process. Effective dissertation advisors are themselves involved in scholarly research and publication, along with graduate-level instruction. They possess a mix of humility and humor to best move students to completion. For the advisor, tension exists between supporting and micromanaging students during the process (Blanchard & Haccoun, 2019). Finding harmony takes experience, considering the strengths of both faculty and students, providing meaningful feedback, along with building mutual trust in the process. Clear communication is needed between advisors and students to structure the process well and provide appropriate developmental scaffolding to facilitate the development of the completed dissertation. Meaningful feedback is critical to keep the doctoral student engaged and to help the dissertator who may fluctuate from confident and excited to intimidated and anxious. The skillful intuitiveness of the faculty member guides students, facilitating a path between emotional rollercoasters and scholarly writing in the dissertation journey.

Advising as Mentoring

Mentoring can take multiple forms. According to Chopra et al. (2019), mentoring archetypes include four roles: traditional, coach, sponsor, and connector:

- **Traditional** - This role requires acute attention to detail and a considerable time investment to ensure the mentee is producing high-quality work and is on track for success. The relationship thrives on respect and trust. The end goal is to ensure the mentee acquires the skills and knowledge to succeed.

- **The Coach** - This does not involve the same degree of time as traditional; It is often a "one-off"; coaches come in to provide specific help for specific issues.

- **The Sponsor** - Sponsors may help mentees land a spot in a national panel or be selected as a speaker at a key meeting. They use political capital to benefit the mentee.

- **The Connector** - Connectors help ensure that their field continues to attract and retain effective and influential people. They are able to tap into their extensive networks in support of mentors.

Mentors can take on multiple roles during the dissertation process. Primarily, the roles of mentorship scale toward ways of supporting concurrently both learning, via research and reflection, and composing, during the writing process. The mentor role must be considered carefully, as the dissertator is often in the unique position of leading and managing complex research. Mentors also are role models, showing adaptability and offering strategies for working through challenging time constraints.

The advising/mentoring relationship can take place in multiple ways including synchronously, through traditional in-person sessions and via video conferencing, or asynchronously through other media. High-quality online advising can respond to timely support needs. In many ways, the dissertation process is about positive collaboration between the advisor and doctoral student, as the former will need to provide a wealth of feedback–likely both in writing and via conversation–as the dissertator advances through each stage of the research and writing process. As a mentor, the advisor will need to provide encouraging written feedback that focuses more on higher-order concerns including content, development, and organization before spending much time on lower-order concerns including spelling and formatting. The student writer needs to remain engaged and understand that feedback is for the benefit of the project and not to make it more complicated.

It is important that advisors have a repertoire of resources to refer students when additional support is needed. Understanding where dissertation skills have been developed in the curriculum is a starting point, to reinforce the confidence and foundational trust needed to conduct a dissertation independently. The following section offers a variety of practices advisors can use to help their students draft and get feedback on their writing in supportive, collaborative environments.

Additional Writing and Advising Practice

Time

Generally, the biggest challenge facing dissertation writers is time. Doctoral students have myriad competing interests as they work to complete their program. Some students are teaching at their universities, some continue to have extensive lab responsibilities, and others are working professionals. Many must also balance family commitments with their doctoral work.

Meeting regularly with doctoral advisors can also pose challenges (see Head, 2008). Advisors are busy with their own professional demands–research, grant writing, teaching, committee work, etc.--and often have multiple students to advise. Consequently, students must manage their own schedules in concert with their advisors' schedules. For example, a student might plan to submit dissertation chapters during the summer term, only to learn that the advisor will be unavailable. This section lists a number of initiatives dissertation writers and advisors can use in order to make their time more efficient. These programs, which can be offered by academic departments/programs or writing and communication centers, can help students learn how to generate text and revise along the way effectively. They can also help advisors reduce the amount of time they spend focusing on lower-order concerns.

Writing and Communication Centers

Writing centers (North, 1984; Rafoth, 2010) or writing and communication centers (Head & Burnett, 2015; Strawser et al., 2019) can provide a variety of opportunities for dissertation writers, from one-on-one consultations to small- and large-group initiatives. Writing centers that provide assistance to dissertation writers often employ professional consultants with advanced degrees who have ample experience working with academic writers and/or graduate-level peer writing consultants who are graduate-level students who have been trained to provide writing assistance. Regardless of their level, consultants can provide assistance to all types of dissertation writers, from those who are doing well to those who are struggling.

Advisors often recommend that a dissertation student visit a writing center for a one-on-one consultation. A recommended practice for this type of situation is that the advisor provides the student with an objective for the consultation, rather than simply saying "work with a consultant." The guided approach can help both the student and the consultant, reinforcing clarity especially since dissertations can be especially long.

Dissertation Accelerators

Dissertation accelerators, sometimes called "bootcamps," are sometimes offered by university writing and communication tutoring centers. The objective of these workshops is to provide dedicated time for students to develop their dissertations along with guidance for best practices in writing and feedback for drafts. These workshops are offered in different formats, synchronous and asynchronous, depending on the availability of the students. Synchronous workshops are often offered in concentrated forms such as week-long, eight hours/per day while asynchronous workshops are generally self-paced. Sometimes, optional dissertation writing groups are coordinated by writing centers to offer students additional feedback from peers.

Dissertation Bootcamps

Dissertation boot camps, often designed as week-long opportunities for students currently writing dissertations to set writing goals, practice disciplined writing habits, learn new strategies, and connect with other dissertation writers inside and outside of their program or field, can be an effective way to infuse skills throughout the writing process as well. Writing or writing and communication centers can offer writing programming to prepare dissertation writers as well (Baillargeon, 2020; Lee & Golde, 2013; Powers, 2014; Simpson, 2013).

Writing Retreats

Writing retreats are similar to bootcamps, but structured more for intense writing time. These retreats may take the form of a time away from home, such as at a cabin or at a university setting, where the outcome is to produce large chunks of writing. They can include other students where social time is spent sharing meals. These facilities may offer walking trails, places for creative reflection along with writing spaces. Writing retreats can often contain agendas that offer opportunities for students to write, socialize, and provide feedback to others. The social interactions are a reminder that each student is part of a larger community with shared experiences and a support unit.

Writing Groups

Writing groups are another alternative, much like a class or seminar, where small groups of students meet weekly or bi-weekly, either in person or online, to offer social support to one another. These groups often have guidelines for interactions. For example, some writing groups meet simply to generate text, where the writers are there simply to write in an environment where they know others are writing, too. Other groups share their work and offer focused critiques on writing products. With these types of social and academic support, it is important for advisors to be culturally sensitive to the writer's needs. Appreciating diverse perspectives for what may work as a support system is an important consideration.

Ongoing Peer Support Groups

It may be beneficial for students to have the opportunity to participate in ongoing peer support groups. These can be formed for students during coursework to prepare for the dissertation phases, as they are drafting and preparing for the prospectus, navigating the writing process, or preparing for the defense or culminating dissertation experience. Ongoing peer support groups can provide students with valuable peer-to-peer networks. These spaces can serve as important and productive sounding boards and authentic opportunities for peer mentoring and critiquing during the complex phases of the dissertation process. These groups can also serve as cohorts, allowing students to form partnerships while supporting and encouraging each other during different phases.

Supplemental Resources

Reflection Prompts

I.   At what points in the curriculum are specific skills related to the dissertation taught or expected to be learned? How does your program assess whether or to what extent students have mastered those skills?

II.   What are the most common challenges faculty advisors face when working with dissertation writers?

III.   What are the most common challenges dissertation writers face throughout their research and writing processes?

IV.   What institutional student support offices are available to assist doctoral students? What partnerships can your academic program build with them?

V.   What resources are needed at your institution to support dissertation writers aspiring to academic fields?

VI.   What resources are needed at your institution to support dissertation writers aspiring to industry or corporate fields?

VII.   Is your dissertation process transparent to students? What might be the advantages of transparency for current or future dissertation writers?

Discussion Activities

I.   Do you have a graduate student advisory board at your institution? If so, how is this body designed? If not, what form(s) might this take?

II.   Map the progress of your dissertation students' academic journeys to date. What do you notice? What experiences stand out to you? How might this information inform programmatic designs and support at your institution?

III.   The alumni perspective can provide important information in ensuring the dissertation process aligns with student learning and intended outcomes. Does your program have an alumni board? What might you learn from gathering alumni input into the dissertation process (at three, five, and ten years post-graduation)?

IV.   What is the typical duration of the dissertation writing process at your institution? How does this align with faculty and institutional expectations?

V.   What does a successful dissertation do? What are the characteristics? Are these apparent to new or emerging dissertation writers?

Activities to Help Develop the Dissertation as Culminating Experience

I.   Invite current dissertation students to reflect on their process at milestone markers along the way. Review and assess these reflective statements and invite further input as needed.

II.   Review dissertations submitted by alumni one to three years out. What information might you glean that can provide information regarding writing and support needed for students?

III.   Gather a group of dissertation advisors (usually faculty) for a discussion focused on their experience guiding and supporting students. How do they see their decisions and processes aligning with capstone and culminating experiences? What might they continue? What might they want to do differently in the future?

IV.   Track the institutions, companies, or organizations where recent graduates have found employment. What does this information tell you about your program and dissertation process?

V.   Examine the dissertations that have been submitted to your program. How many have led to publications, presentations, working papers, grants, or other outcomes?

VI.   Does the dissertation process at your institution include a culminating presentation or defense? Select several to attend over the coming year. How might these experiences align with the intended outcomes of your program? Is it reflective of appropriate culminating experiences?

VII.   Invite graduate students during their coursework to provide a brief reflection on their experiences and the most impactful lessons they have learned about writing and communication to date during the program. Ask them what they think the dissertation will involve. How does this scale to expectations in the program? How might this inform the design of the dissertation process at your institution?

Dissertations have a long-standing tradition as being the significant culminating project for doctoral students. While they vary in length and scope from one discipline to the next, most require a considerable amount of high-level academic writing that is evaluated by an advisor and committee before a student can earn their doctoral degree. Doctoral faculty are encouraged to ensure that skills related to dissertation writing are scaffolded throughout a doctoral program so that students have had ample experience writing in the genres related to their discipline before embarking on their culminating project. Successful dissertations are often the product of a careful, lengthy writing process, one that includes ongoing engagement between the student-writer and advisor, as well as support from various campus support units, such as home departments and writing centers. Advisors and students are encouraged to make these external resources a regular part of the writing process. While dissertations may appear as if they are written by one doctoral student, it is important to recognize that they are actually the products of larger social collaborations that help the student reach a successful end to their culminating experience.

References

Anderson, L. W., & Krathwohl, D. R. (Eds.). (2001). *A taxonomy for learning, teaching, and assessing: A revision of Bloom's taxonomy of educational objectives.* Pearson.

Baillargeon, K. (2020). Dissertation boot camps, writing as a doctoral threshold concept, and the role of extra-disciplinary writing support. *Composition Forum, 45,* https://compositionforum.com/issue/45/boot-camps.php

Blanchard, C., & Haccoun, R. R. (2019). Investigating the impact of advisor support on the perceptions of graduate students. *Teaching in Higher Education, 25*(1), 1-18. https://doi.org/10.1080/13562517.2019.1632825

Carpenter, R., and Dvorak, K. (2022a). Play as a strategy for teaching creativity in communication. *National Teaching and Learning Forum, 31*(6), 6-8. https://doi.org/10.1002/ntlf.30343

Carpenter, R., and Dvorak, K. (2022b). Enhancing career-readiness through creativity in teaching and learning. *National Teaching and Learning Forum, 31*(5), 6-8. https://doi.org/10.1002/ntlf.30336

Carpenter, R., and Dvorak, K. (2022c). Multiplicity as a tenth strategy for teaching creativity in career- and self-development. *National Teaching and Learning Forum, 31*(4), 4-6. https://doi.org/10.1002/ntlf.30328

Chopra, V., Vaughn, V. M., & Saint, S. (2019). *The mentoring guide: Helping mentors and mentees succeed.* Michigan Publishing Services.

Head, K. (2008, June 24). Why aren't you talking? *Chronicle of Higher Education.* https://www.chronicle.com/article/why-arent-you-talking/

Head, K., & Burnett, R. (2015). Imagining it. Building it. Living it. Design and development of the communication center. In Carpenter, R., Selfe, D., Apostel, S. & Apostel, K. (Eds.). *Sustainable learning spaces: Design, infrastructure, and technology.* Computers and Composition Digital Press. https://ccdigitalpr ess.org/book/sustainable/s1/index.html

Lee, S., & Golde, C. (2013). Completing the dissertation and beyond: Writing centers and dissertation boot camps, *Writing Lab Newsletter, 37*(7-8), 1-5, https://wlnjournal.org/archives/v37/37.7-8.pdf

National Association of Colleges and Employers. (2021). Competencies for a career-ready workforce. https://www.naceweb.org/uploadedfiles/files/2021 /resources/nace-career-readiness-competencies-revised-apr-2021.pdf

North, S. M. (1984). The idea of a writing center. *College English, 46*(5), 433-446.

Powers, E. (2014). Dissercamp: Dissertation boot camp 'lite'. *Writing Lab Newsletter, 38*(5-6), 14-15.

Rafoth, B. (2010). Why visit your campus writing center? In C. Lowe & P. Zemliansky (Eds.). *Writing Spaces: Readings on Writing* (Vol. 1). https://wac.colostate.edu/bo oks/writingspaces1/rafoth--why-visit-your-campus-writing-center.pdf/

Simpson, S. (2013). Building for sustainability: Dissertation boot camp as a nexus of graduate writing support. *Praxis: A Writing Center Journal, 10*(2), http://www.praxisuwc.com/simpson-102

Strawser, M. G., Apostel, S., Carpenter, R. G., Cuny, K. M., Dvorak, K., & Head, K. (2019). The Centrality of the Center: Best Practices for Developing a Robust Communication Center on Campus. *2019 Carolinas Communication Association Annual, XXXV,* 98-106. https://nsuworks.nova.edu/shss_facarticles

Winkelmes, M., Boye, A., & Tapp, S. (Eds.). (2019). *Transparent design in higher education teaching and leadership: A guide to implementing the transparency framework institution-wide to improve learning and retention.* Stylus.

Chapter 6

Applied Projects

Ahmet Aksoy

Columbia College-South Carolina

Amber McCord

Texas Tech University

Abstract: Applied projects, specifically service and experiential learning in nature, expose students to professional experiences in their field. With the growing demands of business, students are expected to enter the workforce with the ability to apply the concepts gained in their education. Therefore, instructors are encouraged to develop innovative coursework and assessments that allow students to apply the concepts taught. This chapter discusses the concept of applied projects and how these methods support and prepare students for their future careers.

Keywords: Applied Project, Experiential Learning, Service Learning, Communication Pedagogy, Career Preparation

***

In this chapter, the value of applied projects, specifically experiential learning in the classroom will be outlined to provide readers with a rationale and template for future use. Although a project specific to communication and social media is used, the argument is made that this project is applicable to many disciplines. The chapter begins with an introduction to experiential learning and applied projects. Then, a specific communication project is detailed. Lastly, strategies for effective projects and advising are covered.

Preparing Students for Their Next Journey: The Applied Project

Wanted: Executive experienced in data, digital, social, search, media, creative, PR, events, shopper marketing, programmatic, mobile, print and outdoor. The ability to simultaneously and efficiently handle up to dozens of stakeholders (often with competing interests) a must. Successful candidate is skilled at managing up, managing down and balancing a P&L. Old-school thinker need not apply. (Morrison, 2016)

Coming from *Advertising Age*, Morrison's quote indicates the future direction of the professional and corporate landscape. Businesses' expectations of their current and future workforce challenge higher education learning to adopt new approaches to prepare their students for career marketability. Many businesses expect their incoming workforce to come in not only with knowledge but the ability to apply its educational knowledge in the professional setting. To better prepare students for their careers, instructors must rethink their course curriculum and assignments. They must include components that culminate experiences with course concepts that aid students in their transitions to their future careers.

The applied project teaching method invites learners to partake in a real-world project pertaining to their discipline (Farazmand & Green, 2012). By mixing course concepts with exposure to professional settings, students gain hands-on experiences in their future careers and develop skills that establish them as employable and lifelong learners (Richards & Marshall, 2019). Applied projects have been implemented in courses such as communication (Anderson et al., 2019), public relations (Silverman, 2012), psychology (Peterson et al., 2014), sociology (McKinney & Graham-Buxton, 1993), business (Farazmand & Green, 2012; Gaumer et al, 2022), science (Baum et al., 2012), nursing (Goldsmith et al., 2006), and engineering (Mokhtar & Duesing, 2008; Vallim et al., 2006). As a result, students engaging in an applied project experience personal growth and further understanding of how their education applies to a professional setting (Fraustino et al., 2017; Peterson et al., 2014).

Experiential Learning for Professional Growth

By exposing students to real-world situations, instructors can better prepare their students for their future professions. Experiential learning, as defined by Dewey (1938), is "the idea that there is an intimate and necessary relation between the process of actual experience and education" (p. 19-20). It is recognized as a High Impact Educational Practice (HIEP), which engages students in hands-on experiences where they utilize course content to analyze and solve problems in their societies (Kuh, 2008). Experiential learning is grounded in culminating experiences because it invites students to practice what they are taught in a professional environment. Disciplines should consider integrating experiential learning into their course curriculum because it provides students with attributes that their future employers may seek (Fraustino et al., 2017; Peterson et al., 2014).

According to the National Association of Colleges and Employers (NACE), employers seek candidates with twelve particular competencies (see Table 1). Particularly, NACE (2020) noted that students entering the workforce should highlight problem-solving, analytical, communication, and teamwork skills on their resumes. Thus, instructors should consider coursework that exposes and nurtures these attributes. Teaching from an experiential learning perspective offers several advantages for educators to develop these attributes amongst their students.

Table 6.1. Job Outlook 2022, National Association of Colleges and Employers

Attribute	% of Respondents Seeking for Class of 2022
Problem-solving skills	85.5%
Analytical/quantitative skills	78.6%
Ability to work in a team	76.3%
Communication skills (written)	73.3%
Initiative	72.5%
Strong work ethic	71/0%
Technical skills	64.9%
Flexibility/adaptability	63.4%
Detail-oriented	62.6%
Leadership	60.3%
Communication skills (verbal)	58.8%
Interpersonal skills (relates well to others)	56.5%

Experiential learning asserts a direct connection between a student's learning and experience. It accounts for students' acquisition and development of skills that will prepare them for the experiences they will confront later in life (Dewey, 1938). As such, experiential learning allows for maximum preparation for students' future professional reality. It focuses on how to develop and nurture skills and attributes needed in their future career. If structured adequately, it also encourages students to experience professional growth needed for their future careers.

The most common courses to implement experiential learning are capstone seminar courses (Aldoory & Wrigley, 1999; Allison, 2008; Fraustino et al., 2017). These types of courses tend to have small class sizes and enroll students who are advanced in their particular discipline (Holladay & Johnson, 1998). In these courses, experiential learning projects have reaped positive outcomes in developing students' practical and technical managerial skills (Fraustino et al.,

2017; Werder & Strand, 2012). However, the increased expectation and demand for students to exit college with experiences calls for higher education to adopt new approaches for their students at all levels of educational learning. Therefore, instructors should consider exposing their students to experiential learning projects earlier on in their educational path. Traditionally, introductory and mid-level courses have larger enrollment numbers and may consist of students from different disciplines (Baum et al., 2012). These courses tend to focus on disciplinary concepts rather than exposing students to hands-on experiences. This focus is partly determined by the need to establish foundational knowledge, but also because planning, grading, and managing applied projects in large courses place a heavy burden on instructors.

Despite these obstacles, implementing experiential learning in introductory courses can inspire students to further their scholarship and explore different disciplines. Baum et al. (2012) implemented a semester-long experiential learning project to inform students about environmental issues. Results showed that the project exposed students to professional environmental work and built their interest in environmental sciences (Baum et al., 2012). At the same time, experiential learning projects inform students how course concepts may be applicable to their future career aspirations. As for most college courses, the goal is to develop students' level of intellectual knowledge. However, it is important to create experiences that help students understand the reason behind the content being taught. In introductory engineering courses, Vallim et al. (2006) exposed students to professionals in the field, took a tour of an engineering facility, conducted role-play scenarios, and presented a paper on professional ethics in the engineering space. As a result, students expressed an increased understanding of the subject matter and how they might apply the concepts taught in class within a professional setting.

The literature suggests that not only are experiential learning and applied projects valued and relevant to the professional growth of students, but it also indicates the need to implement projects that culminate in real-world experiences across disciplines and course levels. In doing so, instructors prepare students to transition into their future careers.

Core Competencies

Research has supported the need for college graduates to have competency in both digital technology and communication (NACE, 2018). These skills are now labeled as a necessity in the workplace as career preparation has transitioned, shifting to a knowledge-based and digital economy (Fitzgerald et al., 2018; van Laar et al., 2020). Burning Glass Technologies (2019) projected over the next five years that data analytics and digital marketing skills would be the fastest-growing fields in the UK. These skills require employees to understand and use social media and digital analytic platforms to evaluate an organization's marketing effectiveness. There is also a need for communication skills in STEM degree programs. Akdere et al. (2019) posited teaching interpersonal communication and leadership skills should be essential components of STEM education, along with working in teams and assessing situational contexts. The applied project detailed below allows students to increase awareness of digital communication, while developing competencies such as problem-solving, analytical skills, ability to work in teams, and communication skills that will benefit organizations of all industries.

Case Study: Communication Research & Strategy

The course, *Introduction to Digital and Social Media*, is a high-enrollment, undergraduate course, with multiple sections. It needed a project that provided lower classmen, primarily freshmen and sophomores, a hands-on experience applying the concepts taught throughout the course. Additionally, the project had to be easy to manage and replicable across sections. Two learning objectives guided the development of the project: Students will be able to (a) illustrate and distinguish between content necessary to target and promote messages toward audiences, and (b) create a social media campaign to promote an event or organization's initiative.

Approximately 218 students were enrolled in the course and were divided into groups of four. Students partnered with an on-campus office that needed assistance addressing its social media presence. A representative from the organization held a short presentation in each class prior to starting the project. Students were allowed to ask follow-up questions to help guide their next steps. Students were tasked with researching the organization's digital presence using the questions provided in the Mini Media Audit (see Appendix A). This portion of the project was completed after students were exposed to the strategic communication unit, which detailed how to identify key audiences, set goals and objectives, and identify persuasion strategies used in digital content messaging. After conducting the research, students provided a paragraph detailing their findings and articulating their specific content strategy. The main criterion for this paragraph is that students provided justification for their strategy. Next, students were required to create a month's worth of social media content for at least two social media platforms. They did not need to create a social media profile or post on their own social media accounts. They were just required to provide the content in a document organized by date, time, and platform. This portion of the assignment gave students full creative freedom. Lastly, students provided an assessment plan, which included how they would measure their goals, with specific measurements provided (e.g., reactions, shares, comments, views, clicks).

After completing the project, a survey was sent to all students enrolled in the course to evaluate their perceived knowledge, skills, and abilities as future communication professionals and the overall effectiveness of the project. After one week, students were sent a follow-up email about the survey to improve response rates. After two weeks, 41.7% of students voluntarily participated in the administered survey (n = 91) and were given extra course credit for their participation. Four students were removed from the sample based on their responses to quality-control questions. The final sample consisted of 87 participants.

Overall, students reported moderate to high agreement that the project provided them with the knowledge to support their career preparation and readiness. Specifically, a majority of students strongly agreed that the project taught them how to communicate across a variety of digital tools and technologies (n = 46, 53%), that the coursework provided an understanding of students' future professions (n = 46, 53%), and that allowed them to learn how things can be applicable to the world of work (n = 49, 56%). Most of the students strongly agreed that the project helped them develop problem analysis and critical thinking skills (n = 50, 58%), leadership skills (n = 46, 53%), and oral/written communications (n = 47, 54%).

Students also commented in open-ended responses that the project developed skills that would transfer to the workforce. One student said, "it gives us real world experiences so we can learn to work on social media projects in a team." The project also unveiled the importance of group work and patience. "I had to be patient with my group, not knowing what everyone was going through. I had to be patient in order to be an effective group member," said a student. Others noted this patience taught them about "team management" and effective "teamwork." Others indicated how the element of group work helped them "gain confidence" and "trust" in order "to collaborate with others effectively." There were also some challenges noted such as working within groups and project instructions. The following sections help provide guidance on how to build applied projects that facilitate workplace competencies and avoid the challenges that arose from this project.

Implementing an Applied Project

A project's effectiveness is subject to the specific learning outcomes proposed. Additionally, there are ways to foster student engagement and create a successful student learning experience. Based on instructor reflection and data collected from students, it is important for applied projects to be relatable, manageable, flexible, and evaluated.

Relatable

Students should feel connected to the applied project. In the case of the social media project, students worked with a familiar campus organization. Partnering with local or campus organizations helps students engage in creative thinking and create meaningful content. For this project, most students had been exposed to the specific event used for the project or could potentially be a participant in the upcoming event. By selecting a campus or local organization, one can gain the initial student engagement that is often lacking in other projects taken from a textbook. The connection students have to campus or local organizations gives a sense of belonging that is hard to create artificially. However, if partnering with a campus or local organization is not possible, allow students the flexibility to select their own organization. This again will allow them to feel connected to the project in a way that is not forced by the instructor.

Working with local or campus organizations provides the real-life experience that is a hallmark of applied projects, but it also comes with challenges to consider. As the project progresses, questions may arise that only the participating organization can answer. This can be problematic with larger classes, as the organization may be bombarded with emails or calls from students. To overcome this obstacle, multiple class meetings should be used as an informal Q&A with the organization. To start, an initial presentation should be scheduled. The organization should detail its goals, target audience, and current communication outlets during the presentation, which will set the foundation for students' work. A second meeting should be scheduled midterm to allow for follow-up Q&A. Students should drive this interaction with information found through their own work and proposed strategies. Other inquiries throughout the project should be directed to the instructor who will serve as a mediator with the organization. This will reduce any repeated questions coming from the different student groups.

Manageable

Consider projects that are limited in scope and broken into smaller segments. This can facilitate a greater understanding and application of specific principles without overwhelming students. In the social media project, students were limited to creating a month's worth of content for one event, "Sibling Saturday." Additionally, breaking applied projects into multiple segments that can be completed over a longer period helps students manage the projects more easily. The social media project was broken into three segments: Mini Media Audit, Content Creation, and Assessment Plan. Each of these segments applied different course concepts, which were built on one another. For example, through the Mini Media Audit, students could identify what current platforms were used by the organization, the types of content they had already created, and where the organization could improve. This information was used to inform the content creation segment. Lastly, the assessment plan was based on the content they created.

Flexible

Enabling student creativity within boundaries is critical with applied projects. Finding a balance between real-world autonomy and a structured, gradable project is difficult. Assignments that are balanced between clear instruction and flexibility permit students to be more creative in their work (Al Hashimi et al., 2019). Placing emphasis on required elements and justification for creative materials is one way to find the proper balance. Justification based on course material was a key element for the social media project. Students were required to provide a paragraph detailing their strategy, identifying their purpose, and appropriate platforms and content. The paragraph explained their reasoning behind creating the materials they submitted.

Evaluate

Evaluation can happen at multiple points during the project to gain insight into what is working or what needs to be adjusted. These assessments can be informal check-ins with students during class or more formal evaluations. Questions developed can include Likert-type items and/or open-ended questions. They should be created to measure the learning objectives set for the project. For the social media project, students were surveyed after the project was completed. The survey collected information by assessing students' perceptions of the knowledge, skills, and abilities gained by working on this project. Additionally, open-ended questions were included to measure project objectives. Giving credit for participation could increase the response rate and give additional feedback. The organization should also be included in the evaluation to understand how they perceive the project's effectiveness. Assessing the organization's overall experience will provide further insight into what is expected at an organizational level and how instructors can better prepare students to enter the workforce. This could take the form of a follow-up survey or an interview. All the information collected can be used to revise the project for a future semester.

Guiding Students: Effective Advising Methods for Applied Projects

Outside of developing the applied project, instructors must be keen on their role in the process and how to guide their students through the applied project. This calls on instructors to develop effective advising methods to support their students as they progress. Instructors must manage the way they interact with their students and communicate effectively (Hutson, 2013). To do so, instructors should consider using meetings with their students, check-ins, and informative rubrics.

Mobilizing Your Students – The Effects of Check-Ins

No matter the class size, instructors must carve out times to meet with and guide students through their applied projects. An instructor's office hours serve as a possible space outside of class to address project concerns. Through office hours, students get additional time for student-faculty interaction (Chickering & Gamson, 1999) and permit instructors to build rapport with their students (Starcher, 2011). These student-faculty interactions have been linked to both affective and cognitive learning outcomes (Frisby & Martin, 2010; McGrath, 2014). However, most students likely to attend office hours are apprehensive (Guerrero & Rod, 2013).

To address students' apprehension and effectively capitalize on instructors' time, it is recommended that instructors optimize their office hours. Instructors may choose to have prescheduled meetings with students or email them to encourage visiting during office hours. By scheduling meetings or reminding students of their office hours, students are more likely to attend them (Guerrero & Rod, 2013; McGrath, 2014). As a result, such meeting times have proved not only to increase students' interactions with their instructors but also to improve their learning (McGrath, 2014). This can be vital for an applied project that requires students to apply multiple course concepts. Whether these meetings are one-on-one or group-based, instructors who utilize office hours as a welcoming space can enhance student learning and growth.

Although physical meetings may be preferred, not all students may be able to meet in person. By offering both face-to-face and virtual meeting options, instructors provide their students with more options to interact and build rapport. At the same time, it exposes students to experiences that might prepare them for their future profession. Since the COVID-19 pandemic, eight in ten Americans have used video calling and conferencing. More than 46% of them indicated using video conferencing for their employer (McClain et al., 2021). Through virtual options, instructors can provide students with professional experiences they may face when they enter their future professional settings. Virtual meetings do this by (a) empowering students, (b) developing their communication skills, and (c) enhancing their ability to work collaboratively. In addition, these virtual platforms aid instructors in documenting student progress (Bull Schaefer & Erskine, 2012).

Mobilizing students through meetings increases students' cognitive success, builds rapport, and exposes students to employee-managerial dynamics and expectations. Therefore, optimizing office hours for applied projects is imperative.

The Semester Check-Ins

In addition to opportunities to meet during office hours, purposeful semester check-ins are valued by students. These check-ins should be strategically placed throughout the semester to allow the instructor to utilize time well and observe students' progress on their applied projects.

Instructors should break down these semesterly check-ins into three increments. The first meeting might be near the beginning of the semester after the applied project has been introduced to students. In these check-ins, instructors can gauge how students have planned to tackle their applied project. Prior to the check-in, the instructor might have students fill out an applied project tracking document (see Table 6.2.). In doing so, the instructor will be able to measure the applied project's future development and progress, while helping students plan out their applied project for the semester. In the second check-in, students will update their applied project tracking document and send it to their instructor along with other documents relevant to the applied project. Once received, instructors can evaluate milestones and provide constructive feedback. Students can then use this feedback to adjust their applied project. For the final check-in, students will submit a final draft of their applied project along with their applied project tracking document. At the final meeting between students and the instructor, the instructor will provide feedback to the students.

The applied project tracking document (see Table 6.2) template may be used in individual or group-based settings. Using this template, or something similar, ensures that check-ins between the instructor and student are organized and productive. Planned meetings with a professor followed by time spent evaluating one's progress have proved to enhance students' learning (McGrath, 2014). At the same time, the applied project tracking document serves as a professional alternative to SMART goals planning. These types of templates are valuable for business companies (Lawlor & Hornyak, 2012) because they expose students to attributes employers seek such as problem-solving skills, communication skills, strong work ethic, being detail-oriented, flexibility, and leadership (NACE, 2020).

Table 6.2. Applied Project Tracking Document

Participants		
Name	**Role**	**Contact Information**
John Smith	Team Lead	john.smith@university.edu
Juanita Hess	Researcher	juanita.hess@university.edu
Adam Wood	Content Creator	adam.wood@university.edu
Milestones		
Milestone Name	**Target Date**	**Status**
Research Organization	January	Completed
Mini Social Media Audit	February	Completed
Content Writing Completed	March	Pending
Edits to Social Media Campaign	April	Pending
Calendar		
Event	**Date**	**Time**
Group Meeting	January 12	12:00 p.m.
Semesterly Check-In w/ Instructor	January 20	10:00 a.m.

By creating semesterly check-ins, instructors can oversee the overall progress of their students' applied projects. It serves as a tool that integrates meetings and office hours to produce purposeful learning outcomes. At the same time, these check-ins permit instructors to provide constructive feedback based on the applied project rubrics and objectives.

Presenting Detailed Grading Assessments and Rubrics

Applied projects can be complex; therefore, they demand a progressive means of assessment that invites learning among students. To ensure students' learning and exposure to applied experiences, clear and detailed grading assessments and rubrics are necessary. A rubric is a tool that lists the instructor's criteria and expectations for students' work (Ragupathi & Lee, 2020). It provides students with a visual narrative that breaks down the applied project into components that students can focus on.

The social media project's rubric highlighted five components that students were asked to master (see Table 6.3). First, students needed to illustrate their ability to conduct appropriate research for their social media campaign. Second, students were evaluated on the craft of their campaign. Third, students' creative execution of content was assessed. Fourth, students were challenged to determine how their campaign was applicable to their targeted audience. Finally, students were evaluated on their ability to follow instructional guidelines. Each component was assessed on a scale from poor to excellent.

Table 6.3. Social Media Project Grading Rubric

	Poor **0 -25 Points**	**Fair** **26-50 Points**	**Good** **51-75 Points**	**Excellent** **76-100 Points**
Research	Lacks thorough research and observation of the concept.	Shows research and observations of concept but with minimal effort.	Research and observations of the concept are clear.	Excellent and thorough research, observation, and presentation of concepts that are clear and interesting.
Craft	Crafted very poorly with little to no time or thought put into creating a clear presentation of ideas.	Ideas are presented clearly but with little to no effort.	Executions are presented clearly with some extra details to help further support the idea.	Crafted excellently with obvious care and time put into presenting the ideas in a clear and interesting way.
Creativity/ Originality	Lacks creativity.	Acceptable creativity. The idea has been executed before but is still a great idea.	Admirable creativity. The idea feels new and exciting.	Exceptional creativity. This idea is fantastic! It feels fresh, and exciting, and would make most creatives jealous.
Applicable (Audience Content Fit)	Ideas do not fit within the capability of the medium and/or lack a clear and appropriate brand voice.	Ideas are executable but lack a clear and appropriate brand voice.	Ideas are executable and have a clear and appropriate brand voice.	Ideas have an obvious and appropriate voice that breathes life into the executions. The work could be implemented today and, on the internet, immediately.
Guidelines Met	The content did not meet the guidelines of the assignment.	The content is executable but lacks some guidelines for the assignment.	Content is executable and is clear and appropriate to the guidelines.	The content is excellent and meets the guideline requirements.

Students favor the use of detailed grading rubrics because it provides them with "clear, accessible, and understandable benchmarks for developing and judging their work" (Ragupathi & Lee, 2020, p. 78). At the same time, students' apprehension is reduced since they can view their instructor's expectations through the detailed rubric (Andrade & Due, 2005). Therefore, detailed assessments and rubrics serve as an additional method to guide students through their applied projects.

Conclusion

Applied projects are a beneficial addition to course content at all educational levels and across disciplines. Applied projects with an experiential learning framework expose students to future career scenarios and develop needed attributes that employers seek in the workforce. Additionally, applied projects allow instructors to assess student learning outcomes with coursework that challenges their students to apply course concepts critically. By exposing students to projects that are applicable to a professional environment, students are more likely to grasp the concepts taught in the course (Vallim et al. 2006).

The social media project described in this chapter offers an alternative approach to more familiar applied projects such as capstone projects, internships, and portfolios. Unlike internships or capstone projects, which students complete towards the end of their studies, the social media project can be implemented at any course level and is not discipline-specific. It can also be considered for individual or group-based work. These types of applied projects not only prepare students for their future careers but also expose them to their future professions earlier on in their academic journey. By introducing students to applied projects throughout their curriculum, students can further develop attributes such as problem-solving, teamwork, communication, and many other skills employers seek. Therefore, instructors should consider implementing an applied project to prepare students for their journey after college.

References

Akdere, M., Hickman, L., and Kirchner, M. (2019). Developing leadership competencies for STEM field: The case of Purdue Polytechnic Leadership Academy. *Advances in Developing Human Resources*, 2(1), 49-71.

Al Hashimi, S., Al Muwali, A., Zaki, Y., & Mahdi, N. (2019). The effectiveness of social media and multimedia-based pedagogy in enhancing creativity among art, design, and digital media students. *International Journal of Emerging Technologies in Learning (iJET)*, 14(21), 176-190. https://doi.org/10.3991/ijet.v14i21.10596

Aldoory, L., & Wrigley, B. (1999). Exploring the use of real clients in the PR campaigns course. *Journalism & Mass Communication Educator*, 54(4), 47–58.

Allison, A. W. (2008). A best practices service learning framework for the public relations campaigns course. *Journal of the Scholarship of Teaching and Learning, 8*(3), 50–56.

Anderson, L. B., Gardner, E. E., & Wolvin, A. D. (2019). Constructing narratives of success in the introductory communication course: Using written self-assessments to understand students' perceptions of learning. *Communication Teacher, 33*(2), 164-178. https://doi.org/10.1080/17404622.2017.1400674

Andrade, H., & Du, Y. (2005). Student perspectives on rubric-referenced assessment. *Practical Assessment, Research, and Evaluation, 10*(1), 3.

Baum, S. D., Aman, D. D., & Israel, A. L. (2012). Public scholarship student projects for introductory environmental courses. *Journal of Geography in Higher Education, 36*(3), 403-419. https://doi.org/10.1080/03098265.2011.641109

Bull Schaefer, R. A., & Erskine, L. (2012). Virtual team meetings: Reflections on a class exercise exploring technology choice. *Journal of Management Education, 36*(6), 777-801

Burning Glass Technologies (2019). No longer optional: Employer demand for digital skills in the UK. *https://www.burning-glass.com/wp-content/uploads/no_longer_optional_report.pdf*

Chickering, A. W., & Gamson, Z. F. (1999). Development and adaptations of the seven principles for good practice in undergraduate education. *New Directions for Teaching and Learning, 80*, 75–81. http://doi.org/10.1002/tl.8006

Dewey, J. (1938). *Experience and Education.* Kappa Delta Pi.

Farazmand, F. A., & Green, R. D. (2012). Applied projects: Learning outcome differences between senior and sophomore-junior students. *Journal of Case Studies in Accreditation and Assessment, 2.*

Fitzgerald, B., Barkanic, St., Cardenas-Navia, I., Chen, J., Gross, U., & Huges, D. (2018). Lessons from the Great Recession: A digital recovery rewards digital skills in emerging field. *Industry and Higher Education, 32*(1)57-61.

Fraustino, J., Pressgrove, G., & Colistra, R. (2017). Extending understanding of service-learning projects: Implementing place-based branding for capstone courses. *Communication Teacher, 33(1),* 45-62. https://doi.org/10.1080/17404622.2017.1372609

Frisby, B. N., & Martin, M. M. (2010). Instructor-student and student rapport in the classroom. *Communication Education, 59*, 146–164. http://doi.org/10.1080/03634520903564362

Gaumer, C. J., Ashley-Cotleur, C., & Amone, C. (2022). Use of client-based projects in business education: A comparison of undergraduate and graduate pedagogy. *The Coastal Business Journal, 11(1),* 5.

Goldsmith, M., Stewart, L., & Ferguson, L. (2006). Peer learning partnership: An innovative strategy to enhance skill acquisition in nursing students. *Nurse Education Today, 26*(2), 123-130. https://doi.org/10.1016/j.nedt.2005.08.001

Guerrero, M., & Rod, A. B. (2013). Engaging in office hours: A study of student-faculty interaction and academic performance. *Journal of Political Science Education, 9*(4), 403-416. https://doi.org/10.1080/15512169.2013.835554

Holladay, C. & Johnson, L. (1998). What is a seminar? Two views of the same course. *Teaching Theology and Religion, 1*(1), 27-30.

Hutson, B. L. (2013). Faculty development to support academic advising: Rationale, components and strategies of support. *Journal of Faculty Development, 27*(3), 5–11.

Kuh, G. (2008). High-impact educational practices: What they are, who has access to them, and why they matter. Association of American Colleges and Universities.

Lawlor, K. B. & Hornyak, M.J. (2012). Smart goals: How the application of smart goals can contribute to achievement of student learning outcomes. In *Developments in business simulation and experiential learning: Proceedings of the annual ABSEL conference* (Vol. 39)

McClain, C., Vogel, E., Perrin, A., Sechopoulos, S., & Raine, L. (2021). How the internet and technology shaped American's personal experience amid COVID-19. *Pew Research Center*. Retrieved from https://www.pewresearch.org/internet/2021/09/01/how-the-internet-and-technology-shaped-americans-personal-experiences-amid-covid-19/.

McGrath, A. L. (2014). Just checking in: The effect of an office hour meeting and learning reflection in an introductory statistics course. *Teaching of Psychology, 41*(1), 83-87. https://doi.org/10.1177/0098628313514186

McKinney, K., & Graham-Buxton, M. (1993). The use of collaborative learning groups in the large class: Is it possible?. *Teaching Sociology, 21*(4), 403-408. https://doi.org/10.2307/1319092

Mokhtar, W., & Duesing, P. (2008). Using research and applied projects to enhance learning in mechanical engineering design courses. *International Journal of Learning, 15*(9).

Morrison, M. (2016, May 2). How account management was reborn. *Advertising Age*. Retrieved from https://adage.com/article/agency-news/dad-s-account-man/303804

National Association for Colleges & Employers (2018). *Job Outlook 2019.* https://www.odu.edu/content/dam/odu/offices/cmc/docs/nace/2019-nace-job-outlook-survey.pdf.

National Association of Colleges and Employers (NACE). (2022, January 15). The attributes employers want to see on college students' resume. [Press Release]. Retrieved from https://www.naceweb.org/about-us/press/the-attributes-employers-want-to-see-on-college-students-resumes/.

Peterson, J., Wardwell, C., Will, K., & Campana, K. (2014). Pursuing a purpose: The role of career exploration courses and service-learning internships in recognizing and developing knowledge, skills, and abilities. *Teaching of Psychology, 41*(4), 354-359. https://doi.org/10.1177%2F0098628314549712

Ragupathi, K., & Lee, A. (2020). Beyond fairness and consistency in grading: The role of rubrics in higher education. In C.S. Sanger & N.W. Gleason (Eds.) *Diversity and inclusion in global higher education: A lesson from across Asia* (pp. 73-95). Palgrave Macmillan. https://doi.org/10.1007/978-981-15-1628-3_3

Richards, M. B., & Marshall, S. W. (2019). Experiential learning theory in digital marketing communication: Application and outcomes of the applied marketing & media education norm (AMEN). *Journal of Marketing Development and Competitiveness, 13*(1), 86-9.

Silverman, D. A. (2012). Service learning projects in the public relations writing course. *Journal of Community Engagement & Higher Education, 4*(1), 1–9.

Starcher, K. (2011). Intentionally building rapport with students. *College Teaching, 59*, 162. http://doi.org/10.1080/87567555.2010.516782

Vallim, M. B., Farines, J. M., & Cury, J. E. (2006). Practicing engineering in a freshman introductory course. *IEEE Transactions on Education, 49*(1), 74-79. http://doi.org/10.1109/TE.2005.85615

van Laar, E., van Deursen, A. J. A. M., van Dijk, J. A. G. M., & de Haan, J. (2020). Determinants of 21st-Century Skills and 21st-Century digital skills for workers: A systematic literature review. SAGE Open. https://doi.org/10.1177/21582440199 00176

Werder, K. P., & Strand, K. (2011). Measuring student outcomes: An assessment of service-learning in the public relations campaigns course. *Public Relations Review, 37*(5), 478–484. https://doi.org/10.1016/j.pubrev.2011.09.014

Appendix A: Mini Media Audit Assignment

Mini Media Audit. Students will conduct research and evaluate an organization's communication efforts. First, they will need to identify an organization. Then, they will use the following questions to guide the project.

- What communication platform(s) does the organization currently use?

- What is the mission or overall purpose for each platform?

- What are the top three social media posts in terms of engagement?

    · Look for patterns. Does the organization tend to get the most response when they include photos? Videos? Do people respond to the same kinds of posts on the organization's Facebook Page as they do on the Instagram account?

- How often do they post?

- Who is the target audience for each platform?

- Google your organization/track down their website.

    · What is the organization's purpose and values?

    · Are there upcoming events they want to promote?

    · Who is their target audience?

Based on the information collected above, students will write a paragraph describing a strategy for the organization to use moving forward. In this paragraph, they need to identify the purpose of the content, decide what platform(s) will be best to use for social media content, and what kind of content will be most appropriate. In this paragraph, it is important for students to justify their strategy.

Appendix B: Social Media Campaign Assignment

Learning Objectives:

1. Students will be able to illustrate and distinguish between content necessary to target and promote messages toward audiences.

2. Students will be able to create a social media campaign to promote an event or organization's initiative.

Instructions:

In groups, you will select an event or initiative on the list provided by your client and will create a social media campaign for your client. Students will be expected to create a month's worth of content which they will use to promote your client's event, based on the data and observation you collect (examples: number/type platforms, number of followers, number of posts per week, basic trends of engagement, etc.). You will explain in 250 words why you decided to use the platform in which you chose and possibly the hashtag(s) you used.

On-Campus Potential Clients

· Office of Student Life & Activities

· Department of Parent and Family Relations

· Department of Residence Life

· University Athletics

Appendix C: Group Peer Evaluations

If instructors decide to implement an applied project with groups, the following peer evaluation may serve as an additional measure that may be incorporated with the grading of each student's work.

Instructions:

On a scale of 0 to 2 (0 = "poor;" 1 = "average;" 2 = "excellent") rate the other people in your group on the five criteria listed. **Do not rate yourself.** Provide the name and scores for each member of your group. If you have additional comments, include them to the right of the person's name whom you are evaluating (please keep it brief). At the end of the document, indicate any comments you have about your group as a whole.

Student 1			
1.		Attendance at all group meetings requiring this person	Additional Comments:
2.		Level of commitment to meeting group goals	
3.		Willingness to cooperate and compromise to reach goals	
4.		Ability to meet group-imposed deadlines	
5.		Quality of contributions to the group	
		TOTAL SCORE (Sum the five items – 10 points max.)	
Student 2			
1.		Attendance at all group meetings requiring this person	Additional Comments:
2.		Level of commitment to meeting group goals	
3.		Willingness to cooperate and compromise to reach goals	
4.		Ability to meet group-imposed deadlines	
5.		Quality of contributions to the group	
		TOTAL SCORE (Sum the five items – 10 points max.)	
Student 3			
1.		Attendance at all group meetings requiring this person	Additional Comments:
2.		Level of commitment to meeting group goals	
3.		Willingness to cooperate and compromise to reach goals	
4.		Ability to meet group-imposed deadlines	
5.		Quality of contributions to the group	
		TOTAL SCORE (Sum the five items – 10 points max.)	

Chapter 7

Comprehensive Exams

Cassandra L. Carlson-Hill

City of Madison, Wisconsin

Danielle Johnson

University of South Florida

Abstract: Generally completed towards the end of graduate coursework, comprehensive exams mark a significant turning point in graduate student experiences. In this chapter, we offer a foundation for more effective navigation and advising of student culminating experiences and highlight the general rationale for and utility of comprehensive exams across disciplines. It also identifies best practices for effective comprehensive exams, including the central role that advising plays in ensuring student success.

Keywords: comprehensive exams, comps, advising, graduate student experience, graduate student success

***

Though the thesis or dissertation is arguably the highest-stakes work produced in advanced degrees, comprehensive examinations mark a significant turning point in the mastery of knowledge and skills fostered by graduate study (Kelley, 2014). Often referred to as "comps" or "qualifying exams," they can indicate a student's readiness to move out of academia with the required breadth and depth of knowledge in a specific field of study or to move on to research that will permanently cement a place for them within academia. Broad and centripetal in scope, comprehensive exams may take many forms, including written examinations, oral examinations, and independent conduct of research (Ponder et al., 2004). Despite their ubiquity and utility in graduate study, many programs do not effectively prepare graduate students for the exam process (Kelley, 2014). Indeed, research shows that 40-60% of graduate students do not complete their degrees (Gittings et al., 2018; Zhou & Okahana, 2016). While personal attributes (age, gender, employment status, etc.) influence attrition, students often cite institutional or educational factors such as academic and social integration into a program, satisfaction with advising, communication with committee members, and research experiences (Gittings et al., 2018; Tinto, 2012). This begs the question: How can we effectively assess and advise graduate students through comprehensive examinations?

We offer a foundation for more effective navigation and advising of student culminating experiences within this edited volume. This chapter, specifically, highlights the general rationale for and utility of comprehensive exams across disciplines. It also identifies best practices for effective comprehensive exams, including the central role that advising plays in ensuring student success.

Comprehensive Exams Overview

Historically, institutions began to implement broad, standardized assessments as an accompaniment to doctoral research in the 1930s, after significant boosts in graduate student enrollments (Estrem & Lucas, 2003; Geiger, 1993). Over time, institutions required graduate students not only to complete their advanced coursework but to "pass a comprehensive examination… hand in a satisfactory dissertation and survive a final oral examination"—or any combination thereof (Stanford, 1976, p. 244). North (2000) notes that a student is only ready to join the academy upon completion of these "ritual gauntlets" (p. 250). This system of incremental assessment is common practice across universities today (Schafer & Giblin, 2008). However, what these steps look like and the levels at which students are required to complete them (master's vs. doctoral) differ from institution to institution.

Stemming from Bloom's *taxonomy of educational objectives* (Bloom et al., 1956)—the "holy grail" of frameworks for curriculum and assessment— comprehensive exams specifically test the cognitive domain of learning. Comprehensive exams assess overall knowledge, ability to synthesize, and mastery of breadth and depth in a field of study (Schafer & Giblin, 2008). Per Kuther (2019), "comps could test course knowledge, knowledge of your proposed research area, and general knowledge in the field. This is especially true of doctoral students, who must be prepared to discuss the field at a professional level" (para. 2). Comprehensive exams also evaluate a student's capacity to move beyond each milestone laid out in an academic program (Guloy et al., 2020).

Many institutions identify the purpose of comprehensive exams on their websites and in other graduate student resource materials. For example, one program writes:

Students should not view it simply as a bureaucratic hurdle to pass over on your way to the dissertation. Instead, before embarking on narrowly focused dissertation work, the comprehensive examination establishes that you have the broad familiarity and expertise with the field that is the mark of doctoral education. It is the checkpoint that confirms that you are ready to pass from being a student to a scholar. (Old Dominion University, 2022, para. 1).

Another school notes:

The purpose of the comprehensive examination is to evaluate the ability of a student to formulate an original research problem, to develop an appropriate experimental approach for solving that problem and to demonstrate independent, creative and critical scholarly ability in presenting and defending the proposal. (University of Iowa, 2022, para. 1).

Further, "another purpose of the exam is to demonstrate written and oral mastery of secondary research to qualify the student to move on to conduct primary research" (University of Massachusetts Amherst, 2022, para. 1).

Often these general descriptions explain the overarching goals of the exams, but direct students to individual departments or programs for more specifics. They may slightly vary in purpose depending on the technical nature of a program, but in general, the end goal is to demonstrate the student can critically analyze a particular topic or problem and apply theory to praxis. Ponder et al. (2004, p. 230) reported graduate director perspectives about the purposes of doctoral comprehensive exams (see Table 7.1). Top functions included knowledge acquisition testing, ability to synthesize, and aptitude for conducting original research. More recently, Guloy et al. (2020) reported faculty and student recollection of these same purposes, adding "gatekeeping" and "forming students' identities as part of a particular scholarly community" (p. 283) to the list. A distinction we discuss later in this chapter, some faculty also believe a reconsideration of the comprehensive exam is vital, particularly as many graduate programs no longer prepare most students for a job in the academy (Guloy et al., 2020). Instead, many students need these degrees for industry jobs, and some programs gear their exams towards experiential praxis as a result.

Table 7.1. Purpose of Doctoral Written Comprehensive Exam

Purpose	*Answers from Programs with Closed-Book Exam*	*Answer from Programs with All Other Comp Exam Structures*	*Total*
To test broad-based knowledge, familiarity, and understanding of the literature/research done in the marketing field	15	8	23
To test students' ability to synthesize and integrate literature and find common themes	10	8	18
To test if students can conduct independent research, including the design of original ideas, original models, and dissertation research	4	10	14
To determine if students can think creatively, conceptually, and critically	4	1	5
To motivate and incite students to read/probe the literature	2	2	4
To prepare students for scholarly academic life	2	2	4
To weed out students not previously "caught" by coursework	1	2	3
To ensure that students are well-rounded methodologically	1	1	2
To test students' ability to solve marketing problems and move the field forward	2	0	2
Other			
- Rite of passage	1		1
- To have a standardized mechanism for evaluating students		1	1
Grand total [a]	42	35	77

a. Grand total exceeds sample size due to multiple responses from some doctoral coordinators.

Note. From "Doctoral Comprehensive Exams in Marketing: Current Practices and Emerging Perspectives," by N. Ponder, S. E. Beatty, and W. Fox, 2004, *Journal of Marketing Education, 26*(3), p. 230 (https://doi.org/10.1177/0273475304268778). Copyright 2004 by Marketing Educators' Association. Reprinted with permission.

Typically administered towards the completion of coursework, comprehensive exams involve a series of questions (based on readings assigned ahead of time or throughout coursework) for which students must write quality responses in a fixed amount of time. In many programs, the students do not receive these questions ahead of time. Instead, students are expected to have the foundational knowledge of the topic area(s) ahead of time and respond to questions with that knowledge base and critical thinking skills. This often involves amassing a repertoire of sources in a scholarly field and memorizing the information ahead of time to deconstruct, reassemble, and apply it during the exam.

However, more recent variations of these exams include take-home and/or customizable versions, with questions tailored to a particular student's area of study and expertise (Schafer & Giblin, 2008). They also may include the student submitting the questions for approval, with the professor retaining the right to edit and select questions for the exams (Maddox, 1993). Many schools provide a laptop to students for the written on-campus exams, but some schools are using web-based all-day or several-day exams which students may complete at the time and place of their choosing. Indeed, graduate directors identified several variations in the types of comprehensive exams offered (Ponder et al., 2004, p. 231; See Table 7.2).

Table 7.2. Structures of Doctoral Comprehensive Exams

Type of Structure		Total
Traditional		
Closed book		28
Open book		4
Total traditional		32
Nontraditional		
Original paper		7
Take home, extended time		2
Article critique		1
Combinations	Open book with article critique	3
	Original paper with article critique	2
	Both open and closed book	2
	Both open and closed book with article critique	1
	Either closed or open book	1
	Open book, original paper, and article critique	1
Total nontraditional		20
No exam		1
Grand total		53

Note. From "Doctoral Comprehensive Exams in Marketing: Current Practices and Emerging Perspectives," by N. Ponder, S. E. Beatty, and W. Fox, 2004, *Journal of Marketing Education, 26*(3), p. 231 https://doi.org/10.1177/0273475304268778. Copyright 2004 by Marketing Educators' Association. Reprinted with permission.

When asked why they switched to less traditional forms of comprehensive examinations, graduate directors in marketing offered a myriad of responses (Ponder et al., 2004). First, the faculty wanted to use concentrated questions as a foundation for which students would write various dissertation chapters later (creating more targeted work for students). Additionally, faculty who opted for open-book comprehensive exams felt it might help reduce students' study time and give them better skills for integrating and critiquing literature rather than simply memorizing it. Further, most faculty felt open-book, take-home exams would get students thinking about the dissertation sooner while preparing them to write publications and conference papers. Faculty who opted for no comprehensive exams as part of the graduate study "felt they could achieve a better assessment of students' skills" through classes and seminars (Ponder et al., 2004, p. 232). Thus, while the overall structure and prevalence of comprehensive exams have shifted in recent decades, the purpose behind them remains relatively unchanged. They are one, albeit imperfect, measure of a graduate student's scholarly aptitude, knowledge, and ability to engage with scholarship.

Resources abound for understanding graduate comprehensive exams. If students or faculty want guidance on traditional or discipline or sub-field specific comprehensive exam styles and questions, they need only look on their university's graduate study website, if available, internet forums devoted to comprehensive exams (such as "Ask Academia" on Reddit or "#phdlife" on Twitter), or they can look to others in their program who already completed the process. However, scholars note that resources can be dated and not applicable to specific advisors, which muddies expectations (Boyce et al., 2019). Additionally, even with the resources available, it can be a daunting and confusing process for faculty and students (Cannon, 2020).

Some comprehensive exams are exit exams for graduate students, and the students know exactly which topics or test questions they might be asked ahead of time. Typically, these exams vary based on the level of graduate study and subfield in which they occur. Some master's programs offer optional end-of-degree assessment types (e.g., thesis or comprehensive exam), while others have no exit requirements at all. Additionally, some universities require comprehensive exams to obtain a master's degree and additional qualifying exams to move to doctoral candidate (ABD status). Other institutions only require qualifying exams. In the latter case, if students choose to leave after having passed said exams, they can obtain a master's without a Ph.D. In some cases, exam assessment and evaluation criteria are not made clear to faculty or students until after the exam or when the exam results are challenged (Estrem & Lucas, 2003). When criteria were communicated ahead of time, students reported finding them inconsistent and counterproductive (Golde & Dore, 2001).

Despite the low prevalence of clearly laid out evaluative criteria, many programs have rankings for assessing students on comprehensive exams (such as pass, pass conditionally, pass with honors, etc.). This "don't know what's right or wrong until we see it" approach accommodates novel areas of study or connections between and among fields of study (Cannon, 2020). However, it may also be challenging for many graduate students, especially those educated under the standardized testing of No Child Left Behind (see Klein, 2015) in a system where curriculum and accreditation center on measuring and documenting student learning.

The array of exam types or requirements can produce a considerable amount of stress for faculty and students alike ("Will I...", 2022). Brightman and Lenning (2011) described the process as "months and months of preparation ... rewarded with nothing more than a thumbs up and questions about when our dissertations would be done" (p. 5). One study found that 39% of faculty did not even know if there was a written description for comprehensive exams at their institution or the purpose of the exams themselves (Kostohryz, 2016). Because of this, scholars note the importance of asking questions about the purpose of comprehensive exams and rethinking how they are administered and used in graduate study (Estrem & Lucas, 2003; Hahn & Leslie, 2017; Ponder et al., 2004). When some institutions shifted from a traditional structure to a more novel approach, faculty seemed satisfied with this repositing of purpose, format, and assessment (Ponder et al., 2004). In the following pages, we detail best practices for comprehensive exams based on the multidisciplinary literature, followed by principles for effective advising during the comprehensive exam process.

"Mastering" a Field: Effective Comprehensive Exams

In previous iterations, comprehensive exams winnowed graduate students and marked who was most likely to find success in the academy (Franke & Kahn, 1992; Ponder et al., 2004). In more recent literature, the objective remains fluid. While this fluidity of purpose can be beneficial, it can also be challenging for all involved. In the Carnegie Initiative on the Doctorate (CID) Graduate Faculty Survey, Walker et al. (2008) noted faculty divergence about the purpose of the comprehensive examination—even at the intradepartmental level. Thus, what we consider to be most vital in effective comprehensive exams is the specific program asking questions about the purpose of comprehensive exams and rethinking how they are administered and used in graduate study (Estrem & Lucas, 2003; Hahn & Leslie, 2017; Ponder et al., 2004; Wood, 2004). Kostohryz (2016) contended that given ever-evolving accreditation standards, a primary responsibility of graduate programs is to ensure the purpose of a comprehensive exam reflects the current program goals and foci. Indeed, if program faculty and university administration cannot position this milestone within their overall graduate educational mission and learning outcomes, they will have difficulty fostering an informed, inclusive, and purposeful experience for students.

Although this may be obvious to some well-established graduate programs, not all programs update their information regularly or have consistent program information listed on their websites, let alone offer support for exam completion (Fisher et al., 2020). To ensure comprehensive exams assess what students need to master, graduate programs should keep a few things at the center of their curriculum and assessment development.

Department/program faculty and administrators must guarantee these exams serve a clearly explicated purpose. This purpose is generally established by the faculty who need to keep the changing landscape of advanced degrees in mind. Guloy et al. (2020) emphasized the salience of this task by encouraging graduate faculty to consider whether the questions posed in comprehensive examinations are congruent with their stated purpose. To claim to measure the mastery and synthesis of theoretical concepts in a comprehensive exam when primarily separating the students in terms of scholarly success is disingenuous. Instead, all the comprehensive exam's purposes within a specific program should be clearly identified and each question or type of assessment directly linked to those outcomes. To achieve this, Guloy et al. (2020) suggested a systematic "reflection on why the original foci were considered important, whether they still are, and/or whether there are alternative ways in which the aims might be addressed" (p. 288). Walker et al. (2008) posed the following questions for consideration:

- What is the purpose of the doctoral program? What does it mean to develop students as stewards? What are the desired outcomes of the program?

- What is the rationale and educational purpose of each element of the doctoral program? Which elements of the program should be affirmed and retained? Which elements could usefully be changed or eliminated?

- How do you know? What evidence aids in answering those questions? What evidence can be collected to determine whether change serves the desired outcome?

Answering such questions collaboratively helps establish a clear purpose for all culminating experiences, reducing unproductive anxiety surrounding comprehensive exams for students and faculty alike.

Programs should conduct a periodic, systematic review of expectations and educational goals for students. This could also include performance targets and assessment types by subdiscipline or major. Hahn and Leslie (2017) suggested that business graduate programs consider performance expectations for students of accounting versus students of marketing, as their program entry and coursework requirements differ. Another suggestion for ensuring assessment closely aligns with subdisciplines is based on Patterson's (2006) findings from social work graduate programs. The author suggested that programs consider one common assessment, such as a comprehensive exam or portfolio of coursework after foundation courses are completed to assess general knowledge of the field. This way programs ensure students have a broad base-level shared knowledge of the field broadly, prior to moving into their subdiscipline study. Programs could then administer subfield-specific assessments, such as an oral defense or research study, after specialized coursework to examine a student's ability to engage in scholarship or dissertation research.

Additionally, the long-term career goals of a program's students should be at the center of how those students are assessed—even in the context of comprehensive exams. Guloy et al. (2020) noted that many faculty assume their role as advisors is to guide students toward a research-oriented understanding of a field. Faculty tend to view graduate degrees as solely preparing students for careers within the academy, understandably because that was the faculty member's experience with graduate school. However, the data paints a different picture. Estimates show that only 12-35% of Ph.D. graduates find tenure-track teaching/research positions in the U.S. and Canada (Larson et al., 2014; Peters, 2021). Indeed, 2019 estimates showed—for the first time in history—that private sectors employed an equal number of Ph.D. graduates in educational institutions (Langin, 2019). In business, a master's or doctorate degree offers high-level training necessary for industry senior management positions (North Central University, 2022). Academic careers only accounted for two of the top ten professions for individuals with a master's or Ph.D. in the humanities—with policy advisors, consulting, and the non-profit sector rounding out the list (Sorbara, 2022). Langin (2019) wrote, "The data also serve as a reality check for faculty members who otherwise still assume that tenure track positions are the standard path for today's trainees" (para. 8).

Given how few graduate students are securing tenure track positions, it is more apparent than ever that a traditional approach to comprehensive exams may be outdated. If most graduate students in a program are not likely to work in research-oriented settings, programs should reconsider the purposes and content of comprehensive examinations to match the preferred qualifications of job candidates in a specific field (Guloy et al., 2020; Hahn & Leslie, 2017;

Kostohryz, 2016). Examining program data about student end goals can help programs best tailor what content a comprehensive exam should cover.

There remains the caveat that when obtaining degrees for technical careers, technical and standardized testing might be ideal, and, in some cases, required for certification. For example, Cassuto (2019) noted that in biology, many students use graduate programs as a launchpad for specialized positions in the private sector at biotechnology companies. Effective comprehensive exams may still allow for required standardized testing or traditional testing formats.

When the sole focus is on the winnowing of those who can and those who cannot conduct research or publish in academic venues, this limits the full range of experiences students can have that will prepare them for their careers outside of the academy. Per Silva et al. (2019), the more understanding of the needs of students and where they go after graduate school, the better they can be prepared for their careers. Silva et al. (2019) published a toolkit of sorts to assist programs with this process at their own institutions.

A less common approach to comprehensive exams equips graduate students to communicate about their field with the public (Lindquist et al., 2011). This focuses on assessing students based on their ability to connect and communicate about their research. Indeed, Cassuto (2021) noted that higher education has a public relations problem rooted in distrust and misunderstanding. Graduate programs are beginning to recognize the salience of producing graduate students who can adequately communicate about and beyond their field. "Socially committed work, no matter the size of its audience, demonstrates the connection between the university and the society it serves — and is served by" (Cassuto, 2021, para. 23). Assessing graduate students' preparedness to explain the value of their discipline may begin with comprehensive exams and institutions should identify ways in which this can be incorporated into their programs. For example, some programs at North Dakota State now require graduate students to pass a content-based comprehensive exam and to create something publicly accessible where they explain their proposed thesis or dissertation research in layperson's terms as part of qualifying for candidacy (Cassuto, 2019). Lindquist et al. (2011) at the University of Nebraska highlighted exam prompts asking students to incorporate an essay for the public about a specific topic area. They noted that while the comprehensive written exam is "an important way to assess technical knowledge… for some students we feel that this is an innovative approach to broadening the capacities of a young professional to reach the public" (p. 107). This kind of communication with the public assessment could also be incorporated into other culminating experiences.

As noted earlier in this chapter, many graduate programs list the purpose of and process for comprehensive exams on their program sites. If programs are not already doing so, they should. Programs should also include on their program web pages a manual for graduate students including (sub)discipline-specific purposes and procedures. This is important since, for example, a comprehensive exam in an M.S. of Mathematics program may look wildly different than a doctoral qualifying exam for English.

It seems basic: Have a purpose for comprehensive exams, explicitly state that purpose in writing and to the public, include it in student materials, assess based on that purpose, and reevaluate that purpose every few years. Indeed, many universities have missions or "ideas" (e.g., The "Wisconsin Idea" at the University of Wisconsin-Madison) centered on a purpose. However, this requires faculty buy-in and collaboration, a systematic review and implementation of the new curriculum, and a dedication to excellence and innovation, not just maintaining the status quo. Somervell (2015) contended that the initial purpose discussions and exam restructuring will be the most significant investment of time for departments. The subsequent review, administration, and grading can be achieved semi- or annually, thus, being less work once implemented effectively.

Effective Advising for Comprehensive Exams

Rethinking comprehensive exams in graduate school also means rethinking the ways in which we advise graduate students in the process. Cassuto (2012, 2019) contended that for generations graduate teaching and advising were simply a byproduct of faculty research. Faculty often tailored their course curriculum to their most current writing projects; students hopped onto faculty research projects, and students were matched to advisors with whom could be a symbiotic, at best, relationship based on shared research interests. Few advisors were matched with graduate students based on student needs and other socio-cultural factors associated with graduate student attrition. In fact, students' socio-cultural needs were long ignored in graduate study, privileging the faculty members and programs these students served.

Nerad and Cerny (1997) found that one-third of students leave graduate programs not during the dissertation writing stages, but during the "in-between" period of writing a proposal or completing comprehensive exams. They noted this is sometimes because of a lack of clearly communicated expectations and guidelines for what the process entails. Sometimes, it is directly tied to a dearth of support after coursework completion.

Within the last two decades, much research has highlighted the value of fostering a culture of support—not just intellectual growth—in graduate school (e.g., Walker et al., 2008), particularly in the interim periods post coursework and pre-dissertation. Graduate faculty have become "guides, gatekeepers, advisors, teachers—and often friends and mentors" (Estrem & Lucas, 2003, p.

402). Below we elucidate those findings, connecting them to effective advising before and during comprehensive or qualifying exams.

Open, Timely, and Direct Advisor Communication

Estrem and Lucas (2003) found that few rhetoric and composition programs, for example, publicly listed evaluation measures (less than 31%) or assessment criteria for comprehensive exams (less than 4%). When this information is not readily found on program sites or in program manuals, students rely on their advisors to provide them with this information. Graduate students reported feeling a lack of clarity and consistency in this "middle stage work" (Estrem & Lucas, 2003 p. 400). Many graduate students do not know the kinds of questions to ask when they enter various stages of graduate school. Nerad and Cerny (1997) indicated that students often felt "disappointed … to discover they were given an opportunity to demonstrate only a small part of their knowledge" after acquiring a vast breadth and depth of knowledge in their (sub)fields (p. 342). Guloy et al.'s (2020) findings echoed this, noting that many students reported only receiving one or two comprehensive (context mastery) questions with others geared toward their thesis or dissertation proposal. This was in direct contrast to some graduate study websites, which listed the stated purpose of these exams as assessing mastery of core material covered in coursework.

Faculty note that students' expectations seem vague, and the aura of mystery around comprehensive exams may lead to self-imposed perfectionism and burnout (Nerad & Cerny, 1997). However, faculty may also fail to recognize their role in making those expectations clear. There is a noted disconnect between the expectation and reality of comprehensive or qualifying exams on the parts of students and faculty. Indeed, comprehensive exam structures are most often based on the knowledge and skills valued by faculty in a program; students who acquire a sense of what faculty members value are primed to pass more easily than those who do not (Guloy et al., 2020).

As scholars of communication, we advocate for open, timely, and accessible advisor communication well before and during comprehensive exams, so advisors can "take some of the mystery out of" the process, helping facilitate student success (Nerad & Cerny, 1997, p. 309). Boyce et al.'s (2019) work supports this conclusion, citing the salience of strong communication about and preparation for middle-level graduate work: "Persistent communication of program requirements through formal structures such as orientation sessions, published handbooks, funded assistantships, and annual reviews help students create a more accurate picture of life in a graduate program" (p. 308).

As noted earlier in this chapter, programs must be able to identify the purposes and create strong foundations for evaluating comprehensive exams. Once that is accomplished, advisors must adequately communicate the guidelines, expectations, and desired outcomes before the students begin studying to help eliminate some of the stress associated with the process (Guloy et al., 2020). This will help students identify the clear purposes of these exams, making them seem less arbitrary or unnecessary, in the eyes of students. Without this, programs risk maintaining a status quo in which moving out of coursework is less about mastery of and critical thinking about a field of study, and more about fortitude throughout rites of passage in graduate school.

Student Sociocultural Experiences and Advising

One of this chapter's authors frequently reminds students that graduate school is not for the faint of heart. It requires not only deep-level thinking but the ability also to make novel and meaningful contributions to a field—and resilience when either of those is lacking. It can also have innumerable personal, emotional, and financial costs. These impact student attrition (Burns & Gillespie, 2018). They also mean that faculty advisors must view and relate to their graduate students not just as students or employees to be managed, but as complex humans with unique needs and abilities. As such, advisors are uniquely positioned to meet the students where they stand and support them in getting to where they need to be (Kelley, 2014).

A challenge in advising for comprehensive exams is ensuring that faculty and student perceptions of need align. For example, Burns and Gillespie (2018) found that while faculty perceive coursework as the time to offer extensive feedback, create stringent deadlines for students, and afford structure to the educational process, preparation for mid- and late-level stages of graduate degrees, such as comprehensive exams and dissertating, should be autonomous enterprises. Sudden freedom or newfound autonomy often accompanies the comprehensive exam in the form of completing work on students' own time and at their own pace as well as negotiating when *they* feel ready to complete their qualifying or comprehensive exam (Fisher et al., 2020).

Students may not understand the stages after their coursework in the same way faculty expect they might. If the advisor does not adequately prepare students for the transition into this newfound autonomy as they prepare for degree milestones, they may flounder (Estrem & Lucas, 2003; Guloy et al., 2020). Indeed, students noted the desire and need for continued support after the completion of coursework (Burns & Gillespie, 2018) to lessen the overwhelmingness of sudden freedom. Instead of autonomy, they preferred structure and connection to their advisor and the broader purpose of their advanced degree. Advisors do not need to hold students' hands after coursework, but providing clear next steps, open communication, and accountability may go a long way in supporting student success before and during comprehensive exams. Additionally, students noted the sense of extended community they felt post-coursework, while preparing for comprehensive exams, if they were in regular contact with their advisor and peers. This was particularly salient (Burns & Gillespie, 2018; Guloy et al., 2020; Jiang, 2020; Kelley, 2014) for students on the margins economically, who perhaps need to hold down other jobs or have family dependents at home, racially/ethnically/gender-wise, and in terms of enrollment status with part-time or full-time enrollment. All these students express various needs, and advisors should work to attune themselves and become part of meeting those individual needs.

Another opportunity for effective advising includes an extension of social support for writing beyond coursework. Fisher et al. (2020) cited many students who felt like the comprehensive exam ushered them into a different, more challenging level of writing and positionality within the program. Students struggled with "various aspects of claiming knowledge" (p. 375) and "finding a comfortable position from which to speak" (p. 374) during their comprehensive exams. Some students were stressed by the sheer volume of reading they needed to keep track of, while others felt that coursework had not adequately prepared them for comprehensive exam levels of synthesis and writing. Thus, Fisher et al. recommended: (a) identifying the "hidden genres" (p. 376) that support exam completion, such as reference matrixes, evaluative and assessment criteria; (b) offering workshops for faculty and post-comps students to share unexpected struggles that arise and learn of the resources available to manage them; (c) highlighting informal writing genres that may better prepare students for formal exam writing; (d) offering opportunities to explore disciplinary and personal identity development at various stages in the graduate degree program, and; (e) assessing critical stages and how they impact student transformation not just in knowledge but also in their representations of self and their communities.

The cognitive work of graduate study is inextricable from larger socio-cultural identities and conditions for learning and writing (Fisher et al., 2020; Kelley, 2014). As such, students benefit from advising that offers structure, while also valuing reflexivity and adaptation. Advisors can play a central role in student agility and perseverance by communicating openly and often, taking time to assess student needs and unique circumstances, and providing opportunities for students to learn from faculty and other students about the comprehensive or qualifying exam process.

Future Considerations for Comprehensive Exams

Despite their wide use within the academic community, some scholars question the validity of cumulative or comprehensive exams. At many institutions "comps" or "quals" mark a weeding out of weaker students and ensure those who move forward find success in the end (Schafer & Giblin, 2008). Though this is an ingrained tradition that graduate students may support—some call it "comping out"—others note this inherently privileges institutions. Hinchey and Kimmel (2000) contend that institutions may maintain or grow graduate programs to provide low-paid labor and grant support, earn prestige, and boost institution rankings.

Indeed, Taylor and Gannon (2018) encourage us to "start somewhere else" when considering comprehensive exams, by viewing them as an opportunity to experiment, bearing in mind that comprehensive exams are both performative and productive (p. 3). Each program must revisit the purpose of these exams to ensure they accurately represent the discipline, faculty, and post-graduation landscape for their students. It also means preparing students adequately to understand that while some programs or disciplines have uniformity in comprehensive exams, others may not. Clear communication about expectations for comprehensive exams in program literature, disseminated by advisors, and thoughtfully understood by students, can help to alleviate some of the anxiety surrounding this mid-level form of assessment. Flexibility and adaptability in assessment format may also go a long way in ensuring the validity of the purpose of these exams. Alternative exam styles may also prove more inclusive and equally beneficial for students and faculty alike. When tailored and executed in a supportive community of scholars, comprehensive exams can prove one of the most valuable culminating graduate student experiences. Brooks (2011) cites personal experience elucidating this:

> Of all the benefits that came from preparing for and taking my exams -- identifying the pertinent literature, grappling with and grouping the major arguments, imagining new interpretations and new courses, and experiencing this exercise in sheer discipline -- the biggest was psychological. Field exams helped me to imagine myself as a teacher as well as a lifelong student. I will always see my faculty examiners as my teachers, but exams taught me to see them as colleagues as well (para. 25).

References

Bloom, B. S., Engelhart, M. D., Furst, E. J., Hill, W. H., & Krathwohl, D. R. (1956). *Taxonomy of educational objectives: The classification of educational objectives by a committee of college and university examiners (Handbook I: Cognitive domain)*. Longmans.

Boyce, B. A., Napper-Owen, G., Lund, J.L., & Almarode, D. (2019). Doctoral students' perspectives on their doctoral programs and department. *Quest*, *71*(3), 299–310. https://doi.org/10.1080/00336297.2019.1618070

Brightman, S., & Lenning, E. (2011). Surviving graduate school. In E. Lenning, S., Brightman, & S. Caringella (Eds.), *A guide to surviving a career in academia* (pp. 5–17). Routledge. https://doi.org/10.4324/9780203855904

Brooks, D. (2011, January 6). As smart as I'll ever be. *The Chronicle of Higher Education*. https://www.chronicle.com/article/as-smart-as-ill-ever-be/

Burns, E. M., & Gillespie, C. W. (2018). A phenomenological study of attrition from a doctoral cohort program: Changes in feelings of autonomy and relatedness in the dissertation stage. *International Journal of Doctoral Studies, 13*, 517–537. https://doi.org/10.28945/4158

Cannon, S. O. (2020). Making kin with comprehensive exams: Producing scholar in intra-action. *Social Science Information, 26*(1), 36–50. https://doi.org/10.1177/1077800419869962

Cassuto, L. (2012, March 4). The comprehensive exam: Make it relevant. *The Chronicle of Higher Education*. https://www.chronicle.com/article/the-comprehensive-exam-make-it-relevant/

Cassuto, L. (2019, May 19). Outcome-based graduate school? *The Chronicle of Higher Education*. https://www.chronicle.com/article/outcome-based-graduate-school/

Cassuto, L. (2021, August 26). What's the best way to do public humanities? Ask a philosopher. *The Chronicle of Higher Education*. https://www.chronicle.com/article/whats-the-best-way-to-do-public-humanities-ask-a-philosopher

Estrem, H., & Lucas, B. E. (2003). Embedded traditions, uneven reform: The place of the comprehensive exam in composition and rhetoric PhD programs. *Rhetoric Review, 22*, 396–416. https://doi.org/10.1207/S15327981RR2204_4

Fisher, R., Brock, C. H., Frahm, T., Van Wig, A., & Gillis, V. R. (2020). Reflections on writing and identity: Exploring the role of qualifying exams in the sociocultural development of doctoral students. *Studies in Continuing Education, 42*(3), 365–380. https://doi.org/10.1080/0158037X.2019.1661237

Franke, G. R., & Kahn, K.B. (1992). Comprehensive examinations in marketing doctoral programs: Content, purpose, and outcomes. In R. P. Leone & V. Kumar (Eds.), *American Marketing Association's educators' proceedings* (pp. 526-527).

Geiger, R. (1993). Research, graduate education, and the ecology of American universities. In S. Rothblatt & B. Wittrock (Eds.), *The European and American university since 1800* (pp. 234–259). Cambridge University Press. https://doi.org/10.1017/CBO9780511720925

Gittings, G., Bergman, M., Shuck, B. & Rose, K. (2018). The impact of student attributes and program characteristics on doctoral degree completion. *New Horizons in Adult Education & Human Resource Development, 30*(3), 3–22. https://doi.org/10.1002/nha3.20220

Golde, C. M., & Dore, T. M. (2001). *At cross purposes: What the experiences of today's doctoral students reveal about doctoral education.* The Pew Charitable Trusts. https://www.phd-survey.org

Guloy, S., Hum, G., & O'Neill, D. K. (2020). Voices at the gate: Faculty members' and students' differing perspectives on the purposes of the PhD comprehensive examination. *Assessment & Evaluation in Higher Education, 45*(2), 279–291. https://doi.org/10.1080/02602938.2019.1637819

Hahn, W., & Leslie, B. (2017). The comprehensive business exam: Usefulness for assessing instructional and student performance outcomes. *Journal of Education for Business, 92*(1), 23–28. https://doi.org/10.1080/08832323.2016.1270886

Hinchey, P., & Kimmel, I. (2000). *The graduate grind*. Routledge.

Jiang, X. (2020). Isolation squared? An autoethnography study of the comprehensive examination during the COVID-19 outbreak (ED611617). ERIC. https://files.eric.ed.gov/fulltext/ED611617.pdf

Kelley, A. (2014). Layers of consciousness: An autoethnographic study of the comprehensive exam process. *International Journal of Doctoral Studies, 9*(1), 347–360. https://doi.org/10.28945/2079

Klein, A. (2015, April 10). *No child left behind: An overview. Education Week.* https://www.edweek.org/policy-politics/no-child-left-behind-an-overview/2015/04

Kostohryz, K. (2016). The doctoral comprehensive examination in counselor education: Faculty members' perception of its purposes. *Journal of Counselor Preparation and Supervision, 8*(3). https://doi.org/10.7729/83.1068

Kuther, T. (2019, March 24). *A note about masters and doctoral comprehensive exams.* ThoughtCo. https://www.thoughtco.com/masters-and-doctoral-stud ents-comprehensive-examinations-1686465

Langin, K. (2019, March 12*).* In a first, U.S. private sector employs nearly as many Ph.D.s as schools do. *Science.* https://www.science.org/content/article /first-us-private-sector-employs-nearly-many-phds-schools-do

Larson, R. C., Ghaffarzadegan, N., & Xue, Y. (2014). Too many PhD graduates or too few academic job openings: The basic reproductive number R_0 in academia. *Syst Res Behav Sci., 31*(6), 745–750. https://doi.org/10.1002/sres.2210

Lindquist, J., Wortman, S., & Francis, C. (2011). Adding value to graduate education: The comprehensive examination. *NACTA Journal, 55,* 106–107.

Maddox, E. N. (1993). The use of student-generated examinations: Guidelines, benefits and cautions. In C.M. Vance (Ed.), *Mastering management education: Innovations in teaching effectiveness* (pp. 240–247). SAGE Publications. https://doi.org/10.1177/105256298901400205

Nerad, M., & Cerny, J. (1997). From facts to action: Expanding the educational role of the graduate division. In M. Nerad, R. June, & D. S. Miller (Eds.), *Graduate education in the United States* (pp. 339–350). Garland Press. https://doi.org/10.1002/ir.37019938005

North Central University. (2018, April 20). What types of careers can you pursue with a Doctor of Business Administration (DBA)? https://www.ncu.edu/blog/ what-types-careers-can-you-pursue-doctorate-business-administration-db a#gref

North, S. M. (2000). Refiguring the PhD in English studies: Writing, doctoral education, and the fusion-based curriculum. *National Council of Teachers of English.*

Old Dominion University. (2022). *Student guide: The Ph.D. comprehensive examination.* https://www.odu.edu/intlstudies/gpis/resources/student-gui de-phd-comprehensive-examination

Patterson, D. A. (2006). A large-scale asynchronous, web-based MSW comprehensive exam administration: Outcomes and lessons learned. *Journal of Social Work Education, 42*(3), 655-668. https://doi.org/10.5175/JSWE.2006. 200500519

Peters, D. (2021, March 22). A PhD leads to meaningful employment but seldom in jobs for which they were meant, report finds. *University Affairs.* https://www.universityaffairs.ca/news/news-article/a-phd-leads-to-meanin gful-employment-but-seldom-in-jobs-for-which-they-were-meant-reports-find

Ponder, N., Beatty, S. E., & Fox, W. (2004). Doctoral comprehensive exams in marketing: Current practices and emerging perspectives. *Journal of Marketing Education, 26*(3), 226–235. https://doi.org/10.1177/0273475304268778

Schafer, J., & Giblin, M. (2008). Doctoral comprehensive exams: Standardization, customization, and everywhere in between. *Journal of Criminal Justice Education, 19*(2), 275–289. https://doi.org/10.1080/10511250802137648

Silva, E. A., Mejia, A. B., & Watkins, E. S. (2019). Where do our graduates go? A toolkit for retrospective and ongoing career outcomes data collection for biomedical PhD students and postdoctoral students. *CBE—Life Sciences Education, 18*(4), 1-6. https://doi.org/10.1187/cbe.19-08-0150

Somervell, J.P. (2015). Assessing student outcomes with comprehensive examinations: A case study. *International Conference on Frontiers in Education: Computer Science and Computer Engineering*, 110–115. https://www.proquest.com/openview/f4c2a3fdd27bff8c5570a9aec34bb5c3/1?pq-origsite=gscholar&cbl=1976352

Sorbara, C. (2022). *10 career opportunities for humanities PhDs*. Cheeky Scientist. https://cheekyscientist.com/career-opportunities-for-humanities-phds/

Stanford, N. (1976). Graduate education, then and now. In J. Katz and R. T. Hartnett (Eds.), *Scholars in the making: The development of graduate and professional students* (pp. 243–258). Ballinger.

Taylor, C. A., & Gannon, S. (2018). Doing time and motion diffractively: Academic life everywhere and all the time. *International Journal of Qualitative Studies in Education, 31*(6), 465–486. htpps://doi.org/10.1080/09518398.2017.1422286

Tinto, V. (2012). *Completing college: Rethinking institutional action.* University of Chicago Press. https://doi.org/10.7208/chicago/9780226804545.001.0001

University of Iowa. (2022). *Comprehensive exams.* https://medicine.uiowa.edu/physiology/education/graduate-program/comprehensive-examination

University of Massachusetts Amherst. (2022). *Comprehensive exam guidelines.* https://www.umass.edu/communication/node/861

University of Wisconsin-Madison. (2022). *The Wisconsin idea.* https://www.wisc.edu/wisconsin-idea/

Walker, G. E., Golde, C. M., Jones, L., Bueschel, A. C., & Hutchings, P. (2008). *The formation of scholars: Rethinking doctoral education for the twenty-first century.* Jossey-Bass/The Carnegie Foundation for the Advancement of Teaching.

Will I have to pass comprehensive exams to get a master's degree? (2022). The Best Master's Degrees. https://www.bestmastersdegrees.com/best-masters-degrees-faq/will-i-have-to-pass-comprehensive-exams-to-get-a-masters-degree#:~:text=What%20are%20comprehensive%20exams%3F,takes%20place%20over%20multiple%20days

Zhou, E., & Okahana, H. (2016). The role of department supports on doctoral completion and time-to-degree. *Journal of College Student Retention: Research, Theory & Practice, 20*(4), 511–529. https://doi.org/10.1177/1521025116682036

Chapter 8

Portfolios

Kathleen J. Kennedy
University of Arizona

Abstract: This chapter explores the rationale, uses, and best practices for student portfolios in higher education. Portfolios are purposeful collections of student work that demonstrate learning progress, achievement, and reflection. While portfolios take many forms, they share common goals of engaging students, promoting reflection, and providing evidence of competencies. Portfolios can be used for learning, assessment, and career advancement. Process portfolios track growth over time. Assessment portfolios evaluate achievement of learning outcomes. Showcase portfolios feature the best work. Portfolios promote reflection, knowledge construction, and student ownership of learning. Creating an effective portfolio requires defining the purpose, selecting content aligned to goals, assessing merit using criteria, and student reflection. Portfolio advisors play a critical role in providing frameworks, feedback, and resources to guide students. Assessment incorporates both formative and summative evaluation. Quality feedback throughout portfolio development is essential. Portfolios have expanded with e-portfolios that utilize multimedia formats. Examples demonstrate innovative uses of portfolios like mapping student work in a visual portfolio gallery and replacing theses with graduate portfolios. When thoughtfully implemented, portfolios empower students to make meaning of their education and become self-directed learners.

Keywords: portfolios, reflection, student learning, feedback

***

Portfolios are more than a collection of documents, work samples, or artifacts of learning. They are spaces for learning, knowledge construction, reflection, and self-direction that allow students to share achievements, demonstrate competencies, reflect on experiences, and document their academic preparation and career readiness (Lorenzo & Ittelson, 2005). Portfolios are one of the most versatile and effective tools for assessing student learning outcome achievements (Rezgui et al., 2018) and helping students understand their education in a holistic way.

Students and professionals have used portfolios for decades to showcase their capabilities, particularly in creative areas such as "writing, visual arts, architecture, and graphic design" (Batson et al., 2017, p. 7). As active and inclusive teaching strategies have increased, interest in portfolios and portfolio-based competency assessments and reflection has grown considerably. In the mid-1990s, "the use of portfolios went beyond these [creative] disciplines to address pressures by outside constituents to demonstrate the value of students' education and to create a more learner-centered environment" (Buyarski et al., 2017, p. 15). The introduction of e-portfolios, portfolios created on digital platforms and websites, further encouraged the use of portfolios and expanded how information and artifacts can be organized, integrated, and presented. E-portfolios also promote the use of portfolios as a collaborative tool. Finally, increasing demand for highly skilled employees with special knowledge and skills has popularized the use of portfolios to establish credentials and showcase capabilities.

The process of creating and developing a portfolio engages students in the learning process, encourages reflection on their goals and achievements, and deepens students' understanding of what they have learned. A well-managed portfolio project enhances learning by building students' understanding of their skills and accomplishments and how they align with their academic, career, and personal goals. The artifacts, reflections, and contextual materials that students accumulate in a portfolio can also be used as a course or program assessment of student learning outcomes. Some higher education institutions have broadly implemented assessment portfolio systems across academic programs within general education programs.

This chapter explores the rationale for portfolios, different ways of using them, strategies for building them effectively, assessment methods, and best practices for portfolio advising. It concludes with examples of how portfolios are integral to higher education and the learning process.

What Are Portfolios?

Portfolios represent a diverse set of tools with a wide array of pedagogical intentions (Clarke & Boud, 2018). Portfolios, either physical or digital have different purposes and are used in various disciplines. The latter includes: "reflective portfolios for pre-service teachers in teacher education, portfolios as a licensure requirement in nursing training, and writing portfolios for university freshmen in passing the writing practicum" (Lam, 2017, p. 84). In some situations, the term is used in a limited way to describe a collection of work that provides evidence of certain skills (Bird, 1990; Carroll et al., 1996), representing a student's best work (Lombardi, 2008), as "an archive or a tool that manages these evidences" (Rezgui et al., 2018, p. 521). In a broader and more useful conception, a student portfolio is a learning system that is used to promote a student's "self-assessment and self-confidence" (Wolf & Siu-Runyan, 1996, p. 30).

While the discipline, form, and usage of the portfolio may vary, the definitions of student portfolios and the associated learning process reflect some overarching principles. First, a student portfolio is "more than a repository in which a learner stores a lot of documents" (Rezgui et al., 2018); it is a collection of information and artifacts that have an educational purpose. The conceptualization of a student portfolio developed by a consortium of educators under the auspices of the Northwest Evaluation Association (NWEA) has been widely adopted. Paulson et al. (1991) adopted this portfolio definition: "a purposeful collection of student work that exhibits the student's efforts, progress, and achievements in one or more areas" which includes "student participation in selecting contents, the criteria for selection, the criteria for judging merit, and evidence for student self reflection" (p. 60). The authors noted that a portfolio must provide "a complex and comprehensive view of student performance in context" (Paulson et al. 1991, p. 63). Arter and Spandel (1992) use the same NWEA definition and observe that an assessment portfolio is the result of a purposeful process and "should be continuous, capture a rich array of what students know and can do, involve realistic contexts, communicate to students and others what is valued, portray the processes by which work is accomplished, and be integrated with instruction" (p. 36). The context for a portfolio collection includes "a reflective narrative that not only helps the learner to understand and extend learning but invites the reader of the portfolio to gain insight about learning and the learner" (Porter & Cleland, 1995, p. 154). The conception of a student portfolio as more than a mere collection of work is reflected in contemporary teaching practice. For example, this definition is from an assessment and curriculum training guide: "A portfolio is a systematic collection of student work that represents student activities, accomplishments, achievements, and thoughts over a specific period of time in one or more disciplines" (University of Hawaii at Manoa, n.d.).

Portfolios are an intentional and structured way for students to make connections, develop meaning around what they are learning and experiencing, and engage in a "self-reflective, metacognitive appraisal of how and, more importantly, why learning has occurred" (Zubizarreta, 2004, p. 4). In this way students can actively "construct a view of their learning that is integrated, personal, and relevant to their lives" (Buyarski et al., 2017, p. 17). Portfolios are a purposeful collection of evidence of learning over time and not a comprehensive collection of a student's work. This evidence includes artifacts or work products, contextual information, and self-reflections. The portfolio can be for a specific time period, a course, or an academic program, or can be evidence of learning and accomplishments accumulated over a career.

Program Portfolios

Although the content of a course portfolio and a program portfolio may be similar, the process is different. For a program portfolio, students draw on several courses from the program, relevant extracurricular activities, internships, practicums, and other experiential learning to provide evidence of the program's cumulative effect. Students prepare reflective writings such as essays or cover memos to explain their portfolio and learning (University of Hawaii at Manoa, n.d.). Because a program portfolio covers several courses, program portfolios are typically scored by multiple faculty members, ideally with different areas of expertise, using a structured, analytic rubric. Some academic programs also have external experts provide their evaluations.

Electronic Portfolios

E-portfolios are portfolios created and maintained in digital systems. An e-portfolio can be hosted on a website, within a digital learning system, or through another electronic media platform. The term *e-portfolio* can refer to the basic function of a portfolio—"a digital container capable of storing visual and auditory content including text, images, video and sound" (Abrami & Barrett, 2005, para. 1) or be used to describe the larger pedagogical concept of a portfolio. Generally, an e-portfolio has the same characteristics and benefits as a physical portfolio, but the digital format also facilitates sharing, collaboration, interaction, broad use of multimedia formats, and building interconnections between various artifacts and content within the portfolio (Lorenzo & Ittelson, 2005; Rezgui et al., 2018).

Identity formation and self-authorship were important goals of portfolio pedagogy, even before the digital era (Andrus et al., 2017). With the widespread adoption of e-portfolios in academia and many professions, e-portfolios can form and define a student's digital identity. E-portfolios can help "students self-author their digital identities, exercise control and ownership of their multimodal digital footprints, and hone their transliteracy skills" (Andrus et al., 2017, p. 50).

Uses of Portfolios

Portfolios can promote learning, assess learning, and present evidence of learning achievement in an integrated context that encourages student-centered, active learning. In higher education, portfolios are commonly used to demonstrate academic, career, and professional development.

Categories of Portfolios

Portfolio uses (see Table 8.1) can be classified into three basic categories based on the portfolio's primary purpose: process, assessment, and showcase (Abrami & Barrett, 2005).

Table 8.1. Common Uses of Portfolios

Process portfolios	Assessment portfolios	Showcase portfolios
Goal: Track a student's learning progress and development over time.	*Goal: Assess a student's achievement of specific course or program learning objectives(s).*	*Goal: Demonstrate a student's level of achievement and competencies by highlighting their best work*
Understand the learning process Build meaning from learning experiences Self-discovery and self-evaluation to assist in identifying transferable skills Serve as a point of collaboration Transition between different stages of education Career planning and development tools for workers in transition Document lifelong learning progress	Course portfolio project aligned to course learning outcomes Capstone portfolio aligned to capstone project or course learning outcomes Program exit requirement aligned to program learning outcomes Graduate program portfolio and defense replacing a thesis	Demonstrate competencies, skills, and talents Marketing and self-promotional tools for job seekers Establish a digital identity Marketing to prospective clients Performance appraisal and promotional tools for employees within an organization Document prior learning and skills to gain credit and recognition of their informal learning experiences and related competencies

Process Portfolios

Process, or developmental, portfolios show evidence of growth or change over time by providing a running record of learning. A process portfolio is "a systematic and organized collection of evidence used by the teacher and student to monitor growth of the student's knowledge, skills and attitudes" (Cole et al., 1995, p. 9). Barrett (2006) viewed process portfolios within a constructivist model as a way to foster learning and document growth over time as "a story of learning [that] is owned by the learner, structured by the learner, and told in the learner's own voice" (p. 2). A process portfolio focuses on students' progress, including goal setting, reflection, self-assessment, self-evaluation, collaboration, and feedback as the keys to autonomous learning (Nicolaidou, 2012). It can be used to help the teacher and the student understand the learning process, create new learning methods, and identify learning needs.

To create a process portfolio, students select works that show their growth and integrate those artifacts with reflections and assessments of their learning progress. In creating a process portfolio, learners manage their own learning and focus on personal growth and development. A process portfolio can help students develop lifelong learning skills as a part of their individual improvement (Abrami & Barrett, 2005; Meyer et al., 2010; Zubizarreta, 2004).

Assessment Portfolios

Assessment portfolios are evaluation tools that document student learning and provide evidence of specific curricular content mastery (Williams et al., 2013). An assessment portfolio demonstrates what a student has learned and achieved, based on the intended learning outcomes (Burt & Morris, 2020; University of Warwick, 2020) for summative purposes (Baume & Yorke, 2002; Nystrand et al., 1993). This type of portfolio can be a completion requirement for degree and certification programs.

In this type of portfolio, artifacts are chosen based on the curriculum and specific learning objectives, and reflections tend to focus on how the student's work and associated learning experience align with curriculum objectives. Assessment portfolios are often more formal than process or showcase portfolios (University of Hawaii at Manoa, n.d.), follow a prescribed format and structure (Burt & Morris, 2020), and use multi-criteria performance rubrics for evaluation. Depending on how an assessment portfolio project is defined, it "may be all of the work-in-progress portfolio or may be a selection" (University of Warwick, 2020). While these portfolios may be very useful as evidence of learning to teachers and administrators, an assessment portfolio may be less useful for overall student development or future pursuits (Burt & Morris, 2020).

Showcase Portfolios

A showcase portfolio focuses on final accomplishments and contains a selection of the student's best work (Lam, 2017). Showcase portfolios exhibit the highest level of achievement accomplished and thus build students' pride and self-esteem (Danielson & Abrutyn, 1997). While the final portfolio contains a collection of the student's best work, creating a showcase portfolio engages "self-reflection, revision and metacognition" (Lam, 2017). Creating a showcase portfolio can help students make meaning of their learning through artifact selection, preparation of commentary and supporting information, integration and organization, and reflection.

Showcase portfolios can forward academic and career advancement. They can also "assist with self-marketing, online branding, or building a positive digital footprint" (Burt & Morris, 2020). In higher education, showcase portfolios "can be used to highlight a student's CV or resume to suit a particular purpose, such as attracting potential employers or college admissions officers" (Burt & Morris, 2020). Showcase portfolio preparation can help students transition to the next step in their careers and serve as a transformative culminating experience.

Catalysts for Reflection and Integration

Essential elements of portfolios are reflection and integration. Selecting, labeling, linking, and providing contextual information about the artifacts in a portfolio requires reflection. The portfolio process may also include reflective writing assignments such as journals, essays, and self-assessments. Reflections can also take other forms, such as: video commentary about the learning process, mind maps, photo essays, oral presentations and discussions, and storyboards A student portfolio may contain a descriptive essay or memo to the faculty, assessment committee, reviews, or other viewers to explain the work and reflect on how the collection demonstrates a student's accomplishments. In this descriptive writing, a student explains why they selected the examples and describes changes in their knowledge, abilities, attitude, and feelings during the learning process (University of Hawaii at Manoa, n.d.).

Collaboration Tools

Portfolios can be collaborative learning tools when viewed as "collaborative systems that provide opportunities for assessment, self-assessment, and co-evaluation" (Herrera-Pavo, 2021). Collaborative activities such as peer reviews, portfolio events, and related discussions broaden students' perspectives and further engage students in the portfolio process.

Tools for Improving Pedagogy

A portfolio can capture the learning process itself (Barrett, 2007) as the student's learning progress and achievements are tracked along the way (Gómez et al., 2013; Mohammed et al., 2015). It can include various attempts, unpolished works, and self-reflection on struggles and challenges (Burt & Morris, 2020). An overall evaluation of a selection of portfolios can be used to identify successful practices and projects, gaps in instruction and learning, and opportunities for innovative approaches.

Institutional Assessments

Portfolios can be aggregated and used to evaluate courses, academic programs, and even entire institutions based on the quality of student portfolios. One common approach is to use program portfolios to assess program learning outcomes and identify areas for improvement. Portfolios can support program assessment by: (a) enabling assessment of multidisciplinary learning; (b) helping identify curriculum gaps or a lack of alignment with program objectives and outcomes; (c) providing an understanding of what students have and have not learned and mastered, and (d) indicating career competencies students have acquired.

Effective Portfolios

Portfolios can be used by students to represent their learning and help prepare them for future careers and professional practice (Clarke & Boud, 2018). However, not all portfolio projects are effective learning experiences or accurately reflect student achievements. An effective portfolio should present a purposeful selection of student work to demonstrate the student's progress toward and achievement of specific learning objectives. An effective portfolio must be more than a collection of work products that portray accomplishments or a form of social communication (Lane, 2007). It requires reflection and integration of the student's work and usually includes contextual information about the learner and the learning process.

An effective portfolio encourages students to engage in self-assessment, self-reflection, and self-regulation, all essential in a learner-centered environment. These are skills that students often need to develop as they progress. Exercises, discussions, and feedback that help students develop these skills are essential to students' creating effective portfolios and successfully building meaning from their educational experience.

While portfolios have seen an unprecedented surge in popularity over the past two decades, they are also the subject of some controversy: "learners often perceive little gain from writing reflections as part of their portfolios; scholars question the ethics of such obligatory reflection; and students, residents, teachers and scholars alike condemn the bureaucracy surrounding portfolio implementation in competency-based education." (Driessen, 2017, p. 221).

Portfolio Advising

Portfolio advisors need to help students understand the purpose and benefits of the entire portfolio process. Advisors also should ensure that students understand the importance of reflection and integration in assisting students in deriving meaning from their learning and the portfolio process. Without this mentoring, as well as support from the broader academic program and institution, the value of portfolios is diminished and can become just another task needed to complete an academic program.

Creating a portfolio requires students to go beyond knowledge of facts and engage in deep reflection and critical thinking. This process can be challenging even for the most advanced students. The portfolio advisor plays an essential role in this process by providing a framework to guide portfolio creation and development. The framework should direct students while giving them the freedom and personal agency needed to express what they know, understand, and can do.

A portfolio advisor should define four aspects of the portfolio at the beginning of the project and reiterate and reinforce this throughout the process:

1. The portfolio purpose: This includes providing appropriate, challenging, and specific goals. Appropriate goals are essential to ensuring that the portfolio project is relevant to the students and fulfills the academic objectives. Challenging goals can lead to higher levels of student engagement and self-worth. Specific goals are more effective than general or nonspecific ones, primarily because they focus students' attention, and feedback can be more directed (Locke & Latham, 1984; Hattie & Timperley, 2007).

2. Criteria for selecting content: Building a shared understanding of the portfolio work selection criteria between a student and their portfolio advisor is essential to successful outcomes. Including students in the process of developing the selection criteria is one approach to building this understanding.

3. Criteria for judging merit (assessment): This is typically comprised of an explanation of the overall assessment plan (e.g., use of formative and summative assessments, revise and resubmit, peer and expert reviews) and a detailed review of the final summative assessment rubric.

4. Feedback on content and reflection(s): Understanding and acting on feedback is essential to successful portfolio creation and development. Students often do not understand, know how to respond to feedback, or even use the feedback they receive.

Portfolios can increase students' sense of ownership over their work, help students build connections between parts of the academic curriculum, and help them integrate learning across different subject domains (Nicol & Milligan, 2019). Most students need guidance from the portfolio course instructor or a designated portfolio advisor to achieve this. The portfolio advisor must ensure that students have access to the tools, resources, and instruction needed to complete their portfolio and reflect on the associated learning process successfully.

Students must understand what is expected, why it is expected, and how they will be assessed before they start working on their portfolios. Depending on the portfolio's purpose, it can be appropriate to link the portfolio project to a student-centered goal. For example, if a student is creating a showcase portfolio to be used for self-promotion and career advancement, then the portfolio can be linked to the student's career aspirations. Table 8.2 shows a typical alignment of responsibilities for portfolio creation and development.

Table 8.2. Portfolio Creation and Development Responsibilities

Student contribution	Portfolio advisor/faculty, academic program, or institution
Provide feedback on the portfolio purpose and relevance to future goals	Define the explicit purpose
Participate in selecting work	Provide criteria for selecting content
Create the work (artifacts of learning)	Provide direction, guidance, and feedback on work
Prepare contextual content	Provide direction, guidance, and feedback on contextual content
Participate in developing criteria for judging merit	Provide criteria for judging merit (assessment)
Engage in self-reflection	Provide direction, guidance, and feedback on reflection(s)
Interconnect and link work and content	Recommend approaches for organizing and categorizing work and content

Portfolios are complex projects; time management and project management tools and skills training can aid students in learning how to efficiently and effectively build their portfolios. Dedicated class time for learning to manage a portfolio project is one way to ensure that students acquire these essential skills.

Engaging Students in Portfolio Projects

The full potential of portfolios as a tool for assessment, learning, and career advancement requires that students personally invest in the process, understand the purpose and requirements, and have the guidance they need (Bolliger & Shepherd, 2010; Pegrum & Oakley, 2017). A portfolio is not intrinsically interesting and appealing to students; it takes effort and intention to engage students in a portfolio project. It is essential to communicate multiple benefits and outcomes to students—both functional (e.g., career advancement) and developmental (e.g., deriving meaning from the learning process). Focusing on one functional benefit can result in some students not being engaged because that benefit is irrelevant. For example, if students are preparing a showcase portfolio solely for employment, a student who already has a post-graduation position may not be engaged in the portfolio project.

Integrating a portfolio in class activities can increase student engagement and lead to continual reflection on learning and development. Integrating co-curricular and extracurricular activities into a portfolio project can also increase student engagement. For example, some portfolios incorporate service learning, community engagement, or an independent research project.

Portfolio Feedback and Assessment

Portfolio feedback and assessment are complex, interrelated processes. Portfolio projects have many components, often tackled in sequence in which each assignment contributes to a larger whole. For these complex projects, feedback and assessment results from early stages are likely to be used by students to improve their entire portfolios.

One approach to initiating a portfolio project involves presenting this information along with formal, written material and supporting that with discussions and comprehension checks. Portfolio projects rely on students monitoring and regulating their learning. Students need support in developing self-assessment skills and opportunities to practice reflection on their work to succeed. One common mistake is assuming that students know how to perform reflection and can manage the entire portfolio process alone. Unless students have prior portfolio experience and training, they may "not be able to develop appropriate self-evaluative judgments to assess the quality of exemplar works relating to the rubrics of portfolio tasks" (Lam, 2013). A clear understanding of the portfolio process (e.g., how to select learning artifacts) can be further developed through training, reviews, feedback, and dialog throughout the portfolio creation and development process.

Effective Feedback

A well-planned portfolio project with an explicit purpose and a specific goal that aligns with the criteria for success builds a shared understanding of expectations and a starting point for useful and effective feedback. Once there is a shared understanding of these foundational elements, providing quality feedback throughout the portfolio creation and development process is essential to an advisor's responsibilities. While providing feedback is an advisor's responsibility, students benefit from feedback from multiple sources and perspectives, including other faculty, peers, experts, and external reviewers. Other faculty or an outside expert can provide corrective information, a peer can provide an alternative strategy, research can provide information that clarifies ideas, and a friend can provide encouragement (Hattie & Timperley, 2007).

High-quality feedback is one of the most powerful influences on student learning achievement (Black & Wiliam, 1998; Hattie, 2008; Hattie & Timperley, 2007; Steen-Utheim & Hopfenbeck, 2019). Research shows that feedback can enhance learning (Black & Wiliam, 2018; Evans, 2013; Hattie & Timperley, 2007) when it is timely (Weaver, 2006), specific (Poulos & Mahony, 2008), understandable, and provides information on how to improve (Hattie & Timperley, 2007; Steen-Utheim & Hopfenbeck, 2019).

A model for providing effective feedback is proposed by Hattie and Timperley (2007). Based on this model, effective feedback must answer three major questions asked by a teacher and/or by a student:

1. Feed Up: Where am I going (What are my learning intentions?)

2. Feed Back: How am I going (What does the evidence tell me?)

3. Feed Forward: Where to next (What are the next steps or goals?)

(Hattie & Timperley, 2007)

Each of these questions works at four levels of feedback (task, process, self-regulation, and self) designed to match the content and focus of feedback to the learning stage of individual students (Hattie & Timperley, 2007). When applied to portfolios, effective portfolio feedback can be organized into these four levels (Steen-Utheim & Hopfenbeck, 2019):

- *Task level:* How well are portfolio tasks understood and performed? At this level, feedback is about the task, work product, or artifact. Simple rather than more complex feedback tends to be more effective at this level.

- *Process level:* Does the student have competency in the main processes needed to understand and perform tasks for this stage of the portfolio project? Process-level feedback aims to improve the strategies and methods students employ and can improve task confidence and self-efficacy.

- *Self-regulation level:* How effectively does the student monitor, direct, and regulate actions toward the portfolio goal? Look for signs of autonomy, self-control, self-direction, and self-discipline.

- *Self level:* How effective and insightful are personal revaluations and reflections?

Students report learning from the feedback they received within a portfolio assessment, although, making sense of feedback is a complex process (Pokorny & Pickford, 2010), and students can encounter difficulties when trying to learn from and use feedback. For feedback to be effective and help students learn, students need to want to use the feedback, understand the feedback (Gibbs & Simpson, 2005; Hattie & Timperley, 2007; Price et al., 2010), and be able to use the feedback. If the feedback is received too late in the learning process, it is useless to students (Mulliner & Tucker, 2017; Weaver, 2006) and they may not even read the comments. When students are critical of the feedback they receive or perceive it as a personal critique (Gibbs & Simpson 2005), they may ignore the feedback (Price et al. 2010). Additionally, if students do not have the opportunity to use the feedback, it limits their engagement with the feedback (Taras 2006).

Research shows that the relational dimension of feedback dialogue can be important to the feedback's effectiveness (Blair & McGinty, 2013; Price et al., 2010; Price et al., 2011; Steen-Utheim & Hopfenbeck, 2019). Some research suggests that students prefer oral feedback and can find written feedback challenging to understand (Ferguson, 2011; Higgins et al, 2001; Steen-Utheim & Hopfenbeck, 2019). It is helpful to present written feedback using categories, bulleted text, and tables to organize information and make it easier for students to interpret quickly. No matter how feedback is delivered, advisors should regularly check to ensure that students have received the intended message and work to close any gaps between the current and desired levels of understanding.

Advisors can help students prioritize their efforts by focusing on critical information and actions and eliminating minor refinements and unnecessary information. If many students have similar areas of strengths and gaps, consider initiating a group discussion that incorporates feedback and encourages students to share successful strategies. See Table 8.3 for tips for effective feedback.

Table 8.3. Effective Feedback Checklist

Feedback construction	Feedback format and delivery
· Align feedback with the student's stage in the portfolio process. · Use a framework (e.g., Feed Up, Feed Back, Feed Forward) to structure feedback. · Reinforce understanding of good/desired performance based on the portfolio goals, criteria, and expected standards · Be detailed and specific · Balance positive and negative comments to encourage positive motivational beliefs and self-esteem · Provide high-quality, actionable information about how to improve Construct feedback to reduce the effort required for students to use feedback (e.g., edit to focus on the most important areas).	· Use a combination of written and oral feedback · Provides students with opportunities to close the gap between current and desired performance (e.g., revise and resubmit) · Encourage teacher and peer dialogue around learning · Ask students to reflect on the assignment and feedback · Ask students to rate or comment on the feedback they receive.

Portfolio Assessment

A portfolio can be a useful tool for assessment. The type and structure of the assessment should be based on the portfolio purpose within the academic program and associated learning objectives. Portfolio assessments typically involve both formative and summative assessments. During the portfolio creation and development process, assessments typically shift from formative to summative assessments. Assessments should align with the relevant portfolio objectives and the expected student learning outcomes. Since portfolios can be used in almost any discipline, for many purposes, and over various lengths of time, there is not one standardized approach to assessment. Since portfolios have some common attributes including a purposeful collection, demonstrating student progress and achievement, and incorporating reflection), some assessment practices can be generalized. Lam (2017) observed that "the role of learner agency and the process of reflective thinking remain indispensable when describing the characteristics of portfolio assessment" (p. 85). Thus, portfolio assessments should encompass the whole portfolio and its key components: artifacts, integration, and reflections.

For summative assessments, many educators use a quantitative rubric to ensure everyone has the same expectations. Even when portfolios can be highly individual and assessment includes subjective factors, a structured rubric helps ensure the portfolios are assessed in a consistent, standardized manner.

In a quantitative rubric, the criteria for performance are usually given in the rows of a rubric, and the levels of performance are usually presented in the columns. Portfolio rubrics typically include six to eleven criteria for performance with four or five levels of performance. The criteria for performance comprise the elements that must be present for the student's work to be rated complete and high quality. Portfolio criteria include the selection of artifacts (based on purpose and criteria), reflective commentary (e.g., description of or background about artifacts), reflections on the process, use of research, portfolio structure (e.g., navigation and links), usability and accessibility, portfolio design, and writing and grammar. Other discipline-specific criteria include the use of multimedia, creativity, and professional standards. Rubrics for physical portfolios often include a category related to the quality, condition, and professionalism of the portfolio case, folder, or binder used. Rubrics for e-portfolios often include assessments of integration (e.g., links and interconnections) and the use of interactive media.

Portfolios and Educational Innovation

A Portfolio of Portfolios

Many universities and colleges compile links to students' e-portfolios on department, school, and college websites. The School of Design at Carnegie Mellon in Pittsburgh, PA, USA has taken this one step further. It created an interactive environment where their student portfolios are organized by a student's level (e.g., junior, senior, graduate) and area of work (e.g., communications, social innovation, products). A filter allows users to create a collection of relevant image tiles. The images link to a sample student work with text, visual, and multimedia content and a link to the student's portfolio site (Carnegie Mellon University, 2022).

Using Portfolios to Connect Learning Experiences

Portfolios can be used to help students reflect on and evaluate their own learning outcomes. For example, many universities and colleges incorporate portfolios into the general education program. In 2021, the University of Arizona launched a new general education program where students prepare general education portfolios of their work and reflect on their learning across the general education curriculum. One of the main objectives of the University of Arizona General Education Refresh is to encourage students to reflect, curate, and transfer learning from one environment to another through the creation of ePortfolios. The new program starts with an *Introduction to General Education* course where students learn about developing an ePortfolio. Students then take courses in four disciplinary domains (arts, humanities, natural science, and social science) and multidisciplinary studies. In the context of these courses, students build skills and knowledge in four areas: quantitative reasoning, writing, diversity and equity, and world cultures and societies. The general education program culminates with a capstone course where students reflect on their general education experience and complete their portfolio. This portfolio project is designed to help students reflect upon and make meaning of the general education experience through the refinement of their ePortfolio (University of Arizona, 2022).

Portfolios in Place of a Thesis

A graduate portfolio is a compilation of the accomplishments, skills, and work product obtained in a graduate academic career. A graduate portfolio demonstrates the student's ability to integrate the knowledge attained and apply it to the student's field of interest. Graduate portfolios may be an alternative to a traditional master's thesis. At the University of Arkansas Little Rock, for example, students in the MA in Professional and Technical Writing can choose to prepare a thesis or a portfolio. At the end of the program, students who choose the portfolio option prepare an e-portfolio of their best work written during their time in the program, reflections, and biographical and profile information (University of Arkansas Little Rock, 2022).

Other universities have similar requirements for master's students. At the University of Oxford in the United Kingdom, MSt in Creative Writing students are required to prepare a creative writing portfolio in their first year. All master's level students at San José State University, in California, are required to have a culminating experience and many students have the option to construct an e-Portfolio rather than write a master's thesis.

Conclusion

Portfolios offer an opportunity to help students reflect on their learning, construct meaning from their educational experiences, and navigate the transition from college to their careers. They provide educators with a robust assessment strategy that can help recognize students' broad capabilities and achievements. Effective use of portfolios requires detailed planning and management and student ownership of their learning. The portfolio advisor is critical in providing students with the framework, feedback, support, and resources students need to successfully create a portfolio.

References

Abrami, P. C., & Barrett, H. (2005). Directions for research and development on electronic portfolios. *Canadian Journal of Learning and Technology, 31*(3), 1–15.

Andrus, S., Batchelder, L., Benander, R., Firdyiwek, Y, Gray, E., Refaei, R., Terry, D., & Zeman, E. (2017). Learners and the Digital Era: Digital Identity, Digital Literacy, and Eportfolios. In K. S. Coleman & A. Harver (Des.) *Field Guide to Eportfolio*, AAC&U, (pp. 47-53).

Arter, J. A. (1992). *Portfolios in practice: What is a portfolio?* (ED346156). https://eric.ed.gov/?id=ED346156

Arter, J. A., & Spandel, V. (1992). Using portfolios of student work in instruction and assessment. *Educational measurement: Issues and practice, 11*(1), 36-44.

Baume, D., & Yorke, M. (2002). The reliability of assessment by portfolio on a course to develop and accredit teachers in higher education. *Studies in Higher Education, 27*(1), 7-25.

Barrett, H. C. (2006). Using electronic portfolios for formative/classroom-based assessment. *Classroom Connect Connected Newsletter, 13*(2). http://electronicportfolios.com/portfolios/ConnectedNewsletter.pdf

Barrett, H. C. (2007). Researching electronic portfolios and learner engagement: The REFLECT initiative. *Journal of Adolescent & Adult Literacy, 50*(6), 436-449.

Batson, T., Coleman, K. S., Chen, H. L., Watson, C. E., Rhodes, T. L., & Harver, A. (2017). Field guide to ePortfolio. Association of American Colleges and Universities.

Bird, T. (1990). The schoolteacher's portfolio: An essay on possibilities. In J. Millman & L. Darling-Hammond (Eds.), *The new handbook of teacher evaluation* (pp. 241-253). Sage.

Black, P., & Wiliam, D. (1998). Assessment and classroom learning, *Assessment in Education: Principles, Policy & Practice 5*(1):7-74. http://doi.org/10.1080/0969595980050102

Black, P., & Wiliam, D. (2018). Classroom assessment and pedagogy, *Assessment in Education: Principles, Policy & Practice, 25*(6), 551-575. https://doi.org/10.1080/0969594X.2018.1441807

Blair, A., & McGinty, S. (2013). Feedback-dialogues: Exploring the student perspective. *Assessment & Evaluation in Higher Education, 38*(4), 466-476. https://doi.org/10.1080/02602938.2011.649244

Bolliger, D. U., & Shepherd, C. E. (2010). Student perceptions of ePortfolio integration in online courses. *Distance Education, 31*(3), 295-314. https://doi.org/10.1080/01587919.2010.513955

Burt, R., & Morris, K. (2020). The complete guide to student digital portfolios, https://campuspress.com/student-digital-portfolios-guide

Buyarski, C., Oaks, S., Reynolds, C., & Rhodes, T. (2017). The promise of eportfolios for student learning and agency. In K. S. Coleman & A. Harver (Eds.) *Field Guide to Eportfolio* (pp. 8-13), Association of American Colleges & Universities.

Carless, D. (2006). Differing perceptions in the feedback process. *Studies in Higher Education, 31*(2), 219-233. https://doi.org/10.1080/03075070600572132

Carnegie Mellon University (2022). Design. Student Work. https://design.cmu. edu/content/student-galleries

Carroll, J. A., Potthoff, D., & Huber, T. (1996). Learnings from three years of portfolio use in teacher education. *Journal of Teacher Education, 47*(4), 253-262.

Clarke, J. L., & Boud, D. (2018). Refocusing portfolio assessment: Curating for feedback and portrayal. *Innovations in Education and Teaching International, 55*(4), 479-486. https://doi.org/10.1080/14703297.2016.1250664

Cole, D. J., Ryan, C. W., & Kick, F. (1995). *Portfolios across the curriculum and beyond.* Corwin Press.

Danielson, C., & Abrutyn, L. (1997). *An introduction to using portfolios in the classroom.* Association for Supervision and Curriculum Development.

Danowitz, E. S. (2012). On the right track: Using eportfolios as tenure files. *International Journal of ePortfolio, 2*(1), 113-124.

Driessen, E. (2017). Do portfolios have a future? *Advances in Health Sciences Education, 22*(1), 221-228. http://doi.org/10.1007/s10459-016-9679-4

Evans, C. (2013). Making sense of assessment feedback in higher education. *Review of Educational Research, 83*(1), 70-120. https://doi.org/10.3102/0034 654312474350

Ferguson, P. (2011). Student perceptions of quality feedback in teacher education. *Assessment & Evaluation in Higher Education, 36*(1), 51-62. https://doi.org/10.1080/02602930903197883

Forde, C., McMahon, M., & Reeves, J. (2009). *Putting together professional portfolios.* Sage.

Gibbs, G., & Simpson, C. (2005). Conditions under which assessment supports students' learning. *Learning and Teaching in Higher Education,* (1), 3-31.

Gómez, J. I. A., Meneses, E. L., & Martínez, A. J. (2013). University e-portfolios as a new higher education teaching method. The development of a multimedia educational material (MEM). *International Journal of Educational Technology in Higher Education, 10*(1), 188–209. https://doi.org/10.7238/rusc.v10i1.1333

Hattie, J. (2008). *Visible learning: A synthesis of over 800 meta-analyses relating to achievement.* Routledge.

Hattie, J., & Timperley, H. (2007). The power of feedback. *Review of Educational Research, 77*(1), 81-112. https://doi.org/10.3102/003465430298487

Herrera-Pavo, M. Á. (2021). Collaborative learning for virtual higher education. *Learning, Culture and Social Interaction, 28,* 100437. https://doi.org/10.101 6/j.lcsi.2020.100437

Higgins, R., Hartley, P., & Skelton, A. (2001). Getting the message across: the problem of communicating assessment feedback. *Teaching in Higher Education, 6*(2), 269-274. https://doi.org/10.1080/13562510120045230

Juwah, C., Macfarlane-Dick, D., Matthew, B., Nicol, D., Ross, D., & Smith, B. (2004). Enhancing student learning through effective formative feedback. *The Higher Education Academy, 140,* 1-40.

Lam, R. (2017). Taking stock of portfolio assessment scholarship: From research to practice. *Assessing Writing, 31,* 84-97. https://doi.org/10.1016/j.asw.2016.08.003

Lam, R. (2018). Promoting self-reflection in writing: A showcase portfolio approach. In *International perspectives on teaching the four skills in ELT* (pp. 219-231). Palgrave Macmillan. http://doi.org/10.1007/978-3-319-63444-9_16

Lane, C. (2007). The power of" e": Using e-portfolios to build online presentation skills. *Innovate: Journal of Online Education, 3*(3).

Locke, E. A., & Latham, G. P. (1984). *Goal setting: A motivational technique that works!* Prentice Hall.

Lombardi, J. (2008). To portfolio or not to portfolio: Helpful or hyped? *College teaching, 56*(1), 7-10. http://www.jstor.org/stable/27559345

Lorenzo, G., & Ittelson, J. (2005). Demonstrating and assessing student learning with e-portfolios. *Educause Learning Initiative, ELI Paper, 3.*

Meyer, E. J., Abrami, P. C., Wade, C. A., Aslan, O., & Deault, L. (2010). Improving literacy and metacognition with electronic portfolios: Teaching and learning with ePEARL. *Computers and Education, 55(1)*, 84–91. https://doi.org/10.101 6/j.compedu.2009.12.005

Mohammed, A., Mohssine, B., Mohammed, T., & Abdelouahed, N. (2015). Eportfolio as a tool of learning, presentation, orientation and evaluation skills. *Procedia-Social and Behavioral Sciences,* 197, 328–333. https://doi.org/ 10.1016/j.sbspro.2015.07.145

Mulliner, E., & Tucker, M. (2017). Feedback on feedback practice: perceptions of students and academics. *Assessment & Evaluation in Higher Education, 42*(2), 266-288. https://doi.org/10.1080/02602938.2015.1103365

Nicol, D., & Milligan, C. (2019) Rethinking technology-supported assessment practices in relation to the seven principles of good feedback practice. In Bryan, C., & Clegg, K. (Eds.) *Innovative assessment in higher education: A handbook for academic practitioners* (pp. 64-77). Routledge.

Nicolaidou, I. (2012). Can process portfolios affect students' writing self-efficacy? *International Journal of Educational Research,* 56, 10–22. https://doi.org/10.1016/j.ijer.2012.08.002

Nystrand, M., Cohen, A. S., & Dowling, N. M. (1993). Addressing reliability problems in the portfolio assessment of college writing. *Educational Assessment,* 1(1), 53-70. http://doi.org/0.1207/s15326977ea0101_4

Paulson, F. L. (1991). What makes a portfolio a portfolio? *Educational Leadership, 48*(5), 60-63.

Pegrum, M., & Oakley, G. (2017). The changing landscape of e-portfolios: Reflections on 5 years of implementing e-portfolios in pre-service teacher education. In T. Chaudhuri & B. Cabau (Eds), *E-portfolios in higher education* (pp. 21-34). Springer. https://doi.org/10.1007/978-981-10-3803-7_2

Pokorny, H., & Pickford, P. (2010). Complexity, cues and relationships: Student perceptions of feedback. *Active Learning in Higher Education, 11*(1), 21-30. https://doi.org/10.1177/1469787409355872

Porter, C., & Cleland, J. (1995). *The portfolio as a learning strategy.* Boynton/Cook Publishers.

Poulos, A., & Mahony, M.J. (2008). Effectiveness of feedback: The students' perspective. *Assessment & Evaluation in Higher Education, 33*(2), 143-154. https://doi.org/10.1080/02602930601127869

Price, M., Handley, K., & Millar, J. (2011). Feedback: Focusing attention on engagement. *Studies in Higher Education, 36*(8), 879-896. https://doi.org/10. 1080/03075079.2010.483513

Price, M., Handley, K., Millar, J., & O'Donovan, B. (2010). Feedback: All that effort, but what is the effect? *Assessment & Evaluation in Higher Education, 35*(3), 277-289. https://doi.org/10.1080/02602930903541007

Rezgui, K., Mhiri, H., & Ghédira, K. (2018). Towards a common and semantic representation of e-portfolios. *Data technologies and applications, 52*(4), 520-538. https://doi.org/10.1108/DTA-01-2018-0008

Steen-Utheim, A., & Hopfenbeck, T. N. (2019). To do or not to do with feedback. A study of undergraduate students' engagement and use of feedback within a portfolio assessment design. *Assessment & Evaluation in Higher Education, 44*(1), 80-96. https://doi.org/10.1080/02602938.2018.1476669

Taras, M. (2006). Do unto others or not: Equity in feedback for undergraduates. *Assessment & Evaluation in Higher Education, 31*(3), 365-377. https://doi.org/10.1080/02602930500353038

University of Arkansas Little Rock (2022). *MA curriculum.* https://ualr.edu/rhetoric/graduate/ma-curriculum/

University of Arizona (2022). *Why change?* https://ge.arizona.edu/why

University of Hawaii at Manoa (n.d.). *Using Portfolios in Program Assessment.* https://manoa.hawaii.edu/assessment/resources/how-to/using-portfolios-in-program-assessment/

University of Warwick (2020). *Using portfolios to assess learning.* https://warwick.ac.uk/fac/cross_fac/academic-development/assessmentdesign/methods/labreports

Weaver, M. R. (2006). Do students value feedback? Student perceptions of tutors' written responses. *Assessment & Evaluation in Higher Education, 31*(3), 379-394. https://doi.org/10.1080/02602930500353061

Williams, S., Davis, M., Metcalf, D., & Covington, V. (2013). The evolution of a process portfolio as an assessment system in a teacher education program. *Current Issues in Teacher Education, 6(1),* 1–17.

Wolf, K., & Siu-Runyan, Y. (1996). Portfolio purposes and possibilities. *Journal of Adolescent & Adult Literacy, 40*(1), 30-37.

Zubizaretta, J. (2004). The *learning portfolio: Reflective practice for improving student learning.* Anker Publishing.

Supplemental Resources

Discussion Questions

Discussion questions can be used in a number of ways as part of a portfolio project. Generally, the discussion questions should help students understand the portfolio purpose and requirements, further develop their portfolios, or reflect upon and make meaning of the related learning experience.

- What are your goals for your portfolio project? Why are these goals important to you? How will you reach these goals?

- What are the benefits of sharing unfinished, preliminary, or weak work in a portfolio review?

- What obstacles/challenges did you encounter creating your portfolio? What are your strategies for solving these obstacles?

- What was your most successful project? What strategies contributed to that learning or success?

- How did you show differences and similarities across your portfolio?

- What did you learn about yourself from creating your portfolio?

Reflection Prompts

Reflection is an essential part of any portfolio. Reflection prompts are a helpful way to guide students in understanding their learning process and discovering the meaning of their learning. Reflections should be orchestrated to take students through the portfolio creation and development process and aligned with a student's academic stages and where they are in the portfolio process.

Purpose and Rationale for Portfolios

- Why do you believe we're creating portfolios?

- What are the benefits of creating a portfolio?

Portfolio Development Process

- Were the strategies, skills, and procedures you used to create your portfolio effective? What worked and what did not?

- What did you set out to learn about your topic or subject matter through research?

- What did you learn from creating and assembling your portfolio?

- How did you use your own ideas in your work?

- What ideas are you exploring through your work? How does your work convey meaning?

- Did you use a source for inspiration, then combine it with your own ideas to make it something new and innovative?

- What would you do differently if you could start creating your portfolio from the beginning?

- What did you try that you weren't sure about as part of your portfolio project?

- What did you learn from selecting something that was new or different over something that was familiar?

Portfolio Creation Experience

- Reflect on your thinking, learning, and work on your portfolio. What were you most proud of?

- Where did you encounter struggles in preparing your portfolio, and what did you do to overcome these challenges?

- What about creating your portfolio brought you the most satisfaction? Why?

- What lessons did you learn from the portfolio creation process?

- If you could pass on one message to students starting to prepare a portfolio, what would you share with them?

- How did you help your classmates complete their portfolio projects? How did your classmates help you?

- What knowledge or resources would have made your portfolio project work easier?

- What knowledge or resources would have made your portfolio project even better?

Activities

Portfolio Planning Exercise

A portfolio planning exercise is an excellent way to help students start thinking about their portfolios in a structured way and encourage them to organize their portfolio projects before they create and assemble parts of their portfolios. Start by providing a Portfolio Planner with a portfolio elements plan and a completion plan section. The Portfolio Planner should include both the status of portfolio work and a plan for completion.

Table 8.4. An Example of a Showcase Portfolio Planner

Element	Required?	Description	Existing work?	Status
Example: sample 1	Required	A description of the element; note if it is a course assignment.	Yes, needs to be updated	50% complete
Core Elements: Work to be showcased in the portfolio				
Work 1	Required		Yes	100% complete
Work 2	Required		Needs to be updated	80% complete
Work 3	Required			
Work 4	Required			
Framing Information: Profile and other contextual information about you				
Resume	Required			
Biography	Recommended			
Additional Elements:				
Blog	Recommended			
Contact information	Recommended			

Table 8.5. Plan for Completion

List only the elements that are not started or still require work.

Elements requiring work	What needs to be done	Additional resources or assistance needed?	Planned completion date

Portfolio Process Mapping or Portfolio Flowcharting

Help students visualize the portfolio planning process by having them create a process map or flowchart with all the steps involved in their portfolio project. This is particularly helpful for complex, major portfolio projects. You can use an online whiteboard, a flowcharting application, Microsoft PowerPoint, paper, markers, and sticky notes. Once students have completed their process maps, you may want to have them compare and discuss their work in small groups.

Self-Assessment

Self-assessment can be a useful way to encourage students to improve their portfolios and to make meaning from their learning and portfolio creation process. It is helpful to incorporate self-assessments at critical points in the portfolio creation and development process. A self-assessment can be relatively simple, such as answering two questions: What have I done well? What can I improve on? At the beginning of a portfolio project, it is helpful to have students assess their prior knowledge and, when appropriate, the work they have already completed that might be part of their portfolio. As the project progresses, specific self-assessment of portfolio attributes or quality may be helpful. For example, is your work integrated across the portfolio? What are ways to clarify the organization of your work? After students have a preliminary collection of artifacts for their portfolio, a self-assessment aligned with the criteria for selecting content can help students improve their selections and identify gaps. As the portfolio nears completion, a structured self-assessment aligned with the criteria for judging merit for the overall portfolio project can help students be more successful with their portfolio projects.

Peer Review

Faculty and portfolio advisor feedback is an essential part of student portfolio development but it is typically part of summative assessment and the students' role in the process is to receive feedback and apply it. In a peer review, students take responsibility for the feedback process. Peer feedback encourages rich conversation among students and encourages students to think more deeply about the portfolio creation process, their work products, and new possibilities. In a peer review, students engage in evaluation, analysis, creating feedback, initiating dialogue, and interacting with peers to derive meaning from the feedback. Peer reviews can be conducted in many ways and may be formal or informal sessions. It is helpful to ask students to consider the criteria for selecting content and the criteria for judging merit for the overall portfolio project in their peer review. A peer review can be conducted in groups of two, three, or several students, with one or more review rounds. Groups of three to five students encourage meaningful dialog and new insights while providing all students with an opportunity to participate in the discussion. Some instructors create a peer review assignment and assess the quality of the feedback students provide to their peers.

Portfolio Showcase

In a portfolio showcase a class or cohort of students simultaneously present their portfolios. Students, faculty, or experts are asked to review the portfolios and provide feedback. The session can be followed by discussions between the reviewers and each student about their portfolio or a broader discussion about the overall work.

Expert or Professional Review

An expert review can be set up as a portfolio showcase or a review session.

Student Assessment of Feedback

Students should be given the opportunity to provide suggestions regarding feedback to help instructors reflect on the feedback they give. This feedback can be essential to both helping students understand the feedback they received and improving the portfolio advisor's feedback methods. Students can provide their assessments of feedback in discussions, one-to-one meetings, or by writing a response to the feedback they receive.

Before Adopting a Portfolio Requirement

Here are some questions to consider:

Portfolio Initiative Rational and Support

- Is there support for the portfolio project among the students, faculty, and administration?

- What strategies can ensure continued stakeholder commitment? (Reese & Levy, 2009)

- Will there be one portfolio standard for the entire institution? (Reese & Levy, 2009)

- Is there an alternative to creating a portfolio project that is more appropriate for the students, faculty, and institution?

Portfolio Purpose

- Do you have a common definition of a portfolio?

- What is the purpose of the portfolio?

- What type of portfolio will be instituted (e.g., process, assessment, showcase)?

- How will students come to understand the purpose of their portfolios?

- How will the portfolio align with the curriculum learning outcomes?

Time and Resources

- Will the costs (e.g., time, effort) incurred by students to create their portfolios outweigh the perceived benefits?

- Do students have other similar requirements in other courses or programs?

- Do the faculty have time to supervise, grade, and mentor students through the portfolio process?

- What training is required or would be beneficial?

Portfolio Process.

- How will the students reflect on their learning accomplishments and goals?

- What type of portfolio will be created: physical, digital (i.e., e-portfolio), or hybrid?

- If it will be an e-portfolio, what platform, technology, and support will be required? Will there be any integration with the institution's online learning system?

Portfolio Assessment

- Will the portfolios be graded? Who will be responsible for grading?

- Will a standardized grading rubric be used?

Student Access

- What, if any, modifications are needed for students in special situations (e.g., transfer students)?

Privacy and Ownership

- Who "owns" the portfolios–students or the program/ institution? If the program/institution owns them, how long will the portfolios be retained after the students graduate?

- Who will have access to the portfolios, and for what purposes?

- How will student privacy and confidentiality be protected?

Course and Program Assessment

- Will the portfolios be used for course or program assessment? If so, what standard will be used?

- How will the portfolios be assessed to evaluate and improve the program?

Instructor and Advisor Assessment

- Will portfolio performance be used to evaluate the instructor or portfolio advisor?

- What role will students have in evaluating the portfolio process and learning experience?

Planning a Portfolio Project

Planning a portfolio project is essential to success. Here are some things to consider in designing a portfolio project:

- Will the portfolio be physical or digital? If it is digital, what platform and technology will be used?

- When and how will students be informed about the portfolio requirements? What role will they have in developing these requirements?

- What materials will a student need to create or collect for their portfolio?

- Is there a minimum and maximum number of artifacts for the portfolio?

- Are there any minimum and maximum sizes for each element of the collection or portfolio?

- Who will decide what materials will be included in portfolios, students or students working with faculty advisors or experts?

- How will students participate in creating the criteria for selection?

- What elements will be required in the portfolio? Will it work from one course or multiple courses in the discipline or program?

- Will the collection of works be directly tied to learning outcomes?

- Will the work included in the portfolio be previously graded projects or work with feedback, drafts, and revisions, or final work product?

- What assistance, training, and support will be provided to students, faculty, and portfolio advisors?

- How much freedom will students have in creating their portfolios?

- Who will review and assess the portfolios?

- Will the portfolio process include peer reviews?

References

An, H., & Wilder, H. (2010). A bottom-up approach for implementing electronic portfolios in a teacher education program. *Journal of Computing in Teacher Education, 26*(3), 84-91. http://doi.org/10.1080/10402454.2010.10784639

Reese, M., & Levy, R. (2009). Assessing the future: E-portfolio trends, uses, and options in higher education. *Educause.* https://library.educause.edu/resourc es/2009/2/assessing-the-future-eportfolio-trends-uses-and-options-in-hig her-education

University of Hawaii at Manoa (n.d.). *Using Portfolios in Program Assessment,* https://manoa.hawaii.edu/assessment/resources/how-to/using-portfolios-in-program-assessment/

Zhong, L., & Hartsell, T. (2015). Factors associated with electronic portfolio adoption among pre-service teachers. *Journal of Educational Technology Development and Exchange (JETDE), 8*(1), 1-17. http://doi.org/10.18785/jetde.0801.04

Chapter 9

Internships

Amanda Joyce
Murray State University

Abstract: Internships are individual culminating experiences that allow students to apply theoretical knowledge from their studies to real-world situations while under the direction of faculty and business mentors who can guide them in their transition to post-graduate life. Involvement in an internship can benefit students, universities, and businesses alike. The purpose of this chapter is to explore best practices for internships and their advising so as to maximize their benefit. The exploration draws upon the experiences of many internship stakeholders, across disciplines, in order to provide guidance to faculty members interested in serving a wide variety of students' needs.

Keywords: Internship, soft skills, career preparedness, effective mentoring

***

Internships provide unparalleled opportunities for students to apply the knowledge that they have gained in their academic careers by participating in structured work experiences prior to their graduation (Taylor, 1988). Well-planned internships benefit students, universities, and businesses or organizations alike, so much so that many have openly called for internships to be encouraged or required of students, perhaps even becoming part of the general education curriculum for college students (Busteed & Auteur, 2017; Hora et al. 2021; Kuh, 2008). The purpose of this chapter is to explore the nature of internships and how faculty can support students by constructing and efficiently mentoring effective internship programs.

What is an Internship?

The purpose of an internship is best understood with a bit of historical context. A millennium ago, it was common for young people to pay to participate in an apprenticeship that allowed them to learn a trade under the mentorship of a master craftsman. Perhaps an early iteration of today's unpaid intern, these students would work and study under the master craftsman until eligible to become journeymen who earned their own wages (Sides & Mverca, 2017; Taylor

Research Group, 2014). The apprenticeship model was common for centuries, but it evolved to accommodate changing business needs. For instance, some positions became paid to attract more workers. Most notably, though: (a) it became far less common for students to live with master craftsmen while learning their trade, and (b) the length of the apprenticeship drastically decreased (Taylor Research Group, 2014). In other words, the apprenticeship became similar to the internship experience of today.

The word "intern" was not widely used until the 1900s, when it described the experience of medical students working and learning in the field (Perlin, 2012; Taylor Research Group, 2014). By the 1960s, universities began to see the value of instituting internship programs to allow students to participate in work-based learning experiences, though the prevalence of such programs was low. In the 1970s, there were only 200 university internship programs nationwide, and while that number reached 1000 in 1983, only 3% of college students completed an internship (Haire & Oloffson, 2009; Taylor Research Group, 2014). Still, an explosion of interns was imminent, and by 2012, it was estimated that approximately two million students each year completed internships in the United States alone (Perlin, 2012).

With so many students involved in internships, it became important to begin to standardize a definition of the experience. In response to concerns that interns could be exploited for free labor, The Department of Labor has established seven guidelines that provide insight into the legal definition of an internship (NFIB, 2018), but these guidelines primarily focus on institutional responsibilities and regulations rather than a general spirit of the intern experience. Within the academic literature, there is consensus that student interns are introduced into an environment that allows for a work-based learning experience that is completed under the supervision of both academic and agency personnel (Hora et al., 2021; Konsky, 1982). Internships are also generally discussed as being time-limited, generally lasting for one year or less (Jaeger et al., 2020), often occurring in the last year of study as a capstone experience that ties theory from classes to real-world application (Gibala & Stuhldreher, 2001). Some fields offer further area-specific definitional guidance, such as accounting, which has created the "Statement of Standards and Responsibilities Under Public Accounting Internship Program" (Smith, 1964).

Who Completes Internships?

The Center for Research on College-Workforce Transitions at the University of Wisconsin-Madison maintains data on the prevalence and characteristics of American internships (Hora et al., 2021). The most recent data paints the picture of an internship landscape that has been drastically altered by the COVID-19 pandemic. For instance, while recent research has indicated that as many as 60% of students complete internships, the institution's 2021 report indicates that the number had dropped to 21.5%. Technology has allowed students to explore the option of completing internships virtually during the pandemic and perhaps beyond (Feldman, 2021), but currently, it is still more common for interns to complete their positions in person, with 47.8% of internships occurring in person and 44.9% occurring virtually. The typical internship length remains approximately the duration of one semester, 18.3 weeks (Hora et al., 2021).

Participation in internship programs is influenced by several demographic factors. Men and women are equally likely to report having completed an internship. Status as a first-generation college student is a predictor of no internship participation; 23.4% of continuing-generation students indicate that they have completed an internship, in comparison to just 15.8% of first-generation students. Similarly, Black, Hispanic, and Native Hawaiian/Pacific Islander students are disproportionately less likely to complete an internship than White, Asian/Asian American, or Native American/Alaska Native students (Hora et al., 2021).

Still yet, there may be disproportionate access to internships in other ways, such as through unequal access to necessary transportation. Approximately two-thirds of interns complete an internship in their home zip code, but among those who do not, the average distance traveled is considerable—331 miles on average (Hora et al., 2021). Among those who did not complete an internship, 67.3% indicated that they would have preferred to complete an internship but that they could not do so because of obstacles in their way. Nearly 60% indicated that they did not have knowledge about how to find an internship. Others reported that they had too many other obligations, such as a heavy course load or a paid job. Some could not find a suitable internship, with either no available opportunities or their scheduled internship was canceled due to the pandemic (Hora et al., 2021). These data suggest that a more concentrated effort needs to be made to remove barriers and ensure more equitable access to internships.

Benefits of Internships

The internship literature often explores the insight of stakeholders, those who have a vested interest in the successful implementation of an internship program (e.g., Maelah et al., 2014). Universities, corporations, and students each stand to benefit from well-designed internship experiences.

Benefits to Universities

As many of those reading this chapter may be able to encourage university administrators to begin or continue supporting institutional internship programs, I begin here with the benefits of such a program to universities themselves. Much of the benefit to universities comes in the form of reputation management. Unfortunately, universities are often perceived by the public as bastions of exclusivity rather than places of education. Hoyle and Deschaine (2016) described the public perception that the university sorts students into groups rather than providing learning activities for students. These authors argued that if universities implemented internship programs in cooperation with businesses, sharing programs and curriculum development opportunities, they could combat this stigma. If others outside of the university became part of the process, seeing "how the sausage is made," they could understand and appreciate the process better. Those interested in attending the university could also be attracted to programs with well-designed internship programs. Eighty-one percent of business school deans reported that students are more likely to enroll in schools with strong internship programs (Weible, 2009), implying that internship programs could be used as a recruitment tool.

These cooperative ventures could also better connect the university to the local community. In the study of business deans described above, 87% reported feeling more connected to their community due to their internship program (Weible, 2009). These connections, particularly with local businesses and organizations, are invaluable and can open countless opportunities for research and funding as well as curricular improvements (Cord et al., 2010; Maelah et al., 2014).

Funding opportunities can also be explicitly addressed by the internship itself. In one particularly creative internship program through the University of Michigan's development office, student interns were taught to fundraise for organizations, including student organizations on campus (Strickland & Walsh, 2013). These results suggest that strong internship programs can benefit the university in ways that extend much further than the internship program itself.

Benefits to Organizations

The organizations in which interns serve also stand to benefit greatly from the internship. Organizations may be reluctant to provide an experience to interns because they are afraid of the effort that may be involved in training a student who may only be involved in the organization for a short period of time. However, they may be more receptive after learning that 94% of supervisors believe that interns helped their organization accomplish its goals (Simons et al., 2012). Further, many organizations choose to use the internship as an opportunity to recruit future employees. Students who intern feel better prepared to begin their careers and are more satisfied with their jobs when they start (Gerken et al., 2012) so organizations may secure a strong class of future loyal and well-prepared employees. Of course, hosting the internship program allows the organization to establish a strong relationship with the university (Seibert & Sypher, 1989), which may help create a pipeline for the best students to participate in an internship with the organization.

Benefits to Students

Perhaps of most importance are the benefits of internships to students. Students can explore career options that may not have been detailed in the classes that they took previously (Seibert & Sypher, 1989). In exploring these options in the workplace environment, they can develop professional contacts and technical expertise that can serve them well as they begin their career (Olson et al., 1984; Seibert & Sypher, 1989).

Graduating students must transition from consuming knowledge in a classroom environment to applying their knowledge to real-world workplace situations. Internships facilitate this transition by teaching students how to "learn how to learn in the workplace," which can strengthen learning across the lifetime of a career (Cord et al., 2010, p.5). While there is little evidence that having an internship is a strong predictor of career success (Jaeger et al., 2020), internships in their firm or field are what employers are most looking for in a qualified candidate (NACE, 2017). In fact, 90% of those who return for a second internship at a firm are given a job offer, and 90% of those who are extended the job offer take it. This implies that there is an opportunity for the intern and organization to screen their interest in one another.

Internships can also help students to develop the "soft" skills that employers desire (Stack & Fede, 2017). Students with internship experience report stronger time management skills, communication skills, leadership skills, teamwork, self-efficacy, self-management, and more confidence in their knowledge (Maelah et al., 2014; Muhamad et al., 2009; Olson et al., 1984). They also experience better moral reasoning (Craig & Oja, 2013). When psychology interns worked with community members, they also showed improvements in empathy, particularly toward those experiencing racism (Simon et al., 2012).

Simon et al. (2012) recommended that undergraduate psychology programs offer internships so that students can "apply psychological principles to community problems" and include "personal, civic, and professional development outcomes as assessment benchmarks in the curriculum" (Simons et al., 2012, p. 326). Based on the many benefits of internships described above, I would extend to all fields, not just psychology, the recommendation to offer internship opportunities to students.

Designing Effective Internships

Internships are considered to serve as a "bridge from academia to practice" (Gibala & Stuhldreher, 2001, p. 2). Some consider internships to be a "super capstone" because they both cap the educational experience and bridge to the world of employment (Fernald & Goldstein, 2013, p.3). In comparison to the relatively passive learning that can sometimes occur in the early years of classroom learning, internships allow for active learning (Hoyle & Deschaine, 2016). In fact, one study showed that accounting interns ranked applying what they have learned in a real-world setting as the best benefit of their internship (Maelah et al., 2014). So valuable is this opportunity that some consider the experience to be transformative (Simons et al., 2012). Indeed, this suggests that well-designed internships are a fantastic way for students to celebrate their acquired knowledge and revel in the transition into the professional world.

Of course, simply labeling an experience as an internship is not enough to guarantee a positive experience. Universities have a responsibility to make sure that the internship is an effective learning experience for the students (Muhamad et al., 2009). One of the most effective ways to do this is to listen to its stakeholders (Hoyle & Deschaine, 2016). Even the most well-intentioned faculty internship supervisor may have very little insight into what the learning experience entails for individual interns if they do not ask the students or supervisors with the hosting organization. Thus, faculty wishing to build and maintain a good internship experience should prioritize frequent and detailed communication with these stakeholders to determine how their program and curriculum should be designed (Hoyle & Deschaine, 2016).

Standardization and Course Manuals

While much of the optimization of an internship program is unique to its circumstances, some have identified general factors that faculty, students, and field supervisors desire in their internship experience. For instance, faculty and students in psychology reported wanting more time and money and less paperwork (Simons et al., 2012). Interns in computer science echoed the need for financial support (Jaradat, 2017).

While finding additional funding may be more challenging, it may be possible to create more time and reduce paperwork through careful organization. A standard internship manual with detailed explanations, common forms, and expectations could communicate the expectations for all parties. For instance, as faculty reported wanting students to become more reliable in attending meetings (Simons et al., 2012), spelling out expectations for regularly scheduled meetings would be beneficial.

Internship Timeframe

While the average internship length is approximately one semester in length (Hora et al., 2021), it appears that some may benefit from a longer experience. Interns in computer science have reported a desire for longer internship experiences to allow for the practice of newfound skills and more opportunities for observation (Jaradet, 2017). Similarly, psychology field supervisors were concerned with students getting as much experience as possible (Simons et al., 2012).

In contrast, others may desire a micro-internship option. O'Sullivan (1993) described a community psychology course in which students spent just 30 hours interning as volunteers in their community. Students were referred to an external agency that coordinated volunteer efforts at local agencies such as soup kitchens and then returned to a classroom environment to discuss their experiences through the lens of a community psychologist. Others have suggested that individual internships may also occur on a smaller scale by offering one-credit-hour options to students who work reduced hours and have fewer course assignments than in a three-credit-hour experience (Seibert & Sypher, 1989). These examples suggest that both students and field supervisors may be open to internships that are shorter or longer, with greater or less involvement, than the standard 16-week semester and that faculty might wish to explore alternate formats.

Effective Screening

When designing a program, faculty must determine how they will screen for effective candidates. For a capstone experience, interns will often be nearing the end of their academic journey. Thus, many programs choose to limit their candidates to juniors and seniors who are majoring in that field (Seibert & Sypher, 1989). To maintain strong relationships with field supervisors, many programs also choose to screen for their strongest students by implementing a minimum grade point average for candidates (Seibert & Sypher, 1989).

While more information about the placement process will be detailed later in the chapter, it is worth noting here that student interns believe that their mentor should be involved in placing them at the appropriate site (Muhamad et al., 2009). Departments may want to institute an early application process to allow faculty to work with organizations to find the best matches between candidates and open positions. Applications should also be detailed enough that these organizations have the information needed to make placement decisions. Seibert and Sypher (1989) recommended that an application and resume be submitted one and a half months before the semester and that the application allows candidates to describe explicitly the type of internship that they desire. I would also suggest encouraging applicants to provide references.

This would allow organizations to gather more detailed information about the student's strengths and goals.

Funding

Perhaps the most discussed issue surrounding internships is that of funding. Faculty must deeply consider the funding needs of students. Seventy percent of internships are part-time, and 60% are unpaid (Haire & Oloffson, 2009; Jaeger et al., 2020), meaning that many interns must decide between finances and work experience. This decision frequently prevents students from pursuing internships and those who pursue the internship still have considerable funding concerns (Hora et al., 2021; Jaradet, 2017; Simons et al., 2012). In fact, an entire book has been written on the topic of underpaid interns (Perlin, 2012). So disgruntled have some become with the discrepancy between the hard work of interns and the little or no compensation that they receive, that the issue has been addressed legally. For instance, two hard-working interns on the set of the film "Black Swan" filed a lawsuit that argued that they should be paid for the essential work that they did (Haire & Oloffson, 2009). More recently, the Department of Labor worked to define what constitutes interns and internships to help prevent unscrupulous organizations from exploiting intern labor (NFIB, 2018).

Faculty aware of the struggle of underfunded interns should work to combat some of these difficulties. The College of Business Administration at Watershed University requires that all internships be paid (Hoyle & Deschaine, 2016). While it might not be possible for programs to avoid completely working with organizations that do not provide paid internships, faculty could prioritize paid internship opportunities. Student interns are more likely to be paid if they visit the career center (NACE, 2017), so programs may encourage students to seek assistance there if available. It is also highly recommended that, when possible, faculty award scholarships to help cover the wages a student will lose when working an unpaid internship in place of their typical job (Stack & Fede, 2017). Although it is no small feat to secure funding in the current university climate, administrators and kind benefactors may respond well to the argument that such funding may help combat the disproportionately low access that some groups have to this important capstone experience.

Avoiding Wrongdoing and Pitfalls

While most students report being very satisfied with their internship experiences, approximately 25% report dissatisfaction (Hora et al., 2021). A small minority experience discrimination (3.3%; Hora et al., 2021), which may be a problem difficult for a faculty mentor to handle alone and could require assistance from a Title IX office or other university administrator.

Many other points of dissatisfaction could be addressed by frequent open communication among faculty, students, and site supervisors. These complications often follow common themes so faculty should learn to navigate them to the benefit of all.

The first common theme of dissatisfaction, the location of the internship, is also related to the problem of funding. Many internships require students to either commute a great distance or move to another city entirely (Hora et al., 2021). This can be costly to interns who are already putting themselves in precarious financial positions, and students may not anticipate these difficulties. For instance, many doctoral students in psychology are required to complete an internship, but most of them report not being aware that an internship may require them to move to a new city (Parent & Oliver, 2015). This can also entail losing the social support of their friends, family, and familiar community (Kaslow & Rice, 1985). It is important that faculty communicate the expectations of an internship early and often so that students have time to prepare for this transition.

The second common theme of dissatisfaction involves job duties. One study found that many South Korean interns in the travel and tourism industry were not as satisfied with the internship experience as anticipated (Kim & Park, 2013). The authors of the study posited that the interns were exposed for the first time to the realities of that industry including the day-to-day experience of what the job entailed and how difficult it would be to find a job in their desired area. Interns, especially those without social support, reported finding their jobs less enjoyable and secure, the workload unreasonable, and the starting salary poor (Kim & Park, 2013). Others reported concerns that they had not benefited from gaining experience and technical skills, not having received the traditional employee experience. Instead, they believed, that because they were temporary interns, they were not given the same tasks as regular employees (Muhamad et al., 2009).

Even though these sticking points concern activities happening away from campus, under the supervision of the site supervisor, faculty have a responsibility to address them. Certainly, when students are being given inappropriate duties as part of their internship, faculty should communicate with site supervisors to understand why and to ensure that the problem will be rectified, when appropriate. In response to students who are disheartened by the realities of their industry, faculty could also encourage communication between students and site supervisors to ensure that student perceptions are accurate and to explore the possibility of aligning the internship more closely to permanent positions in the organization. When necessary, faculty mentors could instead help students reframe their internship as an important learning experience to help avoid similar professional environments in the future.

Effective Internship Advising

What is required for different internships varies among disciplines, states, and universities (Hoyle & Deschaine, 2016). The structure of the program, including the number of hours required on-site, the application process, the preferred forms of assessment, and the campus internship supervisor, vary across institutions. Larger universities are more likely to have central internship coordinator roles, whereas smaller universities tend to rely on faculty advisors in the departments of the student interns (Gryski et al., 1987). Despite these differences, one commonality remains: all interns need organized, compassionate, student-centered faculty mentors who are committed to educating those interns throughout their experience.

Scaffolding and Structure

At the center of effective internship advising is an appropriate level of scaffolding and structure. Kaslow and Rice (1985) compared interns to infants and children, who need to individuate themselves from their parents as they get older. The comparison is not meant to demean students; instead, it provides an appropriate analogy to guide faculty advisors and site supervisors as they help interns transition from students-in-training to employees applying their expertise. According to this developmental model, student interns initially experience a chaotic phase in which they feel inundated with information and so need supervisors to provide them with information and guidance in a parental role. Later in the internship, students experience a more adult-like phase in which they are familiar with the demands of the job and feel confident in their abilities to handle their duties. The transition occurs at different speeds for every intern; thus, students need advisors who respond to their unique roles and needs. In addition, faculty should also provide site supervisors with appropriate information about students so they too can meet students where they are.

Faculty mentors can provide structure to students in many ways before and during the internship. Well-defined learning objectives can help faculty to communicate the rationale behind pedagogical decisions. Some fields, such as gerontology, have standard learning objectives (Dras & Miller, 2002). Faculty may provide structure by communicating with site supervisors prior to the semester which is important since many faculty place their students in internships (Muhamad et al., 2009). For example, faculty internship advisors of political science students are historically equally likely to place students at their sites as students are to find the placement themselves (Gryski et al., 1987). When faculty have secured these placements, they may also wish to discuss learning expectations for the coming internship with the site supervisor. One recommended pathway to open this conversation is to share learning objectives (Dras & Miller, 2002).

A faculty mentor can provide a structure through formal meetings with student interns. Recommendations dating to the 1980s (Seibert & Sypher, 1989) suggest that faculty mentors meet individually and meet student interns every other week and three times during the semester with the full group of interns together. Research from that time period suggests that meetings typically occurred much less frequently, perhaps three times per semester (Gryski et al., 1987). Newer research suggests that improvements have been made in that area and so recommendations have been made for weekly hour-long meetings (Dras & Miller, 2002).

Assessments

Despite frequent meetings with students, the fact remains that most of an intern's learning occurs away from the faculty mentor. Thus, many choose to scaffold the learning process through carefully designed assessments. The ways in which students are assessed vary across programs. For instance, one study conducted found that in political science internship programs, 54% assign letter grades to their students, 19% assign a pass/fail grade, and 7% assign some combination of letter grades and pass/fail (Gryski et al., 1987). Regardless of the grading scale, most departments reported that most students received the same high grade.

When creating assessment assignments, it is recommended that faculty mentors create authentic learning activities that have real-world relevance and allow students to reflect on their experiences (Cord et al., 2010). Often this can be accomplished through project-based learning (Johari & Bradshaw, 2008). Traditionally, this learning comes in the form of a portfolio including a journal, a final paper, and an evaluation from a field supervisor (Seibert & Sypher, 1989).

Journal

Journals provide interns with the ability to reflect on their experiences throughout the semester. Interns can write about the work that they did that day but can also reflect on the larger experience. For instance, they can reflect on how their beliefs about the field have evolved while working at their internship site and how the experience has influenced their career goals. They may also reflect on the feelings that arise from their internship (Dras & Miller, 2012). Some recommend that journals be completed at least twice weekly (Seiberg & Sypher, 1989). I prefer to have students reflect on three big questions in journals that they submit to me weekly:

1. Describe your daily experience. What happened each day? With whom? What are you learning from this experience?

2. How did your experiences this week relate to what you have learned in your assigned readings? How else can you relate your experiences to your knowledge of Psychology?

3. Optional: Anything unusual, unique, or an area of concern?

Journals can serve as a strong complement to regular meetings with students. I assign weekly readings from an introductory Psychology course, so that students may reflect each week on the ways in which they are applying their knowledge of the principles of our field in their internship. By having students reflect on this process in their journals, they have an opportunity to organize their thoughts before we discuss their experiences in meetings. The third question provides an opportunity to share and address areas of concern.

Final Paper

While journals serve as an immediate record of students' thoughts throughout the semester, a final paper allows students to reflect on their overall experience of their internship. A final paper may be more substantive and formal than the ongoing journal entries-- perhaps even 20-40 pages and written in a scholarly tone (Dras & Miller, 2012). I require from students a 10-page final reflection including an introduction; reflections on the employer, internship duties, as well as learning and work experiences; and final overall reflections. It is good practice to provide students with detailed discussion questions for each section so that they can thoroughly reflect on their learning.

Evaluation from Field Supervisor

A final component of many internship portfolios is an evaluation from a field supervisor. Soliciting this feedback is in line with recommendations for faculty mentors and field supervisors to communicate to provide the best learning experience for students (Hoyle & Deschaine, 2016). Faculty may wish to draft a formal letter in which they request feedback from supervisors. Open-ended questions allow supervisors to express unique circumstances, whereas standard Likert-type scale questions allow supervisors to quickly provide feedback that can be compared across multiple interns and semesters. In addition to providing the faculty mentor with evaluative information about their students, they can provide a base for letters of recommendation written for the student (Seibert & Sypher, 1989).

Encouraging Beneficial Relationships

Perhaps the most important job of a faculty mentor is to provide an atmosphere for beneficial relationships. Student interns are in vulnerable positions, embarking on a potentially scary transition between their role as students to their role as employees. They are often doing so while working in a precarious financial situation and settling into a new location that lacks their usual social support (Parent & Oliver, 2015). Kaslow and Rice's (1985) analogy comparing interns to children who are growing to learn independence also insightfully emphasizes that while many children have siblings to help them along their journey, interns are not afforded the same privilege. The older siblings of the internship world, those who previously interned, have often moved away and cannot provide support. Thus, a great deal of the social responsibility toward interns falls to faculty mentors and site supervisors.

Therefore, in addition to building strong relationships with their students, faculty supervisors also have a responsibility to facilitate strong relationships between the interns and their sites. Students who have positive social relationships at their internship sites benefit from increased access to information and resources (Kim & Park, 2013). Students rated site supervisors as being high in support (4.2 on a 5-point scale), but task-specific mentoring as only 3.45 on the same scale (Hora et al., 2021). It seems from this that while site supervisors have good intentions for their interns, they could benefit from more guidance from faculty mentors about how to mentor student interns effectively. Some site supervisors may hesitate to invest the time and effort necessary for quality mentorships because they view interns as temporary members of their organization. Faculty mentors may be able to remind them that internships create mutually beneficial situations in which firms can screen for job applicants who can bring value to the firm during the internship period and beyond (Jaeger et al., 2020).

Instead of indicating a problem with the site supervisor's commitment to interns, though, the low task-specific mentoring score from above may instead reflect confusion about what is expected in the internship process. Faculty mentors, site supervisors, and interns should communicate early and often about expectations for learning. This may begin shortly after enrolling in the class with a learning contract that is created between all stakeholders (Seibert & Sypher, 1989). Later communication may be more informal but is equally important. Faculty mentors who remain in contact with site supervisors can address difficulties and adjust their regular meetings with students to best meet their needs.

Conclusion

Internships are phenomenal culminating, work-based learning experiences that encourage students to apply the knowledge that they have accumulated throughout their education to a work setting. They allow students to explore in more depth their future career goals, provide a steady pool of talented future job candidates to organizations, and allow universities to improve their relationships with local community organizations. There is no one correct way to facilitate a positive internship experience but interested faculty can serve their students by listening carefully to the guidance that has been provided to us from interns, organizations, and faculty mentors. Facilitating a positive internship experience is an exciting and rewarding experience that will surely leave an indelible mark on any faculty mentor's soul.

References

Busteed, B., & Auter, Z. (2017, November 27). Why colleges should make internships a requirement. *Gallup*. https://news.gallup.com/opinion/gallup/222497/why-colleges-internships-requirement.aspx

Cord, B., Bowrey, G., & Clements, M. D. (2010). Accounting students' reflections on a regional internship program. *Australasian Accounting, Business and Finance Journal, 4*(3), 47-64.

Craig, P. J., & Oja, S. N. (2013). Moral judgment changes among undergraduates in a capstone internship experience. *Journal of Moral Education, 42*(1), 43-70. https://doi.org/10.1080/03057240.2012.677603

Dras, D. D. V., & Miller, K. M. (2002). Learning outside the classroom: The undergraduate gerontology internship. *Educational Gerontology, 28*(10), 881-894. https://doi.org/10.1080/03601270290099877

Feldman, E. (2021). Virtual internships during the COVID-19 pandemic and beyond. *New Horizons in Adult Education and Human Resource Development, 33*(2), 46. https://doi.org/10.1002/nha3.20314

Fernald, P. S., & Goldstein, G. S. (2013). Advanced internship: A high-impact, low-cost, super-capstone course. *College Teaching, 61*(1), 3-10. https://doi.org/10.1080/87567555.2012.698327

Gerken, M., Rienties, B., Giesbers, B., & Könings, K. D. (2012). Enhancing the academic internship learning experience for business education—a critical review and future directions. In P Van den Bossche (Ed.), *Learning at the Crossroads of Theory and Practice* (pp. 7-22). Springer. https://doi.org/10.1007/978-94-007-2846-2_2

Gibala, D., & Stuhldreher, W. (2001). The internship as a capstone experience: The bridge from academia to practice. *Link, 15*(2), 2-5.

Gryski, G. S., Johnson, G. W., & O'Toole, L. J. (1987). Undergraduate internships: An empirical review. *Public Administration Quarterly, 11*(2), 150-170.

Haire, M., & Oloffson, K. (2009, July 30). Brief history: Interns. *Time*. http://content.time.com/time/nation/article/0,8599,1913474,00.html

Hora, M.T., Colston, J., Chen, Z., & Pasqualone, A. (2021). *National Survey of College Internships (NSCI) 2021 Report: Insights into the prevalence, quality, and equitable access to internships in higher education*. Center for Research on College-Workforce Transitions.

Hoyle, J., & Deschaine, M. E. (2016). A multidisciplinary exploration of collegiate internships: Requirements for undergraduate and graduate programs. *Education+ Training, 58*(4), 372-389. https://doi.org/10.1108/ET-10-2015-0098

Jaeger, D. A., Nunley, J. M., Seals, A., & Wilbrandt, E. J. (2020). *The demand for interns* (Paper No. w26729). National Bureau of Economic Research. https://www.nber.org/system/files/working_papers/w26729/w26729.pdf

Jaradat, G. M. (2017). Internship training in computer science: Exploring student satisfaction levels. *Evaluation and program planning, 63*, 109-115. https://doi.org/10.1016/j.evalprogplan.2017.04.004

Johari, A., & Bradshaw, A. C. (2008). Project-based learning in an internship program: A qualitative study of related roles and their motivational attributes. *Educational Technology Research and Development, 56*(3), 329-359. https://doi.org/10.1007/s11423-006-9009-2

Kaslow, N. J., & Rice, D. G. (1985). Developmental stresses of psychology internship training: What training staff can do to help. *Professional Psychology: Research and Practice, 16*(2), 253. https://doi.org/10.1037/0735-7028.16.2.253

Kim, H. B., & Park, E. J. (2013). The role of social experience in undergraduates' career perceptions through internships. *Journal of Hospitality, Leisure, Sport & Tourism Education, 12*(1), 70-78. https://doi.org/10.1016/j.jhlste.2012.11.003

Konsky, C. (1982). Internships in speech communication: A national survey and commentary. *Association for Communication Administration Bulletin, 41*, 39-51.

Kuh, G. D. (2008). High-impact educational practices: What they are, who has access to them, and why they matter. *Peer Review 14*(3), 29.

Maelah, R., Mohamed, Z. M., Ramli, R., & Aman, A. (2014). Internship for accounting undergraduates: Comparative insights from stakeholders. *Education+ Training, 56*(6), 482-502. https://doi.org/10.1108/ET-09-2012-0088

Muhamad, R., Yahya, Y., Shahimi, S., & Mahzan, N. (2009). Undergraduate internship attachment in accounting: The intern's perspective. *International Education Studies, 2*(4), 49-55. https://doi.org/10.5539/ies.v2n4p49

NACE. (2017). *Job Outlook 2018.* Tech. rep., National Association of Colleges and Employers.

NFIB. (2018, March 26). New and more flexible rules for unpaid internships. *National Federation of Independent Business.* https://www.nfib.com/content/legal-compliance/labor/new-and-more-flexible-rules-for-unpaid-internships/

Olson, R. K., Gresley, R. S., & Heater, B. S. (1984). The effects of an undergraduate clinical internship on the self-concept and professional role mastery of baccalaureate nursing students. *Journal of Nursing Education, 23*(3), 105-108. https://doi.org/10.3928/0148-4834-19840301-05

O'Sullivan, M. J. (1993). Teaching undergraduate community psychology: Integrating the classroom and the surrounding community. *Teaching of Psychology, 20*(2), 80-83. https://doi.org/10.1207/s15328023top2002_3

Parent, M. C., & Oliver, J. A. (2015). Mentoring the earliest-career psychologists: Role models, knowledge of internship issues, and attitudes toward research and science. *Professional Psychology: Research and Practice, 46*(1), 55. https://doi.org/10.1037/a0038839

Perlin, R. (2012). *Intern nation: How to earn nothing and learn little in the brave new economy.* Verso Books.

Seibert, J. H., & Sypher, B. D. (1989, November 18-21). *The Importance of internship experiences to undergraduate communication students.* Annual Meeting of the Speech Communication Association, San Francisco, CA.

Sides, C., & Mrvica, A. (2017). *Internships: Theory and practice.* Routledge.

Simons, L., Fehr, L., Blank, N., Connell, H., Georganas, D., Fernandez, D., & Peterson, V. (2012). Lessons learned from experiential learning: What do students learn from a practicum/internship? *International Journal of Teaching and Learning in Higher Education, 24*(3), 325-334.

Smith, C. A. (1964). The internship in accounting education. *The Accounting Review, 39*(4), 1024.

Stack, K., & Fede, J (2017, August 1). Internships as a pedagogical approach to soft skill development. *National Association of Colleges and Employers.* https://www.naceweb.org/career-readiness/internships/internships-as-a-pedagogic al-approach-to-soft-skill-development/

Strickland, S., & Walsh, K. (2013). Fostering future fundraisers through a model undergraduate internship program. *The Journal of Nonprofit Education and Leadership, 3*(1), 5-17.

Taylor, M. S. (1988). Effects of college internships on individual participants. *Journal of Applied Psychology, 73*(3), 393. https://doi.org/10.1037/0021-9010.73.3.393

Taylor Research Group (2014, February 4). A brief history of the internship. *Taylor Research Group.* https://www.taylorresearchgroup.com/news/2017/4/5/a-brief-history-of-the-internship

Weible, R. (2009). Are universities reaping the available benefits internship programs offer? *Journal of Education for Business, 85*(2), 59-63. https://doi.org/10.1080/08832320903252397

Section 3:
Disciplinary Approaches to Culminating Experiences

In Section 3, each chapter presents a sense of how culminating experiences fit within the goals of their academic disciplines. The multidisciplinary approach of this volume provides an examination of the broad range of historical context, academic objectives, and real-world needs that these experiences fit within.

There are numerous questions that readers may ask as they read through each of the chapters, including the following: How can the culminating experience bridge the gap between academics and the "real" world and make connections from theory to practice? How do employers view the culminating experience and how may they be brought on board to help with those connections? What is or should be the role of the accrediting body in determining objectives? How can the student and mentor both be supported to provide the best experience? How can students best be prepared for the next level of academic life? These and many other questions may guide the reader in determining how best to apply the lessons provided in the following section.

As can be seen, there are many ways to achieve an excellent outcome for students, but how this is done depends upon overarching goals and available resources. Knowing the implications for the decisions that must be made when laying out the structure of the culminating experiences for the students. Understanding the complexity of the process as well as the myriad ways that the experience may have an impact on the student is key to providing a meaningful experience. As Amanda Main puts it, does the capstone experience "cap" the academic program or provide a bridge to the professional world for the student? Realizing that the answer is "both" is important, as it signals a level of understanding that moves beyond the surface level. DiGregorio and colleagues indicate that transformative learning often occurs for the student during the process, changing the student's "frame of reference," indicating a higher-level knowledge and appreciation for the academic discipline and the next steps that they may take. This can also be said for the readers of this volume as the multifaceted role of culminating experiences becomes clearer.

Chapter 10

Business

Amanda M. Main

University of Central Florida

Abstract: This chapter explores the creation of transformative culminating experiences for a college of business that addresses the need for providing a high return on investment to students, a transparent connection between the curriculum and the demands of the workforce, and the inclusion of the stakeholders', voices while maintaining integrity with the broader mission of the university. The chapter recognizes that higher education serves a vital purpose, and the evolving landscape of social challenges necessitates the production of highly skilled workers. The pivotal question of whether culminating experiences mark the closure of a degree program or a launchpad for the next phase of exploration and the fact that business schools often lack a unifying paradigm that causes challenges in integrating theory and practice frames an exploration of various models including faculty-student research collaborations, industry-sponsored projects, and internships; as well the examination of different lenses for creating coherent themes for capstone courses, with an emphasis on globalization and ethics. To illustrate the concepts discussed, an example is provided from a large university where a strategic management course serves as the capstone, featuring an industry-sponsored project that breaks down the competencies acquired by students and aligns them with the needs identified by employers.

Keywords: capstone, management, college of business, models of culminating experiences, industry-sponsored projects, internships, pedagogy

***

The historical purpose of higher education, according to a Humboldtian model, included the pursuit of unbiased knowledge and truth through the activities of teaching and research. The academy sought knowledge for the sake of discovery and to educate students to contribute to the formation of the ideal well-rounded individual (Tomusk, 2007). The largest area of contention around the purpose grew out of the extension of the university into the public sphere. Humboldt envisioned an "ivory tower" where enlightenment was protected from the masses in order to be leveraged by an informed few who would direct society in the best direction for progress. Yet others believed that university education should be expanded to all people in order to further democracy as a form of sustainable citizenship, thereby ameliorating social problems that arise from increasing complexity within developing societies (Zgaga, 2005).

However, given our current status as a society of unprecedented complexities, there is no longer agreement on a core purpose or coherent construct for higher education (Barnett, 2004; McArthur, 2011). Over the past 70 years, pro-democracy efforts have led universities to lower access barriers for students from lower economic strata and under-represented demographic groups; however, over the same period, neoliberal initiatives have persuaded many to question the material value of a civically oriented liberal education (Barnett, 2004; Naidoo & Jamieson, 2005; The National Task Force, 2012; Speight et al., 2013). Conflict abounds now as to whether the academy should focus on enlightenment values, civic engagement, social advocacy, or economic progress (Barnett, 2004).

In the United States, higher education is facing new and daunting levels of challenge regarding financial aid, skyrocketing tuition, intrusion of government policies, and the increasing demands from the workplace for graduates with specialized training and skills (Bastedo et al., 2016; Goodchild et al., 2014). These challenges have pushed universities into a transformed marketplace where they must constantly compete for both reputation and demonstrable value to current and potential students as well as taxpayers who are more concerned with return on investment than with developing the skills for a successful life of public service (Bok, 2003; Suspitsyna, 2012; American Council on Education, 1949). In this marketplace, both public and private institutions are increasingly operating as corporations, with economic goals pushed to the forefront of their mission (Gumport, 2000; Kerr, 1994; Thompson, 2014). Institutions struggle to offer both a workplace development curriculum and a significant load of traditional coursework. They increasingly need to produce highly skilled technical workers who are also nimble enough to adapt quickly to changing environments while at the same time, at least appearing to do so, transforming individuals into informed citizens in a democracy (Fein, 2014; Kirst & Stevens, 2015). This reality greatly complicates the curriculum and pedagogical choices, but for many business programs, this has also opened the curriculum for innovations in service learning and ethics training.

One approach to curriculum innovation is first to gather insights from primary stakeholders. Approximately 91 percent of employers reported that critical thinking, communication, and problem-solving abilities rank as more crucial than the actual major or field that the candidate studied (Hart Research Associates, 2015). Interestingly, 87 percent of employers practice preferential hiring for college graduates who completed a senior project as part of their degree (Hart Research Associates, 2015). These pieces of information, taken together, suggest that a culminating college experience that solidifies student competencies desirable in the workforce should provide the best experience for the current climate. With such experience of these college graduates, employers should observe the honed hard and soft skills of their workers, which are often reported as low by organizations that have difficulty finding qualified employees for openings (Carnevale et al., 2014; Carnevale et al., 2013; Fischer, 2014).

Accordingly, the purpose of this chapter is to explore the creation of transformative culminating experiences for a college of business to address the need for providing a high return on investment to students, a transparent connection between the curriculum and the demands of the workforce, and the inclusion of the stakeholders' voices, while maintaining integrity within the broader mission of the university.

Arguably, the largest impediment to providing a high-quality culminating experience is the hurried way they were widely introduced to the United States. A series of reports published by the Association of American Colleges (AAC) in the late 1980s and early 1990s encouraged universities to adopt both "gateway" and "capstone" courses to ensure that they were in compliance with the 1985 AAC report, *Integrity in the college curriculum: A report to the academic community*, which called for a distinct beginning, middle, and end of the major. With the rapid reconstruction of curriculum and pedagogy, it is not surprising to see the dissatisfaction of employers with our students' skill sets.

One of the foundational conceptualizations of a capstone course was provided by Durel (1993), who wrote "the capstone course typically is defined as a crowning course or experience coming at the end of a sequence of courses with the specific objective of *integrating* a body of relatively fragmented knowledge into a unified whole" (p. 223). However, this has proven to be better thought of as an umbrella under which many different models fall rather than a definition. Some popular models include a synthesis of the content throughout the program curriculum, the introduction of new theoretical concepts, practical application of theoretical knowledge, examination through the lens of ethics or another peripheral focus, internships, and many other conceptualizations. Dickinson (1993) proposes a question that acts as an effective starting point when deciding on a model for a given course: "Should a capstone course "cap" the undergraduate experience, or should it function as a bridge to the world beyond college?" (p. 215). In other words, is the culminating experience a closure of the degree program, or is it a beginning to the next phase of exploration? How one responds will influence the model that works for a particular degree program.

There is no doubt that the integration of materials is a necessary component of any curriculum. Business education is particularly unique as there is less synthesis across core courses as may be found in programs informed by a common set of assumptions for teaching and learning. For instance, in a psychology program, the core courses may include General Psychology, History and Systems of Psychology, Abnormal Psychology, and Developmental Psychology. Such courses are all connected epistemologically by the scientific method and share foundational vocabulary and a history of paradigm development that can provide structure to various applications of psychology. These courses rely on similar skill sets and facilitate the transfer and synthesis of knowledge by students in different tracks within the program. However, in a business college, the core courses will include more disparate subjects such as organizational behavior, finance, accounting, marketing, management, and economics. Each of these requires very different skill sets and would likely not see the same self-selection across all students in a given major. As a lecturer in a college of business who has delivered culminating experiences, I have witnessed many non-finance majors struggle with the math required for standard finance analyses and only begin to gain a holistic understanding of how these equations function when they reach the synthesizing experience.

Spender (2017) argued that business schools because they lack a unifying paradigm, offer models that are generally flawed since they do not successfully integrate theory and practice. Scholarly contributions are important in the curriculum as is the training in economic value creation, and the gap between those activities is not adequately bridged by a set of functioning principles. The challenge is to articulate a "theory of the firm" (ToF) that can function as a framework to evaluate successful businesses that are all radically unique. However, Spender (2017) claimed that business schools "lack even a single ToF on which they can mount a management-oriented curriculum or business model" (p. 192). To address this problem, Spender suggested shifting the model away from theorizing or trying to bridge the theory-practice gap and instead seeing the firm as an "idiosyncratic language" that shapes the practice and pre-defines the management role of a particular firm. This model contains two complementary steps. The first is to articulate in language the core entrepreneurial idea of the firm. The second is to use that language to extend the idea into a set of judgments about productive practices. Such judgments will be unique rather than generic. The resulting apparatus of the firm will never fit a generic ToF but will instead be a coherent synthesis of the core idea and the unique practices. Managers then build a firm's "language" as a set of constraints within a context. Examples include the simple but popular SWOT analysis or the Balanced Scorecard. Logic by itself cannot explain a firm's existence, but logic embedded within a rhetorical situation can. The implication of this approach is that business schools should restore the study of rhetoric and heuristics to their curriculums. One can see the advantage of reframing the study of finance, accounting, marketing, and management from disparate subjects to collaborating discourses. Such a shift requires no expensive technologies or physical resources, instead just a change in attitude towards engaging the uncertainties of creative practice. A successful transformative culminating experience will then be one that uniquely challenges students to engage in rhetorical analysis of a firm's discourse apparatus, to employ logic and reasoning to build arguments for value-creation and to persuade real actors to accept those propositions and to act on them.

Competency-Based Synthesis

Culminating experiences may be in a unique position to accept Spender's (2017) challenge if that becomes the focus of the model selected. The study of strategic management, in fact, responds to the lack of a unifying paradigm for the success of an organization by exploring the business ecosystem as unique and instilling the tools and understanding of the need for critical thinking that calls on all dimensions of one's knowledge and education when evaluating a business. Strategic management as the subject of a culminating business education experience can actually be implemented in the models discussed in this chapter in order to achieve multiplicative benefits, although it may also come with multiplicative challenges.

Strategic management requires students to: (1) utilize knowledge from all areas of their educational program and all of the content from their business core, including the above-mentioned popular SWOT and Balanced Scorecard, (2) see how those tools and theories are applied to solve real-world challenges and how the threads of each analysis tie into one another to create the profile of an organization at a given moment in time, (3) lean deeply into critical thinking, as they realize that each problem is a judgment call that requires a new way of looking at the material, (c) reinforce their statistical analysis skills, (4) reinforce their finance education through the calculation of NPV, WACC, ROI, etc., (5) hone their research skills as they learn to investigate industries using databases and forms such as 10-Ks, (6) practice their written and oral communication skills through their presentations, and (7) receive a bird's eye view of business at the utmost macro level. Depending on the model chosen to overlay with the topic of strategic management, there are other competency benefits as well that come with the approach. A discourse community model is particularly enhanced in a capstone course via the use of teams. Teamwork is one of the top National Association of Colleges and Employers (NACE) (NACE, 2019) competencies, and formal Team-Based Learning (TBL) facilitates the acquisition of disciplinary knowledge and development of skills, as well as reinforcing professional behaviors including conflict management, leadership, customer service, and project management (Mosher, 2014).

Faculty-Student Research Collaborations

Sanyal (2003) proposed a model for business education culminating experiences that serve as a bridge to future inquiry and learning, ensure efficient use of class time, and offer benefits for both the students and faculty in terms of outcomes. The approach referred to is a faculty-student research project where faculty borrow one of their research projects with available data to assist students in formulating a research question and hypotheses, running analyses, and leading to its presentation. Pedagogically, the approach should only require three class sessions, which leaves valuable class time for instruction and other activities, as the majority of the work on the project is done outside of class. Faculty members have the advantage of adhering to their area of expertise so they can build the course readings around the background literature of the project. The faculty-student research model is a rigorous and hands-on approach to teaching. This requires students to utilize and reinforce much of the knowledge and skills they have obtained throughout their time in the program. These include performing statistical analysis to answer their research questions, written and oral communication skills to present their work, and critical thinking in defending their projects. The research model works well in team environments also.

Industry Sponsored Projects

Gorman (2010) notes that many students have great difficulty presenting a solution clearly and precisely, which contributes to the difficulties found by employers who discover that college students are not adequately prepared for the workforce. An industry-sponsored project as a culminating experience offers an opportunity for students to improve their professional communication and for the university to have external and expert input on the curriculum as a validation of learning, meeting accrediting body requirements.

Various methods can be applied when choosing the industry, company, or project to be undertaken, and there are many opinions as to the "best" way to approach this task. Kauffman and Dixon (2011) recommended an approach where faculty are heavily involved in students' selection of projects and help them identify the scope and evaluation, as well as having direct communication with a contact from the sponsoring organization. On the one hand, this design places the onus on the identification of the company on the student, which fits with the Universal Design for Learning approach (UDL; Meyer et al., 2014) that seeks to provide increased access to education for all students through flexibility in the manner of learning and the demonstration of mastery. This empowers students with a sense of autonomy and ownership over their projects and the instructor is relieved of some of the work on the front end of the course development. However, it can be time-consuming and difficult to evaluate diverse projects with different scopes of projects, complexity of company profiles, and industries. The extra cognitive load is shared by students who may have been educated in an environment that has thus far provided a very standardized, "plug and play" approach to projects and assessments. A minimally guided project-based approach may feel overwhelming to the under-prepared students. Another concern is that management of local companies, especially, may become tired of being approached by a multitude of students all wanting to do different projects, and thus choose to discontinue collaboration with the university. A strategic option is for the faculty member to build a relationship with an organizational partner for one or more semesters and to limit the kinds of projects available to student teams. A potential advantage of this approach is that the organization may also be willing to be involved in the evaluation of the projects. This could lead to a secondary benefit for both the company and students by allowing recruiters to identify potential new employees from the results of the projects. The two largest drawbacks to this process would be the time and effort required of the faculty to identify companies and make the deals for the collaborations and that students may not find the industry or company exciting and may be less invested in their project than if they had selected it.

Industry projects are powerful culminating experiences with a focus on building a bridge between universities and employers. Industry-sponsored capstone projects result in increases in student motivation as they provide the opportunity to work with real issues and in real environments. This allows for observation of and feedback for the student outside of the academic setting and often assists with student job placement (Friesen & Taylor, 2007; Magleby et al., 2001). However, this model is not without its challenges. As the university is considered a place of learning, it is often beneficial to encourage risk-taking and making mistakes as learning opportunities, but when working on a sponsored project, there is a much greater impact of the consequences of failure. There are also concerns regarding intellectual property. Protocols and procedures for the administration of the projects must be developed and adhered to, which may create a greater workload. Lastly, faculty may be uncomfortable if working in an area outside of their expertise for the project (Friesen & Taylor, 2007; Magleby et al., 2001).

Internships

One popular model of culminating experiences, especially in colleges of business, is the student internship. Professional internships have long been part of the tradition of many fields, including engineering, medicine, and education. Internships function as the first real professional experience where students begin the life-long process of socializing with practitioners and adapting to the norms of their chosen field. Knowledge and skills are immediately applicable to workplace tasks with real-time feedback on their performance. Internships are now commonplace and perceived by students as having a high value. This perception has grown over the years (Cook et al., 2004; Hite & Bellizzi, 1986). Internship benefits include subsequent success with job acquisition (Scott, 1992). Students report a hiring advantage over students who did not complete an internship (Pianko, 1996). Their readiness for employment is enhanced as they have been able to sample more industries, jobs, and organizational cultures (Cannon & Arnold, 1998; (Knouse et al., 1999).

Internships are popular in business education in the US. The past quarter century has seen a significant rise in offerings from approximately 3% of undergraduate students engaging in an internship in 1980 to almost 50% in 2000 (Coco, 2000). Despite the popularity of the model, care must be taken when implementing a collegiate internship experience to ensure that there is an even distribution of benefits among stakeholders, including the students, the sponsoring organizations, and the universities. When there is a balance of power, the experience becomes synergistic – producing more value than the individual stakeholders were capable of on their own (Starr-Glass, 2006). A well-designed internship program is transformational in that it acts as a rite of passage and liminal space in the transition from student to employee. It is critical that evidence-based practices are followed to create as successful an experience as possible. Starr-Glass (2006) offered six dimensions to apply to institutional learning objectives for internships:: (1) generalizable and transferable learning; (2) discovery of self in work; (3) reflection and process; (4) liminal experiences; (5) challenge and reconsideration of theory; and (6) transformational possibilities. Internships require more resources than other culminating experiences, but they should be seen as long-term investments in human and social capital.

Lenses

Globalization is one of the lenses through which a culminating experience could be presented that both synthesizes the core curriculum and acts as a bridge to the business world. International business tends to be a fragmented component of the business education experience and is often relegated to electives or covered as a module in a business-politics course (Arpon & Kwok, 2001). This makes the integration of international business a prime opportunity for a transformative culminating experience.

Ethics is another common lens to create a coherent theme for capstone courses. Students report finding business ethics interesting but inherently too theoretical to be of any practical value (Giacalone et al., 2003), especially when compared to the so-called "hard skill" courses of the curriculum, such as accounting and finance, which often comprise the core of their education. Given the complexity of ethical dilemmas, it is very challenging for faculty to tackle them in the classroom in a meaningful way. While ethics-based exercises such as case studies and questionnaires can be helpful in delivering the material, they do little to change students' perception of the lack of inherent utility (Knouse & Giancalone, 1998; LeClair & Ferrell, 2000). However, through the implementation of an ethics-centered culminating experience, students are exposed to various ethical dilemmas and learn to identify and anticipate real problems that may occur within a system (West et al., 1998). By packaging the ethics within a more easily recognizable "hard skills" project, students walk away with an applied understanding of the practicality of ethics-informed knowledge. Giacalone et al. (2003) described a business ethics capstone model in which students developed their own ethics training program, requiring them to leverage their knowledge of effective training development and implementation. They achieved a deeper comprehension of ethical issues in their field and the causes of unethical behavior. They learned how to research information regarding ethical issues, the vital connection between practice, and how corporate codes of ethics arise from mistakes.

An Example Project

One implementation of a transformative culminating experience in a business college will next be presented as an example. This is the culminating experience that the author of this chapter uses in a Strategic Management Capstone Course. This may be of particular interest to readers in large institutions, as the enrollment for this course ranges from approximately 600 students in the fall semester to 1,000 students in the spring. As such, many pedagogical dimensions must be carefully considered and implemented to ensure that the experience is: (1) feasible, (2) accessible, and (3) of high quality.

Structure

To accommodate the high enrollment of the course, there are structurally two components for students: a lecture section and a lab section. The lecture section is taught by one faculty member and is live-streamed and recorded so that students may choose to attend the class in person, watch the lecture online and synchronously via the live stream, or watch the video asynchronously online at a time that is convenient for them. All students are encouraged to pause, reverse, and review the lecture recordings to study and for clarification when working on the project. The faculty member oversees a team of graduate students and/or adjunct instructors who facilitate the smaller lab sections using curriculum and content developed by the lead faculty. On-campus attendance in the lab sessions is required (approximately 40 students per lab section). Here the theoretical knowledge presented in the lecture is applied to the industry-sponsored project and feedback on learning and component assessments takes place.

Project

The culminating experience uses the industry-sponsored project model in a way that maximizes benefit for all stakeholders. A sponsoring corporate partner is identified by the college or faculty, and then an agreement is struck that involves an exchange of exposure to students and the university for the real-world experience and incentives to perform provided by the organization. The corporate partner works with the faculty member to present a strategic challenge the company is facing to the students. The students then develop solutions in stages through the lab. The best solutions are advanced to an end-of-the-semester competition where student teams compete for scholarship funds, awards, and prestige. The projects are judged by panels of faculty members, representatives from the higher levels of the sponsoring organization, and executives from a variety of other organizations that deal with the topic of the challenge.

The Competencies

Cognizant of the employee skills gap critique from employers, there is great care taken to integrate the NACE competencies as much as possible to prepare students for the bridge to careers. These competencies include: 1) critical thinking and problem solving, 2) oral and written communications, 3) teamwork and collaboration, 4) digital technology, 5) leadership, 6) professionalism and work ethic, 7) career management, and 8) global and intercultural fluency. These competencies are the result of the work of a task force of members from career services and university relations offices working with employers to identify the skills needed for students to launch successful careers. Developing these competencies in the classroom is becoming increasingly critical due to the skills gap demonstrated between the student and employer perceptions of student level of proficiency. For example, in 2022, approximately 80% of college students rated themselves as very or extremely proficient in critical thinking, while only 56% of employers agreed (Koncz & Gray, 2022). In addition to providing a relevant framework and common vocabulary for developing students' career readiness, NACE offers downloadable support materials for curriculum planning committees.

One of those competencies is teamwork. The sheer number of students necessitates the use of teams for the project and so team-building itself becomes part of the curriculum. As recommended by evidence-based practices in Team-Based Learning pedagogy (Sibley & Ostafichuk, 2014), teams are generated by the instructor rather than student-selected, and their formation is based on several criteria relevant to success in this cognitive apprenticeship approach, including motivation to win the competition, existing competency strengths, and distribution of majors. This capstone course is for all college of business majors, such as finance, management, marketing, real estate, and economics. It provides an excellent opportunity to distribute diversity of perspectives throughout the teams (such as would be found in the real world) and to teach cross-disciplinary collaboration explicitly and in real time. The team is able to practice other competencies such as communication, leadership in the form of the elected team leader, and conflict resolution skills. There are other ways in which the team dynamics in the course mirror that of the workplace, including the ability to fire a low-performing team member and the necessity to provide detailed peer feedback.

Oral and written communication skills are reinforced repeatedly throughout the capstone and are also explicitly taught by leveraging new technologies. As students are preparing their project for their sponsoring company, they are required to practice their presentations through an Artificial Intelligence (AI) platform that provides them with real-time feedback on different dimensions of their performance, such as tone of voice, rate of speech, and eye contact. College courses often expect students to deliver a presentation at the end of the semester with little if any explicit teaching of speaking skills or approaches to overcoming communication anxiety. To address this deficit, the students in the capstone are provided a workshop during the lecture that covers overcoming communication anxiety and skills training for public speaking. Each step of the project involves both a written report and an oral presentation, culminating with the final competition. Students come to appreciate communication skills when dealing with team members in a group they could be "fired" from and on whom they depend for the winning of the competition.

For critical thinking and problem-solving, students must use a new way of thinking about business in order to make judgments about complex and "wicked" strategic challenges. The exercises that build toward the final culminating piece are performed both individually and in group settings to practice solo thinking and the integration of others' perspectives into their analyses. As the course syllabus states, "There are very few absolutes in strategy, and context is always critical. Hence, the solutions you create will not be found in a guidebook, but will require your careful synthesis of information" (Main, 2021, 2022, p. 10).

Overall, the course is run similarly to an organization. While it is a safe environment for students to practice and develop their skills and to receive supportive and formative feedback, a high level of professionalism is expected at all times in order to improve students' work ethic. Students must be present and on time for lab sessions as part of the requirements that affect their grades. All submissions and communications with instructors and other students must be formatted as they would for the workplace. The students must demonstrate the highest levels of professionalism including their attire when presenting themselves to the sponsoring company. In addition to the opportunities presented by the lecture-to-practice interaction with digital technology, the AI platform used for building oral communication skills is also an exposure to a novel digital technology. Students are required to integrate technology in unique, but appropriate ways such as using social media to source information relevant for decision-making and producing content for dissemination through platforms such as Instagram, Tik Tok, and Canva. Finally, students are challenged to find innovative solutions to connect meaningfully with their peers in a virtual environment, given the constraints of space and the number of students.

Students apply for leadership positions on teams for the large company-sponsored project, and each student is provided an opportunity to practice leadership skills by leading their group through one of the formative exercises. This requires emotional intelligence, motivation, time management, delegation, and coaching, which have all been previously covered in the business program content. The students also receive anonymous feedback from their peers on their leadership which allows them to further reflect on and refine their skills. In covering global and intercultural fluency, students are required to examine each element of their industry and strategic analysis through a cultural lens rather than solely a US-centric perspective. Besides cultural fluency, attitudes of openness, inclusiveness, and sensitivity are fostered through course discussions requiring critical thinking, and thus the ability to interact respectfully with all people is promoted.

Finally, throughout the semester, students self-assess their own skills, strengths, knowledge, and experiences relevant to their career, and reflect on how best to position themselves and their unique profile for career success. In other words, they practice strategic management on themselves at a micro-level. At the beginning of the semester, they create a development plan and execute it throughout the semester in ways that reach beyond the classroom so that professional development becomes a way of life that they can leverage into a competitive advantage. Of the several culminating experiences presented here, the sponsored project stands out for facilitating high-quality learning at scale.

Readers who wish to adopt or adapt some of the curricular strategies offered here are urged to consider some general questions in the following culminating experiences planning table:

Table 10.1. Culminating Experiences Planning Table

OVERARCHING QUESTION	EXERCISE
Are you facilitating a culminating experience that spans the entire college or a department only?	If you are teaching for an entire college, describe how you will ensure each major is able to specialize in their chosen field throughout the class. If you are teaching for a single department only, describe how much of the core college-level requirements you will integrate into your curriculum.
Is your primary focus to "cap off" the experiences of the degree program or is it to initiate further inquiry?	How will you ensure that your purpose is in alignment with the topic and the types of assignments? Make explicit connections.
Are you: (a) adding new content, (b) synthesizing the program, (c) examining the content through a new lens, (d) some combination of the above	For each purpose that you are seeking to meet, describe how your materials, structure, and assessment address each of those purposes individually.
What model of culminating experience from this chapter makes the most sense for your application?	For the purpose of exploring new insights that you may wish to integrate, please conduct a thought experiment in describing how you would approach your task if using each of the following models: · Competency-Based Synthesis · Faculty-Student Research Collaboration · Industry-Sponsored Project · Internship · Examination Through Specific Lenses What elements of each of these ideas can you integrate into your curriculum to strengthen and make it more robust? Are there any ideas that you like that you could change and/or adapt to fit your context?
How much of an emphasis do you want to place on career readiness?	What balance do you want to seek between the traditional "academic" focus and ensuring that your students have the competencies necessary to be competitive candidates in the marketplace?
How can you get the most "bang for your buck"?	What competencies will your experience require of students? How can you elevate those competencies for students in order to (a) explicitly teach them, (b) allow students to demonstrate them, and (c) assist students in translating those tasks to broader competency achievements?

Note. This table demonstrates the alignment between helpful prompts and planning suggestions.

References

Arpan, J., & Kwok, C.. (2001). *Internationalizing the business school: Global survey of institutions of higher learning in the year 2000*. University of South Carolina and Academy of International Business.

Association of American Colleges. (1985). *Integrity in the college curriculum: A report to the academic community*. Association of American Colleges.

American Council on Education. (1949). *The student personnel point of view* (SPPV). American Council on Education (ACE).

Barnett, R. (2004). The purposes of higher education and the changing face of academia. *London Review of Education, 2*(1), 61-73. http://doi.org/10.1080/1474846042000177483

Bok, D. C. (2003). *Universities in the marketplace: The commercialization of higher education*. Princeton University Press.

Cannon, J.A., & Arnold, M.J. (1998) Student expectations of collegiate internship programs in business: A 10-year update. *Journal of Education for Business, 73*(4), 202-205. https://doi.org/10.1080/08832329809601630

Carnevale, A. P., Hanson, A., & Gulish, A. (2013). *Failure to launch: Structural shift and the new lost generation*. Center on Education and the Workforce, Georgetown University.

Carnevale, A., P., Jayasundera, T., & Repnikov, D. (2014). *The online college labor market: Where the jobs are*. Center on Education and the Workforce, Georgetown University.

Coco, M. (2000). Internships: A try before you buy arrangement. *SAM Advanced Management Journal, 65*, 41-47.

Cook, S.J., Parker, R.S., & Pettijohn, C.E. (2004). The perceptions of interns: A longitudinal case study. *Journal of Education for Business, 79*,(3) 179-185.

Dickinson, J. (1993). The senior seminar at Rider College. *Teaching Sociology, 21*(3) 215-218. https://doi.org/10.2307/1319012

Durel, R. J. (1993). The capstone course: A rite of passage. *Teaching Sociology, 21*(3), 223-225. https://doi.org/10.2307/1319014

Fein, M. L. (2014). *Redefining higher education: How self-direction can save colleges*. Transaction Publishers.

Fischer, K. (2014, March 12). A college degree sorts job applicants, but employers wish it meant more. *The Chronicle of Higher Education*. http://www.chronicle.com/article/the-employment-mismatch/137625/id=overview

Friesen, M., & Taylor, K.L. (2007). Perceptions and experiences of industry co-operators in project-based design courses. *International Journal of Engineering Education, 23*(1), 114-119.

Giacalone. R.A., Jurkiewicz, C.L., & Knouse, S.B. (2003). A capstone project in business ethics: Building an ethics training program. *Journal of Management Education, 27*(5). 590-607. https://doi.org/10.1177/1052562903252520

Goodchild, L. F., Jonsen, R. W., Limerick, P., & Longanecker, D. A. (2014). *Public policy challenges facing higher education in the American West*. Palgrave Macmillan.

Gorman, M.F. (2010). The University of Dayton operations management capstone course: Undergraduate student field consulting applies theory to practice. *Interfaces, 40*(6), 432- 443. http://www.jstor.org/stable/40931173

Gumport, P. (2000). Academic restructuring: Organizational change and institutional imperatives. *Higher Education, 39,* 67-91. http://doi.org/10.102 3/A:1003859026301

Hart Research Associates (2015, January 20). *Falling short: College learning and career success.* Association of American Colleges and Universities (AAC&U). http://www.aacu.org/leap/public-opinion-research/2015-survey-results

Hite, R., & Bellizzi, J. (1986). Student expectations regarding collegiate internship programs in marketing. *Journal of Marketing Education, 8*(3), 41-49. https://doi.org/10.1177/027347538600800309

Kauffman, P. & Dixon G. (2011). Vetting industry based capstone projects considering outcome assessment goals. *International Journal of Engineering Education,* 27(6), 1231-1237.

Kerr, C. (1994). *Troubled times for American higher education: The 1990s and beyond.* State University of New York Press.

Kirst, M., & Stevens, M. L. (2015). *Remaking college: The changing ecology of higher education.* Stanford University Press.

Knouse, S.B., & Giancalone, R.A. (1998). The six components of successful ethics training. *Business and Society Review, 98,* 10-13.

Knouse, S.B. Tanner, J.R., & Harris, E.W. (1999). The relation of college internships, college performance, and subsequent job opportunity. *Journal of Employment Counseling, 36*(1), 35-43. https://doi.org/10.1002/j.2161-1920.1999.tb01007.x

Koncz, A., & Gray, K. (2022, March 1). *The competency gap: Recruiters and students differ in their perceptions of new grad proficiency.* National Association of Colleges and Employers. https://www.naceweb.org/about-us/press/the-competency-gap-recruiters-and-students-differ-in-their-perce ptions-of-new-grad-proficiency/

LeClair, D.T., & Ferrell, L. (2000). Innovation in experiential business ethics training. *Journal of Business Ethics, 23,* 313-322. http://doi.org/10.1023/A:1006266526120

Magleby, S.P., Todd, R.H., Pugh, D.L., & Sorensen, C.D. (2001). Selecting appropriate industrial projects for capstone design programs. *International Journal of Engineering Education,* 17(4/5), 400-405.

McArthur, J. (2011). Reconsidering the social and economic purposes of higher education. *Higher Education Research & Development, 30*(6), 737-749. https://doi.org/10.1080/07294360/2010.539596

Meyer, A. Rose, D.H., & Gordon, D. (2014). *Universal design for learning: Theory and Practice.* CAST Professional Publishing.

Mosher, G.A. (2014). Enhancing team-based senior capstone projects: Opportunities and challenges. *2014 ASEE North Midwest Section Conference* 2014(1), p. 1-12). https://doi.org/10.10.17077/aseenmw2014.1002

National Association of Colleges and Employers (2019, March 29). *The four career competencies employers value most.* https://www.naceweb.org/career-rea diness/competencies/the-four-career-competencies-employers-value-most/

Naidoo, R., & Jamieson, I. (2005). Empowering participants or corroding learning? Towards a research agenda on the impact of student consumerism in higher education. *Journal of Educational Policy, 20*(3), 267-281. https://doi.or g/10.1080/02680930500108585

Pianko, D. (1996). Power internships. *Management Review, 85*(12), 31-33.

Sanyal, R. (2003). The capstone course in business programs: Teaching the application of international business research skills. *Journal of Teaching in International Business, 15*(2), 53-64. https://doi.org/10.1300/J066v15n02_04

Scott, M.E. (1992). Internships add value to college recruitment. *The Personnel Journal, 71*, 59-62. http://doi.org/10.1177/0273475300221006

Sibley, J., & Ostafichuk, P. (2014).*Getting started with team-based learning.* Stylus.

Speight, S., Lackovic, N., & Cooker, L. (2013). Stakeholder attitudes toward employability in a Sino-British University. *Journal of Teaching and Learning for Graduate Employability, 3*(1), 26-40. http://doi.org/10.21153/jtlge2012vo 3no1art556

Spender, J.C. (2017). BSchools and their business models. *Humanist Management Journal, 1*, 187-204. https://doi.org/10.1007/s41463-016-0016-0

Starr-Glass, D. (2006). Enhancing the transformative potential of business internships. *Managing Global Transitions, 4*, 285-297.

Suspitsyna, T. (2012). Higher education for economic advancement and engaged citizenship: An analysis of the U.S. Department of Education Discourse. *Journal of Higher Education, 83*(1), 49-72. http://doi.org/10.1353/jhe.2012.003

The National Task Force. (2012). *A crucible moment: College learning and democracy's future.* Association of American Colleges and Universities (AAC&U).

Thompson, R. J. (2014). *Beyond reason and tolerance: The purpose and practice of higher education.* Oxford University Press.

Tomusk, V. (2007). The end of Europe and the last intellectual. Fine-tuning of knowledge work in the panopticon of Bologna. In V. Tomusk (Ed.) *Creating the European Area of Higher Education: Voices from the Periphery* (pp. 269-303). Springer.

West, J., Berman, E., Bonczek, S., & Kellar, E. (1998). Frontiers in ethics training. *Public Management, 80*, 4-9.

Zgaga, P. (2005). Higher education for a democratic culture- the public responsibility. In L. Weber & S. Bergan (Eds)., *The public responsibility for higher education and research,* (pp.107-116). Strasbourg: Council of Europe.

Chapter 11

Humanities

North Carolina Central University

University of North Carolina, Chapel Hill

Abstract: In recent years, the educational landscape has witnessed a significant transformation in the assessment of students' knowledge acquisition. This transition has given way to alternate forms of culminating experiences in the humanities. Culminating experiences provide students with opportunities for authentic learning and applying acquired knowledge in real-life scenarios to make a meaningful impact on their communities. This chapter explores a variety of different culminating experiences that may be used in the humanities, including project-based experiences, capstone projects, service-learning experiences, and portfolio projects. Each type of culminating experience provides students with the skills and knowledge to better prepare them for their future jobs and life experiences. In addition, the authors have included some questions that may help both instructors and students alike assess the best culminating experience for their area of study.

Keywords: capstone, humanities, authentic learning, community engagement

***

In recent years, the need for different methods of assessing students' acquisition of knowledge that goes beyond standardized testing has affected academic communities and given rise to culminating experiences or senior projects that focus on students' abilities to apply the knowledge they have acquired in a variety of circumstances and scenarios (Education Commission of the United States, 2004). Culminating experiences may be defined as a High Impact Practice (HIP) in which students have opportunities for authentic learning, using knowledge gained in their studies to impact their communities (Kinzie, et. al. 2021, p.11). In the humanities, culminating experiences take many forms, including service-learning projects, project-based experiences, portfolio projects, and others which provide opportunities for students to make connections between what they have learned in the classroom and real-world experiences to more readily understand the impact their studies may have in real-world contexts.

In higher education, the intention of the culminating experience is to provide undergraduates an opportunity to show mastery of their subject area. These experiences help prepare learners for the job market and for continued study in graduate school. There are many types of culminating experiences that can be developed depending on the specific discipline and the interest of the student involved. In accordance with this, Brown University states that,

> A senior capstone experience can be any kind of project that draws on what you have learned in your concentration. It is usually completed in close consultation with an advisor. An honors thesis or independent study is one obvious type of capstone. A performance or art opening is another. And, depending on one's goals, a focused internship or other kind of educational work experience could be another, especially if carried out in consultation with a faculty mentor. Many concentrations at Brown, particularly interdisciplinary and joint concentrations, require a senior capstone experience. Even if such a culminating project is not required by a student's concentration, we encourage all juniors to include such a project in their senior-year planning. (Brown University, n.d., para.1)

In other words, while many colleges and universities recommend that students complete a culminating experience, such as the senior capstone project referenced at Brown, these are not always required. However, the proliferation of these programs across universities displays the concerns of students and instructors alike in ensuring that the student's culminating experience is one that will provide support to the student's career goals and life plan.

For this chapter, the authors focus on different types of culminating projects in the humanities and how these are carried out in different disciplines with the goal of providing insights into best practices for a variety of culminating experiences. We have also provided a guide and checklist for use in the development of a culminating experience for specific students and/or programs.

Identifying the best type of culminating experience in the Humanities

Broadly understood, the humanities refer to the study of human culture and society which include academic disciplines and interdisciplinary programs that delve into the ideas, words, stories, symbols, and expressions that provide meaning and sense to the human experience. Thus, culminating projects in the humanities are important as they will further institutional goals while allowing the student to meet the primary objectives of their discipline in a meaningful way. In academia, the humanities encompass a variety of different programs that have at their core inquiry and critical thinking about humanity. In the 2013 report *The Heart of the Matter*, the Commission on the Humanities and Social Sciences reminded Congress that,

> "The humanities remind us where we have been and help us envision where we are going. Emphasizing critical perspective and imaginative response, the humanities - including the study of languages, literature, history, film, civics, philosophy, religion, and the arts - foster creativity, appreciation of our commonalities and differences, and knowledge of all kinds." (p.9)

Others find the term "humanities" somewhat more difficult to define due to its overarching inclusiveness, as Rens Bod states in *A New History of the Humanities: The Search for Principles and Patterns from Antiquity to the Present*, "What are the humanities? It is like the notion of 'time' in St. Augustine: if you don't ask, we know, but if you ask, we are left empty-handed. Since the nineteenth century the humanities have generally been defined as the disciplines that investigate the expressions of the human mind." (p.1) What the humanities hold as its central inquiry, "the expressions of the human mind," is a vital component when assessing culminating projects for courses and programs.

Considering the multitude of programs housed under the humanities, first and foremost, one must take into consideration the best culminating experience for students based on the program and the student's strengths and abilities. Humanities disciplines require a variety of skills and abilities to complete; student learning outcomes in history, for instance, may be different than student learning outcomes in a foreign language. For this reason, it is important to consider not only a student's strengths and areas for improvement but to also ensure that the culminating project is in line with the major goals of the discipline. In addition, for students who have cross-disciplinary training, devising a culminating project that shows expertise in both fields may mean that the advisor and/or advisors lead students to create projects that show mastery in both fields.

Types of culminating experiences in the humanities

Project-based experience

A project-based experience may be best for humanities disciplines that require a heavy amount of public speaking and/or the development of professional projects post-graduation. In this instance, a project may take the form of something in which the student is a stakeholder. The project-based model provides students the ability to perform a complex investigative inquiry and explore themes related to their discipline. According to Dr. John Thomas (2000), the project-based model should meet the following criteria:

1. Be central to the curriculum.

2. Focus on problems or questions that "drive" students to encounter (and struggle with) the central concepts and principles of a discipline.

3. Involve students in a constructive investigation.

4. [It should be] student driven to some significant degree.

5. [It should be] realistic, not school-like. (Thomas, pp.3-4)

Projects in this model require the completion of an intellectual task that incorporates the discipline's inquiry methods to produce a piece of knowledge consistent with practices in the discipline. In such cases, the goal is to provide students with an opportunity to demonstrate the meeting of required learning outcomes in their specific majors. The following examples provide an overview of the most common project-based culminating experiences in the humanities.

The Capstone Project

The capstone project is central to humanities programs. It can take different forms, but its purpose remains the same: to provide students the opportunity to carry out independent research in order to propose an innovative and original solution to real-world problems. The most common model is the capstone. Students enrolled in a capstone course will focus on issues in their field. In this case, the course is designed purposefully as a space where students are challenged to demonstrate mastery of their major. In this version, all students enrolled in the course would complete the same tasks such as a research paper along with reflections on a journal and a final poster presentation, to mention just a few ways in which students may carry out the project. Depending on the discipline, a capstone project may require students to present findings of their independent research-based project, featuring a set of solutions for a problem within the field, and showcase a community service project or learning activity, among others.

The capstone project can also take the form of an interdisciplinary, campus-wide initiative. In 2019, for instance, York University introduced the Cross-Campus Capstone Classroom (C4), a year-long initiative that groups students from different degree programs together in interdisciplinary teams. The goal is to create projects that address real-world challenges proposed by companies, businesses, and non-profit organizations. The purpose of this model is not only the academic and professional development of the students involved but to also consider the social impact of their education. ("C4: The Cross-Campus Capstone Classroom: FAQ," general FAQ 1).

Literally, a capstone refers to the final stone placed at the top of a wall or building signaling the successful completion of such a structure (Smith, para 1). Likewise, the capstone project, as Dr. Jeff Czarnec from Southern New Hampshire University states, is "the apex of all a student's work done throughout their college career." (Smith, para. 3) As a culminating experience, a capstone project is an alternative way for students to prove, through the presentation of new ideas or questions, their understanding of a specific subject within the discipline. It not only departs from the traditional testing model (quizzes, tests, and exams) but also provides opportunities for students to apply knowledge and experience in a way that is similar to what they will find in their careers.

Independent Studies Project (ISP)

Immersing into a self-paced and autonomous research and performance experience is a great opportunity for students to showcase their academic skills while obtaining experience in the discipline that they can apply in their careers post-graduation. ISPs allow students to choose a topic of study that suits their interest, participate in the course design, and work with a faculty member or advisor who may be a specialist in their topic of choice. The topic of an ISP is generally not offered in the institution's curriculum and constitutes an innovative approach to the topic, including representing a completely new field of study.

Students engaged in ISPs are responsible for designing and carrying out the course work, implementing any suggested changes from the faculty advisor, and submitting work for evaluating the progress of the project. The faculty advisor makes suggestions and evaluates the student's deliverables.

ISPs feasibility and success rest on the key aspect of interest. Both student and faculty members must have sufficient interest in the topic to take the project to a safe port. On one hand, the student's interest must be enough to convince the incumbent faculty to work with the student on the project. On the other hand, the faculty member will identify the student with whom the project will reach a successful end.

Service-learning Experience

Service-learning experiences provide students the ability to take what they have learned in the classroom and apply it to real-world situations. At the University of Kentucky, the Center for Service-Learning and Civic Engagement provides students with assistance in service learning initiatives which, according to their website, is due to changes in higher education that have resulted in, "shifting to active, collaborative, experiential modes of teaching and learning that engage students with diverse perspectives, focus on purposeful tasks, and build connections between the classroom and the rest of their lives." (University of Kentucky, n.d.,) In addition, according to Mitchell (2008), "Critical service-learning programs encourage students to see themselves as agents of social change and use the experience to address and respond to injustice in communities," (p.51).

Service-learning projects as culminating experiences in the humanities allow students to apply the knowledge they have gained in their course of study to remedy social problems. In this type of culminating project, a student may take a year or a semester to make meaningful connections with their community by using critical thinking and problem-solving skills to connect with their community in a meaningful way. Students can enhance communication skills, work in a team environment, and take ownership of their own learning (Barton, 2020). According to Elon University's Center for Engaged Learning, there are three effective types of service-learning projects in which students can engage: community-based service, class-based service project, and community and class-based model ("Service Learning," para. 9). A community-based service is, "completed in partnership with a community organization" (para. 9) and executed in conjunction with the community member's goals in mind. A class-based service project is normally conducted in the classroom and may involve organizing a website or other project that does not involve physically going to a community location. Finally, a hybrid model provides opportunities for students to engage in a community-based approach as outlined above while also integrating components of the class-based approach (para. 9).

Designing an effective service-learning project requires multiple steps by both the student and their faculty mentor. The first step in this process will be to investigate the community in which they would like to work. Once this research has been completed, the students and instructor involved should identify a project that will best support their community and devise a plan with an end goal in mind. By having a solid end goal, the students and instructor can conceive of a project that will have the most positive impact on their community. At the culmination of the service-learning project, students should have an opportunity to reflect upon their experience, both on the process as well as the impact their involvement with the community had and how this connected to their schoolwork. In reflecting on the project and their studies, students will be able to more clearly understand how their studies may have a real-world impact.

The best way for instructors to plan service-learning projects with their students is through official university programs. Instructors may also become involved through initiatives that provide them with the necessary tools for implementing service learning into their courses while also providing additional instruction and feedback on implementing such programs.

Senior thesis

A senior thesis may be the best culminating experience for students who wish to show mastery of a topic and demonstrate the ability to conduct research on an area of interest. Through a completed thesis students can show mastery of the content area while also gaining experience writing longer research papers that are necessary in academic environments. During the thesis process, students can expand on research that piques their interest while requiring a certain amount of originality. Many universities and colleges use the senior thesis as a culminating project for honors programs due to the academic rigor needed to complete such a project.

The senior thesis may take a variety of different forms, however, many colleges and universities see this as an opportunity for students to demonstrate their skills in academic writing. For instance, at the University of Notre Dame, students enrolled in the Department of American Studies may write a senior thesis that is a year-long project which can be, "a scholarly paper, narrative nonfiction essay, journalistic article or series of articles, documentary film or museum exhibition; it can reflect personal interests and career goals," ("Senior Thesis," para. 2) What stands out in this approach to the senior thesis is the possibility for students to perform long-form writing that requires a considerable amount of research but also provides students the opportunity to approach the written project creatively.

Other institutions may take a different approach to the senior thesis, and rather than extending this to more creative forms of writing, continue using the essay format as the final product. A prime example of such an approach takes place at Dickinson College, where students must conduct independent research and are provided with support from faculty and other students in writing a thesis of approximately 50 pages. The written thesis is read and evaluated by peers throughout a year-long course. ("The Senior Experience," 2017, pg. 1). In this case, the senior thesis not only prepares students for future careers in writing and research, but also bolsters students' abilities to collaborate with others, receive and provide feedback on written work, and enhance presentational skills. This set of skills is necessary for future positions students may hold, regardless of what the position may be. In other words, while the senior thesis is an individual research project conducted by the student, this takes place in a collaborative environment in which students learn how to work alongside others, receive critical feedback on their projects, and learn how to best argue their perspective with the end goal that others will understand their primary arguments. Thus, the senior thesis is an outstanding culminating project for students who are interested in researching a specific idea in-depth and presenting their findings to others.

The senior thesis has many positives for students, such as conducting in-depth research on topics of interest and honing students' research abilities. Including a presentational element also helps students develop better argumentative skills and comfort with public speaking and orally defending their findings. In addition, students work closely with an advisor which helps build stronger student/professor relationships.

Portfolio

Another possibility for a culminating project in the humanities may take the form of a portfolio. Portfolios can be used in a variety of ways and present themselves differently in areas covered under the humanities. Rolheiser, Bower, and Stevahn (2000) discuss different types of portfolios that may be used in assessing student work. They break them down into two different general categories – the best works portfolio and the growth portfolio – while explaining that the best way to implement the portfolio project is by determining student learning outcomes and the audience for whom the portfolio is made. Most importantly for the portfolio project, one must keep in mind assignment criteria and how these expectations fit into the department's and/or institution's strategic planning (p.4).

There are many positives to using a portfolio as a culminating project for students. A portfolio provides students the ability to look back at their work over a period of time and reflect on their progress in their area or areas of study. For students, the portfolio may be a positive as they will have the opportunity to compile work that may be useful for job applications and continuing education, either in the transition from high school to college or the transition from undergraduate to graduate work. The portfolio also affords the opportunity for students engaged in interdisciplinary work to demonstrate proficiency in multiple areas. For example, a student who is double majoring in language and music may be able to write an essay regarding musical productions in the culture of the target language and include a performance piece as part of their portfolio.

There are also many long-range benefits to the portfolio for instructors. The portfolio provides access to information over time, helping instructors to assess student progress and learn more about individual students' strengths and weaknesses, which in turn will enhance an instructor's ability to serve student populations more equitably. Teachers are also better able to assess how their program aligns with departmental and institutional goals and adjust assignments as needed.

However, there are some drawbacks to the portfolio that instructors should keep in mind. The main drawback for students is that those who have transferred into a program that uses a portfolio for a culminating project may find it difficult to catch up to peers. In addition, they may not be able to provide documentation for the portfolio depending on the portfolio's requirements and previous work the student has completed. Instructors will also have to determine how to assess the portfolio project and keep in mind that portfolio projects tend to be time-intensive. Ensuring that the portfolio project takes into account the busy lives many students lead is important to its success.

Different types of portfolios provide opportunities for instructors and students alike to understand their growth by different measures. Below, the authors have used the division suggested by Rolheiser, Bower, and Stevahn (2000) to introduce different types of portfolios. Their breakdown of and assessment of different types of portfolios is comprehensive and provides useful details for instructors to consider with developing portfolio projects.

The Best Works Portfolio.

According to Rolheiser, Bower, and Stevahn (2000), the best works portfolio most effectively measures student achievement and may provide a glimpse of a student's performance that is helpful for future employers and post-secondary institutions (p. 4). This type of portfolio will showcase a student's performance on assessments that showcase their mastery of content via assessments such as exams, tests, and research papers. While this shows a student's best efforts and work, it may also lack a comprehensive view of the student's weaknesses and progression on strengthening those weaknesses over time.

The Growth Portfolio.

A growth portfolio, in contrast to the best works portfolio, showcases a student's learning over an extended period, thus showcasing the accumulation of knowledge and experiences that have guided a student's learning journey. Considering that the growth portfolio is aimed at showing a student's progress throughout a program of study, it is not necessary that this portfolio include all of a student's best works. On the contrary, to show growth and learning, there may be items in the portfolio that provide insights into areas in which the student may have experienced learning blocks and/or challenges. However, a positive of this type of portfolio is the potential to show how a student has improved upon their weaknesses in a subject area (p.4).

Portfolio Examples.

Examples abound of portfolios in the humanities, with many programs requiring a portfolio as a final project to complete their undergraduate degrees.

In the English Department at Winona State University, students are required to enroll in ENG 490 – Portfolio ("Undergraduate Portfolio", para. 1). The portfolio project serves the purpose of gathering together the projects students have completed during their undergraduate work, with the portfolio including an introductory statement as well as, "at least two papers, projects, or other documents," (para. 8) which demonstrate the departments' goals. This type of portfolio project is useful for students as it engages them with already completed work and provides an opportunity to edit their written work. In addition, the portfolio is intended to serve as a tool useful for future employers to assess a graduate's writing abilities (para. 2).

At the University of California, Los Angeles, graduate students in the Digital Humanities program are tasked with creating a portfolio that shows how research in the digital humanities has impacted their studies. Accordingly, the Digital Humanities portfolio is published as a website accessible to the general public and provides information regarding how the student plans on applying what they have learned in the Digital Humanities program to their future research ("Digital Portfolio", para. 2). What stands out in this program is the different major disciplines from which students enrolled in the Digital Humanities program come. The online portfolio falls under the best works portfolio, as students are not only showcasing the culmination of their research in digital humanities but also applying what they have learned to their major area of study, providing insights into how the digital humanities positively impact their research.

Conclusion

A range of culminating experiences in the humanities exists. For students, the culminating project will have implications for their future research and work. For instructors, culminating projects provide necessary feedback on student acquisition of required skills and abilities in their major. The authors have chosen to focus on the project-based experience, service-learning experience, senior thesis, and portfolio as these are the most common culminating experiences found in the humanities and have applications for the variety of programs that humanities encompass. Continuing in this vein, we have compiled some questions that educators can use in assessing their programs and deciding which culminating experience works best for their program's objectives and individual courses.

Questions for instructors and/or program directors considering culminating projects

1. What are the primary goals of my program? What should students achieve by the time they graduate from this program?

2. What resources does my institution have to support my students and my department in implementing this culminating experience?

3. What are the pros and cons of this type of culminating experience? Does this fit in with the culture of my institution? If not, how might this provide opportunities for growth in my institution?

4. Is this a culminating project that all students in my program will achieve? Or is this a culminating project intended for an honors program?

5. What are the time constraints under which the culminating project will take place? Will students need to enroll in a course or courses aimed at preparing for this type of project? Or will students and instructors work together outside of class meetings to complete the project?

Questions for students and instructors in considering a culminating project

1. What is the student's area of interest?

2. What is the best type of culminating project for the student's area of interest? How will projects the student has been involved in previously impact or form part of the culminating project?

3. What will be the time commitment for the student and instructor? Is this possible given the students' and instructors' other commitments?

4. How will this culminating project provide a basis for the student's future career plans?

5. In what ways does my institution provide a support network for this type of project? With what programs may I need to be in contact with and/or involved with to bring about the best culminating experience for my students?

References

Barton, Kathleen Dugan (2020). *Student Ownership: The Missing Link in Education.* Trek Publications.

Bod, Rens (2013). *A New History of the Humanities: The Search for Principles and Patterns from Antiquity to the Present.* Oxford University Press.

Brown University (n.d.) *Capstones* https://college.brown.edu/design-your-education/complete-your-degree/culminating-experiences/capstones

Commission on the Humanities and Social Sciences. (2013). *The Heart of the Matter: The Humanities and Social Sciences for a vibrant, competitive and secure nation.* https://cola.unh.edu/sites/default/files//hss_executivesummary.pdf

Dickinson College (2017). "The Senior Experience" https://www.dickinson.edu/homepage/197/the_senior_experience

Elon University (n.d.) *Service-Learning.* https://www.centerforengagedlearning.org/resources/service-learning/

Education Commission of the States (2004). *Senior and Culminating Projects* https://files.eric.ed.gov/fulltext/ED484972.pdf

Kinzie, J., Silberstein, S., McCormick, A. C., Gonyea, R. M., & Dugan, B. (2021). Centering racially minoritized student voices in high-impact practices. *Change (New Rochelle, N.Y.), 53*(4), 6.

Mitchell, Tanya D. (2008). Traditional vs. Critical Service-Learning: Engaging the Literature to Differentiate Two Models. *Michigan Journal of Community Service Learning.* 2008, pp 50-65.

Rolheiser, C., Bower, B., & Stevahn, L. (2000). *The portfolio organizer: Succeeding with portfolios in your classroom.* Association for Supervision & Curriculum Development.

Thomas, John W (2000). "A Review of Research on Project Based Learning" *The Autodesk Foundation.* https://tecfa.unige.ch/proj/eteach-net/Thomas_researchreview_PBL.pdf

Smith, Laurie (2021). "What is a Capstone Project in College?" https://www.snhu.edu/about-us/newsroom/education/what-is-a-capstone-project

University of California, Los Angeles (n.d.) *Digital Portfolio.* https://dh.ucla.edu/graduate/digital-portfolio/

University of Kentucky (n.d.). *Welcome to the Center for Service Learning and Engagement.* https://servelearnconnect.uky.edu/

University of Notre Dame (n.d.) *Senior Thesis.* americanstudies.nd.edu/the-major/senior-thesis/

Winona State University (n.d.) *Undergraduate Portfolio.* https://www2.winona.edu/english/portfolioinformation.asp

York University (n.d.) *C4: The Cross-Campus Capstone Classroom* https://www.yorku.ca/c4/

Chapter 12

Natural and Applied Sciences

Jacob Moore
Penn State Mont Alto

Abstract: This chapter focuses on the culminating experiences for students at both the graduate and undergraduate levels in the natural and applied sciences. The natural and applied sciences refer to a wide variety of fields including but not limited to physics, chemistry, biology, geology, engineering, computer science, agricultural sciences, and medicine. Matching the breadth of the fields themselves, the culminating experiences in these programs also vary greatly. The natural sciences tend to focus on graduate-level research as the capstone experience, without any consistent capstone experiences at the undergraduate level. Because graduate education is so common among practicing scientists and because so many scientists wind up in academia, graduate research programs serve as the last step to transition from science student to practicing scientist. In the applied sciences, where graduate work is less common, at least excluding medicine, capstone experiences are more often included in undergraduate programs. These culminating experiences include things like capstone design in engineering and computer science, fieldwork in agricultural programs, or residency programs in medicine. While the exact nature of these culminating experiences can vary greatly from one field to the next, they all serve as a sort of onramp into professional practice in that domain, and will often involve actual stakeholders, clients, or patients. Additionally, many of these applied fields will have more regimented and consistent capstone requirements within the field as driven by active and powerful accrediting bodies.

Keywords: Natural Science, Applied Science, Physics, Biology, Chemistry, Engineering, Computer Science, Agriculture, Medicine

***

This chapter focuses on culminating experiences for students at both the graduate and undergraduate levels in the natural and applied sciences. A wide variety of degrees are contained within the natural and applied sciences, along with differing approaches to capstone student experiences.

Defining the Natural and Applied Sciences

It is important to first define what we mean when we talk about the terms natural and applied sciences. These terms do not have a universally defined or definite boundary, but there are some generally accepted attributes for each. For the purposes of this chapter, the following definitions will be used for natural sciences and applied sciences.

Natural sciences refers to the branch of knowledge dealing with the understanding of the natural or physical world. Subjects such as biology, chemistry, physics, and geology/geosciences are all usually considered to be natural sciences. The natural sciences are focused on an understanding of the system rather than applications (separating them from the applied sciences) and they are focused on physical systems rather than social systems (separating them from the social sciences).

Applied Sciences refers to the branch of knowledge dealing with the application of previously developed understanding in order to manipulate or enact change within an existing system. Subjects such as engineering, computer science, agricultural sciences, and medicine are all considered applied sciences. The term "applied science" is also often used to refer to social science subjects, but for the purposes of this chapter applied social sciences will not be discussed.

The Purpose of Education in the Natural and Applied Sciences

Now that we have defined what we mean by natural and applied sciences, we will next discuss the purpose of college education in those fields, and how capstone experiences fit into that purpose.

Natural Sciences

With the pursuit of knowledge and furthering our collective understanding of the universe serving as the driving force behind the natural sciences, being a researcher at the cutting edge of the field is generally considered to be the pinnacle of achievement in these fields. As such, the purpose of education for students in those fields is to prepare students to conduct research. Though research at the undergraduate level is usually not required in these fields, conducting empirical research in the form of master's theses or doctoral dissertations is almost universally required and serves as the capstone experience in these fields.

Applied Sciences

With the application of knowledge and the improvement of existing systems serving as the focus for applied sciences, the fields are much less centered on research and more centered on industrial or commercial ventures. The pinnacle of achievement in these disciplines is still about the cutting edge, but it is more about cutting-edge design, processes, or procedures made in industry rather than in academia. With preparation for industry or professional practice being the focus of education in the applied sciences, we can naturally see a progression from the basic knowledge taught in the early classes to more of an internship-style experience serving at the capstone experience. Whether this occurs at the undergraduate level or at the graduate level, the purpose is to smooth the transition from academia to industry.

Capstone Experiences in the Natural Sciences

As alluded to earlier, research and discovery are considered to be the culminating activity within the natural sciences. When some people think about physicists, biologists, chemists, or geologists, they correctly imagine that the primary focus in these fields is research that pushes the boundaries of our current understanding. College education in these fields trains people toward the end goal of producing researchers in these fields, and the capstone programs should reflect that.

Undergraduate Capstone Experiences

Though research on the cutting edge is the focus of any natural science student pursuing a graduate degree, there are no consistent requirements for a capstone-style research project in undergraduate physics, chemistry, biology, or geology degrees. Students simply progress through specialized courses as they move their way toward a focus area within their degree. This does not mean that capstone experiences cannot exist within these programs, simply that they are not uniformly required and therefore are not consistent from one university to the next when they are implemented.

If we look at the accrediting bodies in natural sciences, we can see some of the reasons behind this inconsistency at the undergraduate level. Physics programs in the US are not generally accredited. Biology programs in the US, with the exception of biochemistry and molecular biology programs, are similarly not generally accredited. Without program-specific accreditation in these fields, a great variety can exist within the curriculum requirements.

If we look at chemistry programs in the US, which are typically accredited by the American Chemical Society, we also still see much of the same. Looking toward the guidelines for accreditation, we see the requirement for a capstone experience, but there is great flexibility in that requirement as shown in the language.

These integrative experiences could be provided in an existing upper-level, designated capstone course (e.g., senior seminar) or distributed among several courses taught in the chemistry department. Typically, a stand-alone capstone course could not be used to fulfill the in-depth course requirement. Mentored teaching also provides an excellent opportunity for students to integrate their knowledge and skills, as does an independent research experience that also requires a research report and presentation of the student's results. (American Chemical Society Committee on Professional Training, 2015).

Finally, we can look towards geology/geosciences, which is in the midst of a possible shift toward accreditation. Though far from universal, ABET, which has long accredited engineering programs, has made gains in serving as the primary accrediting body for geology and geoscience programs. If we look at the accreditation guidelines on the curriculum for applied sciences, we see a required capstone experience, but again great flexibility in how that is administered. "Students in baccalaureate degree programs must also be prepared for applied science practice through a curriculum culminating in comprehensive projects or experiences based on the cumulative knowledge and skills acquired in earlier course work." (Applied and Natural Science Accreditation Commission ABET, 2017, p. 5).

Though there is a lack of uniformity in how these programs are conducted, it should be noted that both of these accrediting bodies specifically call for a culminating experience of some sort that brings together the curriculum. These could be research assignments in high-level technical courses, seminar courses that bring in current researchers, or undergraduate thesis projects as discussed in the ACS guidelines. Though examples of these approaches could be addressed, there is currently no comprehensive inventory of these programs, so it is hard to determine their widespread implementation. Additionally, as all of these avenues for the capstone experience mimic their graduate-level counterparts, the implementation style of each of these will be discussed in the next section with capstone experiences in graduate natural science programs.

Graduate Capstone Experiences

Graduate capstone experiences in the natural sciences consist of thesis or dissertation projects. These are almost always original research projects furthering the field. Though not exactly the same as the peer-reviewed research process for professionals in the field, there is significant overlap. Students start by proposing an idea, then conduct an experiment or gathering data that they need to interpret using established frameworks, and finally, they present the research in written or oral form. Throughout this process, they are subjected to multiple rounds of peer- or supervisory review. In the end, many theses or dissertations are also converted into traditional published research turning what is a training exercise into a legitimate contribution to the field.

Theses and dissertation projects in graduate school for the natural sciences can be viewed as part of a larger strategy of legitimate peripheral participation as a method for bringing new researchers into the community of practice (Hasrati, 2005). In the legitimate peripheral participation framework (Lave & Wenger, 1991), the learners (new graduate students in this case) are trained in the field by starting at the periphery of a social group (the research lab in this case), where they are expected to perform simple but authentic activities. As the students learn, they become more central and senior members of the lab who can in turn begin to mentor other newer students in basic research tasks. The thesis or dissertation project is then the culminating activity for the senior graduate students, showing that they are capable of going through all stages of the research process, and are ready to conduct research professionally as a full-fledged member of the community of practice.

Capstone Experiences in the Applied Sciences

Unlike the natural sciences, the applied sciences are much more focused on preparing students for industry and less on research, at least at the undergraduate level. This affects how capstone experiences are implemented in the applied sciences generally, though what industry looks like varies greatly across disciplines. Engineering is much different from medicine which is much different from agriculture. In the following section, we will look at what capstone experiences look like in a few of the applied sciences.

Capstone Experiences in Engineering and Computer Science

The engineering department, which often contains computer science, constitutes the largest applied science program at many universities. Whereas research is the central goal of the natural sciences, design is the central goal of engineering. Though there are many engineering jobs that do not involve design directly, there are very few engineering firms that do not engage in design as a whole. Because of this, the design activity is usually the central pillar of the capstone experience in most engineering and computer science programs.

Undergraduate Capstone Experiences

At the undergraduate level, a capstone design course is the culmination of the vast majority of the engineering degree programs in the US. Unlike the natural sciences, engineering programs in the US are almost all accredited by a single entity, ABET, formerly the Accreditation Board for Engineering and Technology, as graduation from an accredited program is required for professional licensure as an engineer. As described in the ABET accreditation criteria for the undergraduate engineering curriculum, programs must include:

A culminating major engineering design experience that 1) incorporates appropriate engineering standards and multiple constraints, and 2) is based on the knowledge and skills acquired in earlier coursework. (Engineering Accreditation Commission ABET, 2021).

Though it is not explicitly required as a stand-alone course, the capstone design accreditation requirement is usually implemented as such as it is the easiest way to prove to accreditors that all students have engaged in this requirement. In this course, student teams engage in an authentic design project, often with industrial sponsors and partners, to design and prototype a product or process. This activity mimics how teams of engineers work in industry and challenges students to apply the technical knowledge and soft skills they have developed over the prior semesters.

In the capstone design setting, a project-based learning framework replaces traditional lecture and lab-based activities with the student teams leading the way under instructor mediation. Though too much to include here in detail, Pembridge and Paretti (2019) provided a useful overview of instructional strategies used by experienced capstone instructors.

Despite commonly being included in the College of Engineering, computer science degree programs ascribe to a separate set of ABET accreditation criteria. Though design is not explicitly required, there is still a requirement that all students engage in a capstone experience. As described in the ABET accreditation criteria for the undergraduate computer science curriculum, programs must include a major project that requires integration and application of knowledge and skills acquired in earlier course work (Computing Accreditation Commission ABET, 2020).

Though design is not mentioned as part of the capstone course, the project will almost inevitably involve significant software development because of the nature of the field. Though the software development process has some differences from the traditional engineering design process used for physical artifacts, it shares many aspects with the design process used in other engineering fields.

Graduate Capstone Experiences

Though many engineers go directly from an undergraduate degree to industry, some pursue a master's degree in engineering to advance a career in industry. Students who pursue a graduate degree in engineering will shift from a design focus towards a research focus more similar to what was discussed in the natural sciences. Though not all master's degrees involve a thesis, even non-thesis master's programs in engineering involve some sort of culminating research project, albeit at a smaller scale. The project, thesis, or dissertation will serve as the culminating, research-centric activity for the student. Though research becomes the focus of the graduate degree, engineering is an applied science, and the research questions will have a decidedly applied science focus. Unlike in the natural sciences, establishing how the research might be used later is an important part of the research process.

Additionally, though design is often still a key aspect of graduate-level work, the design space differs. Whereas more routine aspects of design are often incorporated into undergraduate projects, such as the design of a building or the redesign of an existing product, graduate-level design projects are often focused on design within an unfamiliar space, such as the design of an entirely new type of engine or the implementation of a new material for road surfaces. This shifts the focus from a project with near-term commercialization potential to something more long-term.

Capstone Experiences in Agricultural Sciences

The agricultural sciences, including subjects such as agriculture, forestry, food science, and animal science, form the other half of the applied science mission of many of the original land grant universities in the US. This is exemplified by the A&M (Agricultural and Mechanical) moniker still attached to many of these colleges. Broadly, the purpose of the College of Agriculture is to prepare students to manage better land for crops, forests for forest products, stocks of animals, and all the agricultural products that come from these lands and crops. Though not as design-focused as engineering, the agricultural sciences are focused on using science to an end as opposed to just developing understanding. The development of new agricultural products and the necessary processes associated with these products are central to the agricultural sciences and serve as the core of these programs.

Undergraduate Capstone Experiences

There is no one accrediting body that covers all the agricultural sciences, but rather a patchwork of bodies accrediting the programs. This does not mean that there is a lack of capstone experiences, but instead that there is a patchwork of approaches.

To gain some insight, however, we will look to forestry programs that are fairly uniformly accredited in the US by the Society of American Foresters (SAF). According to the SAF criteria for accreditation:

> The program must identify and facilitate opportunities for students to complete a work experience, internship, or related experience related to the type(s) of career opportunities available to program graduates. These may be, but are not required to be, for course credit. (Society of American Foresters, 2021, p. 50)

The required internship or fieldwork experience makes sense in forestry and in the wider agricultural sciences, as much of the professional work of the agricultural sciences is done in the literal and figurative field. Students can engage in the management of forests and engage in contemporary real-world challenges alongside practicing professionals, again harkening back to the idea of legitimate peripheral participation (Lave & Wenger, 1991). Though not uniformly required across all of the agricultural sciences, fieldwork is common, particularly later in the program.

Another unique aspect of the educational system in agricultural sciences is the agricultural extension offered through many land-grant institutions. These extension programs, funded by the US Department of Agriculture, have a mission of bringing research and education to the public. As stated by the National Institute of Food and Agriculture (part of USDA):

> Through extension, land-grant institutions reach out to offer their resources to address public needs. By educating farmers on business operations and on modern agricultural science and technologies, extension contributes to the success of countless farms, ranches, and rural business. (National Institute of Food and Agriculture, n.d., para. 4)

Though these programs are not focused on the students at the university, they do provide a longstanding relationship that connects professors and students to the local agricultural practitioners. This allows the agriculture programs to communicate with farmers and other members of the agricultural community who may not have college degrees. Thus, the agricultural extension offices serve not only the community but also as a conduit for students to practice being a leader in the agricultural community.

Graduate Capstone Experiences

Much like in engineering, the focus of education shifts at the graduate level in the agricultural sciences from a mostly application-based education to more of a research focus. As agricultural sciences are applied sciences, this research is fundamentally defined by how it might be used in the future. Masters' degrees will often culminate in thesis- and non-thesis options, but again, even the non-thesis degree options often incorporate some amount of research as the capstone experience. The project, thesis, or dissertation in the subject area will require students to move beyond learning about the current state of the art and have them work to extend the state of the art with the new knowledge they contribute to the field.

Capstone Experiences in Medicine

Medicine here is defined as training for future doctors, nurses, physical therapists, occupational therapists, veterinarians, and others working to diagnose and treat patients. This goes beyond the typical college of medicine at many universities, but the central goal of all of these programs is to diagnose and treat ailments in patients. This common focus results in commonalities in the approaches taken in capstone courses.

Medicine at its core is an applied science with a high impact on people's lives. Medical professionals make daily decisions with literal life-and-death consequences; thus the field is highly regulated. Mirroring practice, medical education is also highly regulated, with well-established and stringent accreditation processes. Diagnosing and treating patients is the central activity for medical practitioners and will also serve as the central pillar of the capstone experience for students in the medical field through clinical experiences.

Undergraduate Capstone Experiences

While many professions in medicine require a graduate degree, there are also several options, such as nursing, physical therapy assistant, and occupational therapy assistant that do not require a graduate degree for professional practice. These professionals will be working with and treating patients for a number of routine procedures. As such, the capstone experience in the education of these individuals involves getting the students to work with actual patients in supervised clinical experiences. In this way, the students are performing many of the same tasks they will be performing as professionals and applying the classroom knowledge they have gained as part of their degree. As discussed with the natural sciences and with the agricultural sciences, this apprenticeship-like model best matches up with the idea of legitimate peripheral participation (Lave & Wenger, 1991).

Looking at the accreditation criteria set forth by the Commission on College Nursing Education, the autonomous accrediting arm of the American Association of Colleges of Nursing, we can see that clinical experience is a required part of the degree program for accredited nursing programs. The accreditation criteria require that:

> The curriculum includes planned clinical practice experiences that: enable students to integrate new knowledge and demonstrate attainment of program outcomes; foster interprofessional collaborative practice; and are evaluated by faculty. (Commission On Collegiate Nursing Education, 2018, p. 16)

Mirroring nursing, bachelor's and associate degree programs in physical therapy and occupational therapy also require clinical experience as part of the accreditation requirements (Accreditation Council for Occupational Therapy Education, 2018; Commission on Accreditation in Physical Therapy Education, 2020).

In addition to the traditional clinical fieldwork, which is a longstanding requirement in the field, simulation has also been making inroads as part of medical education. Using electromechanical dummies or other technologies, students can diagnose and treat simulated patients. Though this will never be a full-fidelity fieldwork experience, the simulated patients offer several advantages. First, this, of course, reduces the risk for real patients, allowing students to practice treatment in a lower-stress environment. As a result, this also allows students to practice these skills earlier than they would with real patients since the consequences of an error are reduced. Second, these simulated experiences can be scheduled in a way that real clinical experiences cannot. The obstetrics ward for example cannot simply schedule a difficult birth at a given time. Furthermore, it cannot even ensure that all students will experience this at all due to the random nature of the patients coming in. Simulation however can provide this experience in a scheduled fashion, ensuring that all students will get that particular experience. Though simulation is unlikely to replace clinical experiences in the field completely, some research has shown that simulation in conjunction with traditional fieldwork can lead to higher scores on licensing exams (Curl et al., 2016).

Medicine is somewhat unique, in that the "medical degree," the degree that doctors have, is only offered as a graduate degree. Students need to complete an undergraduate degree before even starting their medical degree. There are programs at the undergraduate degree level specifically to prepare for the graduate degree in the form of pre-med degrees, usually housed in the College of Science, but other undergraduate degrees such as biology could just as easily be a path to medical school. To prepare for medical school though, students must provide evidence of some level of preparation in the sciences, preferably with a science-based degree.

Unlike an undergraduate degree in nursing though, these pre-medicine degrees do not contain significant clinical experience and they are generally not accredited by a central body. These programs are usually housed within the College of Science and have varied capstone experiences most similar to degrees in biology or chemistry, as discussed earlier in the chapter.

Graduate Capstone Experiences

At the graduate level, the medical degree is also unique in that what many would consider the capstone experience, the residency, is done after graduating from medical school. In the residency, a three- to seven-year process completed after graduating from medical school but before being eligible to be board-certified (American Board of Medical Specialties, n.d.), the residents go through an extensive clinical experience that brings together everything they have learned and represents the culmination of their training. Like the graduate schools themselves, these residency programs are accredited by the Accreditation Council for Graduate Medical Education (Accreditation Council for Graduate Medical Education, n.d.) signaling that they are also an important part of doctor education. In this residency experience, the residents are working alongside other doctors, completing authentic tasks in the real-life context, all under the supervision of more experienced doctors, called faculty in the accreditation literature. This clinical experience is not all that different in terms of the approach discussed earlier in undergraduate programs such as nursing but is much more expansive in terms of the time spent and scope.

Graduate medical programs in pharmacology and veterinary medicine generally follow a similar path to medical schools. Both of these are graduate degree programs started only after completing another undergraduate degree, usually with the same science focus as a medical degree. They both involve some classwork but focus more on clinical experience as the degree moves on, and finally culminating with residency programs which are common though not required as with doctors. Regardless of the optionality of the residency, though, significant clinical experience is written into the accreditation criteria for pharmacy and veterinary medicine programs (Accreditation Council for Pharmacy Education, 2015; American Veterinary Medical Association, 2021).

Conclusions

The capstone experiences in the natural and applied sciences vary in purpose and in structure across the various disciplines, but each centers around preparing the graduates for the transition to the professional workforce. The natural sciences prepare students by having them conduct research, at least at the graduate level, while under the supervision of other more experienced researchers. Engineering and computer science prepares students to engage in design by having them work in a team on a collaborative design project, under the supervision of faculty and often industry sponsors. The capstone experience in the agricultural sciences most often centers around internships or fieldwork, having students apply their knowledge to real-world problems. And finally, the capstone experiences for the medical fields have students working in hospitals through clinical and residency programs. Each experience varies, but these experiences have evolved over time to better serve not only the students but also their future professions.

References

Accreditation Council for Graduate Medical Education. (n.d.). What we do— Accreditation council for graduate medical education. https://www.acgm e.org/what-we-do/overview/

Accreditation Council for Occupational Therapy Education. (2018). ACOTE accreditation standards. https://acoteonline.org/accreditation-explained/ standards/

Accreditation Council for Pharmacy Education. (2015). Accreditation standards and key elements for the professional program in pharmacy leading to the doctor of pharmacy degree. https://www.acpe-accredit.org/pdf/Standards 2016FINAL2022.pdf

American Board of Medical Specialties. (n.d.). ABMS Board certification requirements. https://www.abms.org/board-certification/board-certificatio n-requirements/

American Chemical Society Committee on Professional Training. (2015). ACS guidelines and evaluation procedures for bachelor's degree programs. htt ps://www.acs.org/content/dam/acsorg/about/governance/committees/trai ning/2015-acs-guidelines-for-bachelors-degree-programs.pdf

American Veterinary Medical Association. (2021). Accreditation policies and procedures of the AVMA Council on Education. https://www.avma.org /sites/default/files/2021-09/coe_pp-July-2021.pdf

Applied and Natural Science Accreditation Commission ABET. (2017). Criteria for accrediting applied and natural science programs, 2018 – 2019. https:/ /www.abet.org/accreditation/accreditation-criteria/criteria-for-accrediting -applied-and-natural-science-programs-2018-2019/

Commission on Accreditation in Physical Therapy Education. (2020). Standards and required elements for accreditation of physical therapist assistant education programs. https://www.capteonline.org/globalassets/capte-docs/c apte-pta-standards-required-elements.pdf

Commission On Collegiate Nursing Education. (2018). Standards for accreditation of baccalaureate and graduate nursing programs. https://ww w.aacnnursing.org/Portals/42/CCNE/PDF/Standards-Final-2018.pdf

Computing Accreditation Commission ABET. (2020). Criteria for accrediting computing programs, 2021 – 2022. https://www.abet.org/accreditation/accr editation-criteria/criteria-for-accrediting-computing-programs-2021-2022/

Curl, E. D., Smith, S., Chisholm, L. A., McGee, L. A., & Das, K. (2016). Effectiveness of integrated simulation and clinical experiences compared to traditional clinical experiences for nursing students. *Nursing Education Perspectives, 37*(2), 72–77. https://doi.org/10.5480/15-1647

Engineering Accreditation Commission ABET. (2021). Criteria for accrediting engineering programs, 2022 – 2023. https://www.abet.org/accreditation/acc reditation-criteria/criteria-for-accrediting-engineering-programs-2022-2023/

Hasrati, M. (2005). Legitimate peripheral participation and supervising Ph.D. students. *Studies in Higher Education, 30*(5), 557–570. https://doi.org/10.10 80/03075070500249252

Lave, J., & Wenger, E. (1991). *Situated learning: Legitimate peripheral participation.* Cambridge University Press.

National Institute of Food and Agriculture. (n.d.). Extension. http://www.nifa. usda.gov/about-nifa/how-we-work/extension

Pembridge, J. J., & Paretti, M. C. (2019). Characterizing capstone design teaching: A functional taxonomy. *Journal of Engineering Education, 108*(2), 197–219. https://doi.org/10.1002/jee.20259

Society of American Foresters. (2021). Procedures, standards, and guidelines for accrediting educational programs in professional forestry, urban forestry, natural resources and ecosystem management, and in forest technology. https://www.eforester.org/Main/Certification_Education/Accreditation/Cri teria_and_Documents/Main/Accreditation/Criteria%20and%20Documents .aspx?hkey=b337bccf-b946-4038-8667-108442c69e22

Chapter 13

Social Sciences

Nikki DiGregorio
Towson University

Amanda J. Rich
York College of Pennsylvania

Laura Evans
Penn State Brandywine

Abstract: Research has established a positive correlation between applied learning experiences and student outcomes. Given the social sciences' examination of human interactions, relationships, and behavior, applied experiences within these degree programs are essential. Social science programs are charged with preparing students for whatever comes next in their respective journeys as the spectrum of career opportunities continues to expand. As such, the social sciences must be able to dovetail the acquisition of knowledge with application, while allowing space for students to make meaningful connections across diverse contexts. Culminating student experiences often serve as the mechanism through which these transformations become palpable. Culminating experiences refer to specific components of curricula that typically occur at the end of a student's degree program, wherein students are expected to integrate and apply the theory and skills they have learned over the course of the program. Applied learning pedagogies present students with opportunities to bridge theory and practice while learning in novel contexts. The interdisciplinary nature of the social sciences serves as both a strength and an opportunity with respect to developing and implementing meaningful culminating experiences for students. Within the social sciences, great diversity exists with respect to how culminating student experiences are developed, integrated, and assessed. This chapter explores extant culminating student experiences across the social sciences and highlights components of well-designed culminating experiences that have demonstrated their effectiveness in supporting learning. Lastly, suggestions for adaptation and replicability within individual disciplines are offered, as well as considerations for interdisciplinary culminating experiences rooted in the social sciences.

Keywords: transformative learning, applied learning, social sciences

***

Context

Research has established a positive correlation between applied learning experiences and student outcomes (Trolian & Jach, 2020); as such, applied learning experiences continue to extend across disciplines in higher education. Given the social sciences' unique foci surrounding the examination of human interactions, relationships, and behavior, applied experiences within these degree programs are essential. Social science programs are charged with preparing students for whatever comes next in their respective journeys as the spectrum of career opportunities continues to expand. Thus, the social sciences must be able to dovetail the acquisition of knowledge with application, while allowing space for students to make meaningful connections across contexts. Culminating student experiences often serve as the mechanism through which these transformations become palpable. More specifically, culminating experiences refer to "those curricular experiences that typically occur at the end of a student's degree program, in which students are expected to integrate, extend, and apply the theory and practical skills they have gained over the course of the program" (Goodsett, 2018, p. 95).

Uniquely, applied learning pedagogies present students with opportunities to "connect theory and practice, to learn in unfamiliar contexts, to interact with others unlike themselves, and to practice using knowledge and skills" (Ash & Clayton, 2009, p. 25). As globalization increases, students must be prepared to engage with diverse populations across professional, industry, and/or academic settings. The multidisciplinary nature of the social sciences serves as both a strength and an opportunity with respect to developing and implementing meaningful culminating experiences for students. Within the social sciences, great diversity exists with respect to how culminating student experiences are developed, integrated, and assessed. This chapter will explore extant culminating student experiences across the social sciences as well as components of well-designed culminating experiences that have demonstrated their effectiveness in supporting learning. Lastly, the chapter will offer suggestions for adaptation and replicability within individual disciplines, as well as considerations for multidisciplinary culminating experiences rooted in the social sciences.

Theoretical Background

Transformative Learning Theory

Transformative learning (Cranton, 1996; Mezirow, 1991) has been conceptualized as the actions involved in changing one's frame of reference. With respect to education, Mezirow (1996) posited that the central goal of adult education is to support autonomous responsible thinking. Social sciences program graduates go on to work in varied arenas, serving others and society through careers in areas such as economics, political science, human services, family science, and psychology, necessitating the ability to function as autonomous and socially responsible thinkers. As such, culminating student learning experiences have the potential to foster transformative learning. Furthermore, Taylor and Cranton (2013) recognized empathy, or the ability to experience the feelings of another subjectively, as a necessary component of fostering transformative learning; "Transformational learning shapes people; they are different afterward, in ways that both they and others can recognize" (Clark, 1993, p. 47). Fundamentally, transformative learning involves more than skill acquisition. Transformative learning occurs in three stages (Taylor, 1997):

1. Learners engage in critical self-reflection about assumptions and present approaches;

2. Learners transform or revise their perspective;

3. Learners actually adopt new ways of behaving, consistent with their renewed perspective.

Transformative learning is an approach that enables learners to assess critically their own perspective and through education experience a palpable shift (Duncan & Goddard, 2017). Research has demonstrated that it is often discrepant experiences that challenge past experiences that prompt reflection (Taylor & Cranton, 2013). Thus, transformative learning theory provides social sciences educators a foundation from which to build student-centered pedagogies that provide conditions for cultural, social, and contextual applied learning experiences that facilitate transformative learning among students.

Self-Efficacy

The concept of self-efficacy emerged from the combined work of Rotter (1966) and Bandura (1977). Rotter (1966) contended that individuals establish general expectations about their ability to exert control over their environment and Bandura (1977) added to this foundation by integrating the role of social cognition in perceived self-efficacy. The new environments presented by experiential learning opportunities can pose unprecedented challenges to students. Research has indicated that students who experience imposter syndrome may observe a decrease in their self-efficacy within this new setting (Ferguson, 2021); within the context of applied learning experiences, students' perceived self-efficacy is often threatened initially. However, these are unique and important teachable moments, as instructors can aim to motivate their students to engage in tasks in meaningful ways, enhance students' self-concept and self-efficacy about learning, set appropriate challenges, and aim for both surface and deep outcomes (Hatie & Yates, 2014). Gregg et al. (2021) noted that "applied experiences such as internships will help students [sic] respond appropriately in different settings in the future," (p. 3); illustrating the vital importance of applied learning experiences, as they provide necessary opportunities for increasing students' perceived self-efficacy. Concisely, the concept of self-efficacy provides a framework through which social sciences educators can support students as they come to understand that specific behaviors generally lead to similar outcomes within particular contexts (DiGregorio & Liston, 2018).

Applied and Experiential Learning

Colleges and universities in the United States utilize applied learning approaches that incorporate both in-class and out-of-class experiences for students, including, but not limited to, internships and practica, undergraduate research, study abroad opportunities, service-learning, and capstone experiences (Ash & Clayton, 2009; Trolian & Jach, 2020). Applied learning is often referred to as "learning by doing" (Schwartzman & Henry, 2009, p.4) and requires students to engage in collaborative learning alongside others in a variety of settings. Moreover, collaborative learning encapsulates a wide range of activities, but is often student-centric with students' application of course material as the foundation for design, as opposed to the instructor's presentation of said material (Loes, 2019).

Research has indicated that a significant portion of academic programs within the social sciences have consistently required some form of culminating learning experience for the past three decades (Hauhart & Grahe, 2010; Perlman & McCann, 1997). More recently, a number of institutions have worked intentionally to create applied learning experiences (Kennedy et al., 2015), with some moving towards an applied learning mandate for all students (Isaak et al., 2018). The shift towards offering applied and experiential learning experiences rests on a burgeoning body of research documenting their correlated benefits. Several common applied and experiential learning approaches have been identified as high-impact practices, a reflection of their concomitance with deep learning (Kuh, 2008). For example, capstone experiences can foster students' capacity to demonstrate problem-solving and communication skills (Young et al., 2017 as cited in Trolian & Jach, 2020). Similarly, undergraduate research experiences have been shown to support critical thinking, and in-depth learning, as well as to help shape career goals (Hensel, 2018). More generally, providing students with opportunities to engage in complex, problem-based learning can advance students' capacity for innovation and leadership skills (Barkley et al., 2014).

It is important to scaffold applied learning experiences throughout curricula and to assess culminating experiences to ensure they are inclusive and support critical reflection. As Ash and Clayton warn (2009), "Experiential learning can all too easily allow students to reinforce stereotypes about difference, to develop simplistic solutions to complex problems, and to generalize inaccurately based on limited data" (p. 26). Therefore, the process of integrating applied learning experiences must be intentional to help offset the risk of inadvertently strengthening student biases. Scaffolding requires individualized and scaled guidance, providing students with increased support as they learn new or complex skills that are then systematically decreased to foster mastery of content and skills (Chu, 2020).

As the student population continues to diversify, social science programs must adapt to evolving learning needs and preferences. For example, interest in online learning continues to increase (Nguyen, 2015). Student engagement with coursework remains a core goal of social science programming, regardless of the mode of content delivery. Moreover, academic motivation has a propensity to lessen during college and research indicates that programs that incorporate applied learning may help enhance students' motivation (Trolian & Jach, 2020).

Results from a multi-institution longitudinal study in the United States suggest a positive correlation exists between specific types of applied learning and students' fourth-year academic motivation, particularly experiences that foster the translation of knowledge into action, irrespective of whether they were situated in-class or out-of-class (Troilan & Jach, 2020). Findings such as these provide justification for augmented backing of applied learning experiences, as evidence indicates that along with catalyzing deep learning, they may also support latent institutional goals, such as academic retention and progression by increasing or helping to maintain student motivation levels.

Internships

The social sciences intrinsically necessitate application. For example, within the field of family science, the majority of academic program content is designed to support individuals and families in the community (Gregg et al., 2021). Students in family science programs intern with a wide variety of programs, including 4-H and cooperative extension, social services, non-profit organizations, assisted living facilities, advocacy programs, child development programs, childcare technical assistance agencies, and other related services (Gregg et al., 2021). Gonyea and Kozak (2014) noted that students' internship experiences can directly shape their career choices and influence their perceived ability to effectuate change in the broader community. Given the importance of the internship experience for students, organizations, and communities, some programs have developed processes matching students to internship placements (Taylor et al., 2017). The Eastern Carolina University-Linking Interns and Community Services (ECU-LINCS) involves 10 steps for internship placement. The steps ultimately connect students with community organizations but also provide students to practice professional skills like making first impressions, creating and updating a resume, and interviewing (Taylor et al., 2017). Simply put, institutions of higher education utilize internships within their curricula to help ensure students are prepared for employment upon graduation (Ballard & Carroll, 2005), whether targeting professional and industry or academic career settings. Moreover, research has indicated that internship opportunities can create cost-effective pathways to employment after graduation (Gregg et al., 2021).

Service-Learning

Service-learning is similar to other forms of applied learning but incorporates civic engagement within the context of a collaborative relationship with community partners (Flecky & Gitlow, 2010). Notably, service-learning efforts are fundamentally different from other forms of experiential learning in that they are focused on identified concerns at the community level (e.g., women's health programs, housing insecurity, and social programming targeting individuals with intellectual and developmental disabilities). This exclusive feature of service learning creates an opportunity for the development of unique culminating experiences for students. Moreover, service learning is distinct from volunteering because of its concentration on student learning objectives. Additionally, the development of service-learning should include a reflective component for students, which has been shown to strengthen the connection between theory and practice (Flecky & Gitlow, 2010). Incorporation of service-learning can take numerous forms. For example, service learning can be integrated as part of a course, a requirement for completion of an academic program, or part of a larger internship experience that engages students in community-level service (Goodsett, 2018). Additionally, collaborating with community partners on fundraising and grant-writing projects can be mutually beneficial for student learning and community needs (Jorgensen et al., 2017). Service-learning provides students with opportunities to develop professional skills and can also provide support and resources to community organizations.

E-Portfolios

Electronic portfolios, or e-portfolios, are often used in the social sciences as a culminating experience (Hockley & Duneney, 2018). Generally, they refer to a digital compilation of students' work, experiences, videos, photographs, and other artifacts that allow students to review and reflect upon their learning experience (Lam, 2020; Yancey & Terrel, 2019). Beyond reflecting upon past experiences, e-portfolios often require students to connect their past experiences to their future professional goals and think about the perspective of their target audience (Yancey & Terrel, 2019). In addition to being an active learning experience for students, e-portfolios can be used to evaluate student's achievement of program-level learning objectives (Banta et al., 2009).

E-portfolios can involve students identifying the skills and other learning outcomes they believe to be most relevant to their future academic or professional paths as they select artifacts from their strongest work to support their achievement of such outcomes. It allows students to reflect clearly on how particular assignments, academic experiences, and co-curricular activities weave together to support their learning, identify areas for future growth, and construct a professional narrative and professional identity (Cordie et al., 2019). Though more research on the effectiveness of e-portfolios with respect to student learning outcomes is needed, several studies have found that their use supports meta-cognition, skill development, and reflective practice (Cambridge, 2010; Nguyen, 2013).

Capstone Courses & Senior Seminars

Capstone courses, sometimes referred to as senior seminars, often serve as culminating experiences for students and are common requirements for the completion of an undergraduate social sciences degree. These courses, alongside the comprehensive projects that are typically central, serve multiple educational goals, as well as provide a space for the integration of knowledge in a way that supports students in their aspirations beyond completion of the program. Moreover, Hauhart and Grahe (2010) considered completion of a capstone course to be a "rite of passage" that signifies the transition from the status of undergraduate student to another (p. 4). Capstone courses may require students to complete a senior thesis or a capstone project requiring the integration of content from throughout the undergraduate curriculum.

Major Field Tests

Some social science programs use objective examinations as a final experience to measure student's mastery of the program's content (Szafran, 1996). Many programs use Major Field Tests (MFTs) as an end-of-program assessment (Garris et al., 2019). MFTs were initially developed by Educational Testing

Services (ETS) in 1989 to address the need to measure program efficacy (Garris et al., 2019). In social sciences, ETS is often used to meet the needs of external accreditors and guide program development, identifying strengths and areas for improvement (Bush et al., 2008). Although many programs use MFTs, there is a dearth of research on their efficacy (Garris et al. 2019). Stoloff and colleagues (2015) found that scores on MFTs were positively correlated with high-impact practices, which could make MFTs useful in measuring the efficacy of other types of cumulative experiences.

Critical Self-Reflection

Culminating experiences within the social sciences involve interactions with numerous groups of people (e.g., peers, instructors, community members, mentors) and are collaborative by nature. In fact, Loes (2019) posited collaborative learning as a dimension of applied learning. Thus, it is important to consider learning goals that include developing skills necessary for successful collaboration, such as students' abilities to communicate with diverse groups, hold themselves and others accountable, and develop shared visions (Ash & Clayton, 2009). "Students in applied learning pedagogies may have a vague sense of the impact their experiences have had on them but not be fully aware of the nature of their own learning, its sources, or its significance" (Ash & Clayton, 2009, p. 26). Ash and Clayton (2009) continued, "Students may, in other words, miss the opportunity to learn about their own learning processes – to develop the meta-cognitive skills required for life-long, self-directed learning that applied learning is so well suited to cultivate" (p. 27). The challenge of helping students identify specific changes in their own attitudes or knowledge bases, or help them articulate what precipitated those shifts, is one that is met by self-reflection.

Critical self-reflection has been established as a best practice in social work and other human serving fields within the social sciences, with the understanding that it is a "necessarily and profoundly relational process" (Adamowich et al, 2014, p. 141), requiring supportive interactions with others along the way. Student-centered academic programs within the social sciences can leverage their foundational strengths to foster critical self-reflection among students by scaffolding it into culminating projects. Further, critical self-reflection can challenge students' traditional ways of viewing diversity, the social world, and themselves. In alignment with transformative learning theory (Cranton, 1996; Mezirow, 1991, 1997), it is through critical self-reflection that frames of reference are able to be transformed. Notably, this is a lifelong process (Rosen et al., 2017), but curating applied learning experiences that facilitate and support critical self-reflection promotes the development of skills necessary for application well beyond graduation.

However, "a critical reflection process that generates, deepens, and documents learning does not occur automatically – rather, it must be carefully and intentionally designed" (Ash & Clayton, 2009, p. 28). Therefore, when designing critical reflection activities within applied learning contexts it is important to consider best practices, as illustrated by the DEAL model (Clayton & Ash, 2004):

1. Determining the desired outcomes: learning goals and associated objectives;

2. Designing reflection to achieve those outcomes, and;

3. Integrating formative and summative assessment into the reflection process.

The DEAL model provides students with a mechanism through which they can use written expression or verbal communication for learning, as opposed to recounting and describing learning retrospectively (Clayton & Ash, 2004). The effectiveness of the DEAL model has been examined in multiple disciplines within the social sciences (Jameson et al., 2008 and McGuire et al., 2009) and is an adaptable framework that focuses on the intentional design of critical reflection within applied learning opportunities. More specifically, the model provides instructors with a starting point and guideposts for the development of culminating learning projects that incorporate critical self-reflection through scaffolding and ensure alignment to student learning outcomes and is well suited for further application across the social sciences.

More broadly, there is an increasing need for self-reflection among instructors of social sciences with respect to the way we think about pedagogy, our beliefs about students and student learning, and how these ideas shape the development and implementation of applied learning experiences. Self-reflective practice is a tool that can benefit students and instructors alike and assist in documenting what works well and what challenges exist within and between culminating experiences situated in social sciences programs. The supplemental resource located at the end of this chapter provides instructors with reflective prompts for developing culminating student experiences.

Assessment of Culminating Experiences

Increasingly, higher education has emphasized the importance of program assessment. Culminating projects, such as capstone courses and senior seminars, facilitate program assessment (Sum, 2015). Culminating student learning experiences can provide vital data on student learning outcomes in an interactive fashion and present an opportunity for faculty to work collaboratively.

Moreover, the intrinsic flexibility of culminating student experiences allows for their development to accommodate myriad approaches to assessment and diverse student learning outcomes. Assessment of culminating projects also fosters accountability at the program level through the need to demonstrate that students receive the very skills and knowledge programs seek to provide. Applied learning within the social sciences affords faculty with room to engage directly students in the process of assessment by tapping into their reflections on their own learning and experiences (Sum, 2015). Indirectly, assessment efforts may include course mapping exercises wherein students identify courses where they acquired specific skills or mastered content, solicit student feedback related to what perceive to have been "pivotal learning moments" (Sum & Light, 2010, p. 255), or include learning activities such as having students lead substantive discussions synthesizing what they have learned (Sum, 2015).

Considerations for Moving Forward

Culminating experiences provide opportunities to bridge the gap between theory and practice within the social sciences. Given that the social sciences encapsulate numerous areas of study, these experiences can take many forms depending on the goals of the faculty and students. For example, culminating experiences can take the form of teaching assistantships for students in programs centered around preparation for academic careers. Other general options include collaborative research projects and various forms of action research. More specifically, they can be integrated into the curriculum via internships, service-learning, e-portfolios, capstone courses, and MFTs. Across all of these approaches, one commonality is evident: culminating experiences that take students into the very communities they will serve are positively correlated with students' perceiving themselves as better prepared (Goodsett, 2018).

Culminating student learning experiences are unique, not only due to the intentional scaffolding of learning opportunities throughout, but also because of their ability to foster transformative learning and to augment students' self-efficacy beliefs, both of which shape their ability to perform in professional, academic, and industry settings. Importantly, instructional scaffolding should include self-reflection components throughout. Culminating experiences have the capacity to inform students' perspectives of themselves, others, and the very social world they have spent years learning about in an academic setting.

Ultimately, social sciences programming strives to cultivate a meaningful correlation between academic achievement and learning. Considering the public purposes of higher education (Boyer, 1996), developing applied learning experiences that foster lifelong learning benefits not only students and institutions of higher education but also the broader communities that they serve. The design of any culminating learning experience with the social sciences is, intrinsically, a form of collaborative civic learning. By developing applied learning experiences with intentionality and utilizing best practices for scaffolding learning and critical self-reflection, instructors of the social sciences can foster the professional, academic, and personal growth of students.

Supplemental Resource

Reflective Prompts for Developing Culminating Student Experiences

What are the key, program-level learning outcomes to be assessed?

How is the experience student-centered?

How will the experience allow students to reflect on prior learning?

How will the experience contribute to the development of the student's present academic and professional identity?

How will the experience support a student's future professional goals?

How will the student be supported during the experience?

Pre-experience: How is curriculum scaffolded toward culminating experience?

Are all courses or specific courses designed to support experience?

What is the knowledge base needed for the experience?

What specific skills and resources do students need to prepare for and complete the experience?

How will faculty/programs handle student missteps during the experience?

What is the intention of the experience - academic, professional, etc.?

References

Adamowich, T., Kuwee Kumsa, M., Rego, C., Stoddart, J., & Vito, R. (2014). Playing hide-and-seek: Searching for the use of self in reflective social work practice. *Reflective Practice, 15I*, 131- 143. http://dx.doi.org/10/1080/146239 43.2014.883312

Ash, S. L., & Clayton, P. (2009). Documenting learning: The power of critical reflection in applied learning. *Journal of Applied Learning in Higher Education, 1*(1), 25-48. https://files.eric.ed.gov.fulltext/EJ1188538.pdf

Ballard, S. M. & Carroll, E. B. (2005). Internship practices in family studies programs. *Journal of Family and Consumer Sciences, 97*(4), 11-17.[MS2] https://eric.ed.gov/?id=EJ737027

Bandura, A. (1977). Self-efficacy: toward a unifying theory of behavioral change. *Psychological review, 84*(2), 191-215. https://doi.org/10.1037/0033-295X.84.2.191

Banta, T. W., Griffin, M., Flateby, T. L., & Kahn, S. (2009). Three promising alternatives for assessing college students' knowledge and skills. *NILOA*

Occasional Paper, 2. https://www.learningoutcomesassessment.org/wpcont
ent/uploads/2019/02/OccasionalPaper2.pdf

Barkley, E. F., Cross, K. P., & Major. C. H. (2014). *Collaborative learning techniques: A handbook for college faculty,* Jossey-Bass.

Boyer, E. L. (1996). The scholarship of engagement. *Bulletin of the American Academy of Arts and Sciences, 49*(7), 18-33. https://www.jstor.org/stable/3824459

Bush, H. F., Duncan, F. H., Sexton, E. A., & West, C. T. (2008). Using the major field test-business as an assessment tool and impetus for program improvement: Fifteen years of experience at Virginia Military Institute. *Journal of College Teaching & Learning, 5*(2). doi:10.19030/tlc.v5i2.1314

Cambridge, D. (2010). *ePortfolios for lifelong learning and assessment.* Jossey Bass.

Chu, S. K. W. (2020). *Social Media Tools in Experiential Internship Learning.* Springer.

Cordie, L., Sailors, J., Barlow, B., & Kush, J. S. (2019). Constructing a professional identity: Connecting college and career through ePortfolios. *International Journal of ePortfolio, 9*(1), 17-27. http://www.theijep.com

Cranton, P. (1996). Types of group learning. *New Directions for Adult and Continuing Education, 71*(1), 25-32. https://onlinelibrary.wiley.com/doi/pdf/10.1002/ace.36719967105

DiGregorio, N. & Liston, D. (2018). Experiencing technical difficulties: In C. Hodges (Ed.), *Self-efficacy in instructional technology contexts.* (pp. 103-117). Springer International Publishing.

Duncan, S. F., & Goddard, H. W. (2017). *Family life education: Principles and practices for effective outreach* (3rd ed.). Sage Publications.

Evans, R., Scourfield, J., & Murphy, S. (2015). The unintended consequences of targeting young people's lived experiences of social and emotional learning interventions. *British Educational Research Journal, 41,* 381-297. doi: 10.1002/berj.3155

Ferguson, S. N. (2021). Effects of faculty and staff connectedness on student self-efficacy. *Journal of the Scholarship of Teaching and Learning, 21*(2), 58-78. https://doi.org/10.14434/josotl.v21i2.28597

Flecky, K., & Gitlow, L. (2010). *Service-learning in occupational therapy education.* Jones & Bartlett Publishers.

Garris, B. R., Ko, K., & Novotny, B. A. (2019). If it exists, it can be measured: Piloting a major field test for human services academic programs. *Journal of Human Services, 39*(1), 47-60. https://link.gale.com/apps/doc/A679900116/AONE?u=anon~61717c9f&sid=googleScholar&xid=b1d27ebe

Gregg, K., Dove, M., & DiGregorio, N. (2021). Instructional scaffolding in internships: Supporting future professionals in family science. *Syllabus, 10*(2), 1-14. https://www.syllabusjournal.org/syllabus/article/view/271

Goodsett, M. (2018). Exploring culminating experiences: Bridging the gap between theory and practice in LIS education. In *Re-envisioning the MLS: perspectives on the future of library and information science education* (pp. 91-108). Emerald Publishing Limited.

Gonyea, J. L. J., & Kozak, M. S. (2014). Scaffolding Family Science student experiences to increase employment options and preparedness. *Family Science Review, 19,* 26-36. https://www.familyscienceassociation.org/wp-content/upl

oads/2021/07/2014-19-1-Scaffolding-family-science-student-experiences-to-increase-employment-options-and-preparedness_-Gonyea.pdf

Hattie, J. A., & Yates, G. C. (2014). Using feedback to promote learning. *Applying science of learning in education: Infusing psychological science into the curriculum*, 45-58.

HauHart, R. C., & Grahe, J. E. (2010). The undergraduate capstone course in the social sciences: Results from a regional survey. *Teaching Sociology, 38*(1), 4-17. Doi: 10.1177.0092055X09353884

Hensel, N. H. (2018). *Course-based undergraduate research: Educational equity and high-impact practice.* Stylus.

Hockly, N., & Dudeney, G. (2019). Current and future digital trends in ELT. *RELC Journal, 49*(2), 164-178. https://doi.org/10.1177/0033688218777318

Isaak, J., Devine, M., Gervich, C., & Gottschall, R. (2018). Are we experienced? Reflections on the SUNY experiential learning mandate. *Journal of Experiential Education, 41*(1), 23- 28. http://dx/doi.org/10.1177/1053825917740377

Jorgensen, B. L., Ballard, S. M., Baugh, E., Taylor, A., & Carroll, E. (2017). Teaching grant writing to undergraduate students: A high-impact experience. In T. Newman & A. Schmitt (Eds.), *Field-based learning in family life education: Facilitating high impact experiences in undergraduate family science programs* (pp. 51-60). Palgrave Macmillon. doi:10.1007/978-3-319-39874-7

Kennedy, M., Billett, S., Gherardi, S., & Grealish, L. (2015). Practice-based learning in higher education: Jostling cultures. In *Practice-based learning in higher education* (pp. 1-13). Springer.

Kuh, G. D. (2008). *High-impact educational practices: What they are, who has access to them, and why they matter.* Association of American Colleges & Universities.

Lam, R. (2021). E-Portfolios: What we know, what we don't, and what we need to know. *RELC Journal, 1*(1), 1-8. doi: 10.1177/0033688220974102

Loes, C. N. (2019). Applied learning through collaborative educational experiences. *New Directions for Higher Education, 188*, 13-21. doi: 10.1002/he.202341

Lowe, P., Whitman, G., & Phillipson, J. (2009). Ecology and the social sciences. *Journal of Applied Ecology, 46*, 297-305. doi: 10.1111.j.1365/2664.2009.01621.x

Mezirow, J. (1991). *Transformative dimensions of adult learning.* Jossey-Bass.

Mezirow, J. (1996). Contemporary paradigms of learning. *Adult Education Quarterly, 46*, 158- 172. doi:10.1177/074171369604600303

Mueller, A., Perlman, B., McCann, L. I., & McFadden, S. H. (1997). A faculty perspective on teaching assistant training. *Teaching of Psychology, 24*(3), 167-171. https://doi.org/10.1207/s15328023top2403_3

Nguyen, C. F. (2013). The ePortfolio as a living portal: A medium for student learning, identity, and assessment. *International Journal of ePortfolio, 3*(2), 135-148. https://eric.ed.gov/?id=EJ1107805

Rosen, D., McCall, J., & Goodkind, S. (2017). Teaching critical self-reflection through the lens of cultural humility: an assignment in a social work diversity course. *Social Work Education, 36*, 289-298. http://dx.doi.org/10.1080/02615479.2017.1287260

Rotter, J. B. (1966). Generalized expectancies for internal versus external control of reinforcement. *Psychological monographs: General and applied, 80*(1), 1-28. https://doi.org/10.1037/h0092976

Schwartzman, R., & Henry, K. B. (2009). From celebration to critical investigation: Charting the course of scholarship in applied learning. *Journal of Applied Learning in Higher Education, 1,* 3-23. https://files.eric.ed.gov/fulltext/EJ1188538.pdf

Stoloff, M. L., Good, M. R., Smith, K. L., & Brewster, J. (2015). Characteristics of programs that maximize psychology major success. *Teaching of Psychology, 42*(2), 99-108. doi:10.1177/0098628315569877

Sum, P. E. (2015). Capstone courses and senior seminars as culminating experiences in undergraduate political science education. In J. Percell (Ed.), *Handbook on Teaching and Learning in Political Science and International Relations.* Edward Elgar Publishing.

Sum, P. E., & Light, S. A. (2010). Assessing student learning outcomes and documenting success through a capstone course. *PS: Political Science & Politics, 43,* 523-31. Doi: 10.1017/S1049096510000764

Taylor, E. W. (1997). Building upon the theoretical debate: A critical review of the empirical studies of Mezirow's transformative learning theory. *Adult Education Quarterly, 48*(1), 34-59. doi:10.1177/074171369704800104

Taylor, E. W. (2007). An update of transformative learning theory: A critical review of the empirical research (1999-2005). *International Journal of Lifelong Education, 26,* 173-191. doi:10.1080/02601370701219475

Taylor, A. C., Carroll, E. B., Ballard, S. M., Baugh, E. J., & Jorgensen, B. L. (2017). Effectively placing family studies majors at internship sites: The ECU-LINCS match process. In T. Newman & A. Schmitt (Eds.), *Field-based learning in family life education: Facilitating high impact experiences in undergraduate family science programs* (pp. 51-60). Palgave Macmillon. DOI 10.1007/978-3-319-39874-7

Taylor, E. W., & Cranton, P. (2013). A theory in progress? Issues in transformative learning theory. *European Journal for Research on the Education and Learning of Adults, 4,* 33-47. doi: 10.3384/rela.2000-7426.rela5000

Trolian, T. L., & Jach, E.A. (2020) Engagement in college and university applied learning experiences and students' academic motivation. *Journal of Experiential Education, 43,* 317-335. Doi: 10.1177/1053825920925100

Yancey, K. B., & Rhodes, T. L. (2019). *EPortfolio as curriculum: Models and practices for developing students' EPortfolio literacy.* Stylus Publishing, LLC.

Contributors

Ahmet Aksoy (Ph.D., Texas Tech University, 2022) is an assistant professor of communication at Columbia College - South Carolina. He teaches undergraduate-level courses in public speaking, intercultural communications, business and professional communication, and digital media. His research primarily focuses on communication education and how our cultural identities are shaped and communicated within our society.

Javier Alvarez-Jaimes (Ph.D. University of British Columbia) is an Associate Professor of Spanish language, literature, and culture at North Carolina Central University. In addition, Dr. Alvarez-Jaimes serves as Program Advisor and Commissioner of Human Relations at the City of Durham, NC. He has taught undergraduate courses at Eastern Kentucky University, the University of Georgia, and the University of Arkansas. His research is primarily focused on structural violence and marginal discourses in both literature and the arts of Latin America. He is also an artist and teaches about graffiti and street art.

Cassandra (Carlson) Hill Cassandra Carlson-Hill, Ph.D. (University of Wisconsin-Madison) was an Associate Professor of Communication. After 15 years in higher education, she now works in the public sector as the City of Madison, Wisconsin's Digital Inclusion Coordinator.

Russell Carpenter (Ph.D., University of Central Florida) is Assistant Provost and Professor of English at Eastern Kentucky University. He serves as editor-in-chief of the Journal of Faculty Development. Recent articles have appeared in the International Journal for Students as Partners, Journal on Excellence in College Teaching, Journal on Centers for Teaching and Learning, and Academic Leader, among others. He is also a columnist for the National Teaching & Learning Forum.

Nikki DiGregorio (Ph.D., University of Delaware), is an Assistant Professor of Family Studies & Community Development at Towson University. Dr. DiGregorio's scholarship examines the interplay between social policy, language appropriation, and the experiences of underrepresented gender and sexually diverse communities, as well as engagement in the scholarship of teaching and learning.

Kevin Dvorak (Ph.D., Indiana University of Pennsylvania, 2006) is the Executive Director of the Nova Southeastern University Writing and Communication Center. In addition, Dr. Dvorak is a Professor in the NSU Department of Communication, Media, and the Arts and Coordinator of the NSU First-Year Experience Program. His research focuses on writing and communication centers, course-embedded consulting, pedagogy, and faculty development.

Laura Evans (Ph.D., University of Maryland, 2011) is an Associate Teaching Professor of Human Development and Family Studies at Penn State Brandywine. She teaches undergraduate courses on a variety of topics including research methods, family relationships, and interventions for challenges experienced by individuals and families. Her research focuses on therapy processes and common factors in relational therapy, the scholarship of teaching and learning (SoTL), and gender and language.

Nisha Gupta (Ph.D. Syracuse University, 2005) is the Director of the Center for Teaching and Learning and assistant professor of philosophy and gender studies at Centre College. She teaches undergraduate courses in topics such as theories of knowledge, anti-racism, queer theory, and peace studies. Her research is focused on epistemic humility, learning theory, and anti-oppression organizing.

Karen J. Head (Ph.D., University of Nebraska, Lincoln, 2004) is a Professor of English & Technical Communication and Director of The Center for Arts & Innovation at the Missouri University of Science & Technology. Dr. Head is also an adjunct Professor in the School of Literature, Media, and Communication at the Georgia Institute of Technology where she founded and was Executive Director of the Naugle Communication Center. She teaches a variety of communication courses at the undergraduate and graduate levels and pioneered a course on dissertation writing at Georgia Tech. Her research spans several disciplinary lines, often as multidisciplinary work, to include work in the fine arts, education, social science, and broad-based humanities; her scholarship about higher education rhetoric, especially in the area of technology-based pedagogical practices, has been internationally recognized.

Danielle L. Johnson (M.A., Coastal Carolina University, 2022) is a doctoral student in the Department of Communication at the University of South Florida. As a health communication scholar, her research centers around illness and end-of-life (EOL) care as they intersect with media studies and fandom studies.

Amanda W. Joyce (Ph.D., Virginia Tech, 2014) is an associate professor of psychology at Murray State University. She has also served as the undergraduate internship coordinator for the department. She teaches several courses at the undergraduate and graduate levels including lifespan development, research methods, and statistics. Her research is primarily focused on cognitive and self-regulatory development in both early childhood and college years.

Kathleen J. Kennedy (MBA, University of Miami (FL), 2004) is an associate professor of the practice of retailing and consumer science in the Norton School of Human Ecology at the University of Arizona and a 2022 CUES Distinguished Fellow. In addition, Ms. Kennedy is a post-graduate researcher at the University of Manchester (UK) in the DBA Programme. She teaches undergraduate courses in business strategy and retailing management, digital retailing, and sustainable consumption. Her SoTL research is primarily focused on personalized, adaptive learning methods.

Sharrah A. Lane (Ph.D., University of Kentucky, 2020) is an Assistant Teaching Professor in the Department of Romance Studies at the University of North Carolina, Chapel Hill. She has taught a range of introductory to intermediate courses in Spanish language and Latin American literature, film, and culture. Her research lies at the intersection of film studies, childhood studies, and neoliberalism and capitalism.

Amanda M. Main (Ph.D., University of Central Florida, 2017) is the associate department chair and a lecturer of management in the College of Business Administration at the University of Central Florida. In addition, Dr. Main serves as the Assurance of Learning Coordinator for the college. She teaches several courses at the undergraduate and graduate levels including conflict resolution and negotiation, professional and executive leadership, and strategic management. Her research is primarily focused on workplace mistreatment, gender equality, leadership, and culture.

Amanda R. Martinez (Ph.D., Texas A&M University, 2011) is an associate professor of communication studies and sociology at Davidson College, a highly selective small liberal arts college in North Carolina. Dr. Martinez is the chair of the communication studies department and the director of the Speaking Center in the Center for Teaching and Learning at Davidson. She teaches foundational required courses for the communication studies major and minor, such as Principles of Oral Communication, Introduction to Communication Studies, as well as depth electives within her research areas of expertise, such as Stereotypes and Humor, Media Effects, and Gendered Communication in Society. Dr. Martinez regularly advises undergraduates pursuing independent research for their thesis projects and she teaches the senior capstone course for communication studies majors.

Lindsay M. McCluskey (Ph.D., Louisiana State University, 2016) is an assistant professor of public relations and advisement coordinator in the Department of Communication Studies at SUNY Oswego. Dr. McCluskey teaches courses online and in person at the graduate and undergraduate levels, including surveys of public relations, public relations writing, public relations research, crisis communication, social media strategy, public relations case studies, and strategic communication management. Dr. McCluskey has also developed courses in arts, entertainment, and sports public relations as well as lifestyle, beauty, and fashion public relations.

Amber McCord (Ph.D., Texas Tech University, 2017) is an assistant professor of practice in the College of Media and Communication at Texas Tech University.

In addition, Dr. McCord serves as a graphic designer for the Office of Research Development and Communication. She teaches courses at the undergraduate and graduate levels including introduction to digital and social media, production of digital media content, and data visualization for media. Her research and professional work are primarily focused on visual design and understanding how design influences knowledge and attitude.

Jacob Moore (Ph.D., Virginia Tech, 2013) is an associate professor of engineering at Penn State Mont Alto. Dr. Moore teaches introductory courses on engineering design, engineering mechanics, and thermodynamics. His primary research interests center around engineering education, with a focus on open educational resources, concept mapping, and student assessment. He is also the lead author of the Mechanics Map Open Textbook Project, an open textbook for engineering mechanics classes.

Shirley P. O'Brien (Ph.D., University of Kentucky, 2008) is a Foundation Professor in the Department of Occupational Science and Occupational Therapy at Eastern Kentucky University. Dr. O'Brien serves as the Post Professional Occupational Therapy Doctoral Coordinator at EKU. She teaches courses in leadership, policy, and research. Her research is in leadership, online teaching, and policy initiatives.

Patricia Payette (Ph.D., Michigan State University, 2001) is the executive director of the Quality Enhancement Plan (QEP) at the University of Louisville and senior associate director of UofL's Delphi Center for Teaching and Learning. In these positions, Dr. Payette brings her expertise in faculty development, instructional/curriculum design, critical thinking, and higher education training and development. She is a consulting editor for the journal College Teaching and her research centers around best practices in fostering teaching innovation and collaboration in higher education. She has authored numerous articles, essays, and book reviews in publications both inside and outside of the academy.

Andrea M. Hamilton (Ph.D. Ohio State University, 2013) is a civilian employed for the Department of Defense at Wright-Patterson AFB, Fairborn, OH.

Amanda J. Rich (Ph.D. University of Delaware, 2012) is an associate professor of Human Services at York College of Pennsylvania where she teaches coursework related to direct practice, administration, and public policy affecting human service organizations. In addition, Dr. Rich is the director of the Institute for Social Healing at the Center for Community Engagement and owner of Open Roads Inclusive Community Consulting, LLC. Currently, her professional work focuses on the health and well-being of the human service workforce, trauma-informed and healing-centered leadership, community engagement, and community-based support services for families with developmental disabilities.

Michael G. Strawser (Ph.D., University of Kentucky, 2015) is an associate professor of communication at the Nicholson School of Communication and Media at the University of Central Florida. He teaches several courses at the undergraduate and graduate levels including business and professional communication, advanced public speaking, and teaching communication. His research is primarily focused on matters relating to instructional communication and communication education.

Susan M. Wildermuth (Ph.D., University of Minnesota, 2010) is a professor of communication at the University of Wisconsin-Whitewater. In addition, Dr. Wildermuth serves as a 2022 Center for Teaching and Learning Fellow at UW-Whitewater, and as assistant chair of the UWW Communication department. She teaches courses in intercultural communication, organizational communication, interpersonal communication, and research methods. Her research is focused on intercultural competency, disability and communication, and the scholarship of teaching and learning.

Robin G. Yaure (Ph.D., University of Maryland, College Park) is a Professor of Teaching, Human Development, and Family Studies at Penn State Mont Alto. Her research focuses on pedagogical issues such as student persistence, exam preparation, social justice and the COVID-19 pandemic, infant sleep, and translational research. She is coordinator of the Penn State HDFS in Florence summer study abroad program and coordinator of the Penn State Mont Alto HDFS and Psychology baccalaureate programs. She is also the coordinator of the Civic and Community Engagement minor